Creating a Social Network

by Angela Crocker

ALPHA

A member of Penguin Group (USA) Inc.

With love for Brian and Yvonne for getting me started, and for Paul and Sean, who keep me going.

ALPHA BOOKS

Published by the Penguin Group

Penguin Group (USA) Inc., 375 Hudson Street, New York, New York 10014, USA

Penguin Group (Canada), 90 Eglinton Avenue East, Suite 700, Toronto, Ontario M4P 2Y3, Canada (a division of Pearson Penguin Canada Inc.)

Penguin Books Ltd., 80 Strand, London WC2R 0RL, England

Penguin Ireland, 25 St. Stephen's Green, Dublin 2, Ireland (a division of Penguin Books Ltd.)

Penguin Group (Australia), 250 Camberwell Road, Camberwell, Victoria 3124, Australia (a division of Pearson Australia Group Pty. Ltd.)

Penguin Books India Pvt. Ltd., 11 Community Centre, Panchsheel Park, New Delhi—110 017, India

Penguin Group (NZ), 67 Apollo Drive, Rosedale, North Shore, Auckland 1311, New Zealand (a division of Pearson New Zealand Ltd.)

Penguin Books (South Africa) (Pty.) Ltd., 24 Sturdee Avenue, Rosebank, Johannesburg 2196, South Africa

Penguin Books Ltd., Registered Offices: 80 Strand, London WC2R 0RL, England

Copyright © 2011 by Angela Crocker

All rights reserved. No part of this book shall be reproduced, stored in a retrieval system, or transmitted by any means, electronic, mechanical, photocopying, recording, or otherwise, without written permission from the publisher. No patent liability is assumed with respect to the use of the information contained herein. Although every precaution has been taken in the preparation of this book, the publisher and author assume no responsibility for errors or omissions. Neither is any liability assumed for damages resulting from the use of information contained herein. For information, address Alpha Books, 800 East 96th Street, Indianapolis, IN 46240.

THE COMPLETE IDIOT'S GUIDE TO and Design are registered trademarks of Penguin Group (USA) Inc.

International Standard Book Number: 978-1-61564-060-7
Library of Congress Catalog Card Number: 2010910369

13   12   11   8   7   6   5   4   3   2   1

Interpretation of the printing code: The rightmost number of the first series of numbers is the year of the book's printing; the rightmost number of the second series of numbers is the number of the book's printing. For example, a printing code of 11-1 shows that the first printing occurred in 2011.

Printed in the United States of America

Note: This publication contains the opinions and ideas of its author. It is intended to provide helpful and informative material on the subject matter covered. It is sold with the understanding that the author and publisher are not engaged in rendering professional services in the book. If the reader requires personal assistance or advice, a competent professional should be consulted.

The author and publisher specifically disclaim any responsibility for any liability, loss, or risk, personal or otherwise, which is incurred as a consequence, directly or indirectly, of the use and application of any of the contents of this book.

Most Alpha books are available at special quantity discounts for bulk purchases for sales promotions, premiums, fund-raising, or educational use. Special books, or book excerpts, can also be created to fit specific needs.

For details, write: Special Markets, Alpha Books, 375 Hudson Street, New York, NY 10014.

Publisher: *Marie Butler-Knight*
Associate Publisher: *Mike Sanders*
Senior Managing Editor: *Billy Fields*
Acquisitions Editor: *Tom Stevens*
Development Editor: *Jennifer Bowles*
Senior Production Editor: *Janette Lynn*
Copy Editor: *Amy Borrelli*
Cover Designer: *William Thomas*
Book Designers: *William Thomas, Rebecca Batchelor*
Indexer: *Brad Herriman*
Layout: *Brian Massey*
Proofreader: *Laura Caddell*

Contents

Part 1:   Figuring Out Social Networks 1

1   What Are Social Networks? 3
   It's a Social Thing 4
      Meaningful Connections 5
      Etiquette and Protocol 6
      Strategic Alliances 7
   How Social Networks Differ from Social Media 8
   Why Not Use Facebook? 9
   Three Types of Social Network Services 12
      Generic Label 12
      White Label 13
      Custom Label 13

2   How Social Networks Are Used 15
   Making Connections 15
      Business to Business 15
      Business to Consumer 16
      Peer to Peer 16
      Community 17
      When Things Get Fuzzy 18
   What Are Your Social Network Objectives? 19
      Influencing 19
      Organizing 20
      Education 21
      Rallying 22
      Evangelizing 23
      Fundraising 25
      Sales 25
      Convenience 27
      Eliminating Geographic Borders 27
      Just for Fun 27

Part 2: Shopping for a Social Network Service 29

3 Social Network Services 31
Review of Types of Social Network Services 32
The Six Featured Social Network Services 32
Generic Labels... 33
    Ning... 35
    Wall.fm 36
White Labels 39
    SocialGO 40
    BuddyPress 42
Custom Labels 42
    KickApps.. 44
    ONEsite 46
Comparing Network Services 48

4 Social Network Features 49
Features 49
The Activity Feature 51
The Members Feature.. 52
The Photos and Videos Features.. 53
The Tagging Feature 55
The Forums Feature 56
The Events Feature 57
The Groups Feature... 59
The Polling Feature 59
The Ratings Feature 60
The Blog Feature... 61
The Chat Feature 63
The Music Feature 64
The Description Feature 64
The Notes Feature 64
The Text Box... 65

	The RSS Feature	66
	Import	*68*
	Export	*68*
	The Badges Feature	68
	The Birthdays Feature	70
5	**What's This Going to Cost?**	**73**
	What Will You Pay For?	74
	Spending Money	74
	Free	*75*
	Bare-Bones Budget	*75*
	Spend Some	*75*
	Sky's the Limit	*76*
	Other Costs	76
	Back Office Costs	76
	Hosting	77
	Volume of Storage	*79*
	More Bandwidth	*80*
	Backups and Restoration	*81*
	Fault Tolerance	*82*
	Other Costs	83
	Additional Functionality	*83*
	Mobility	*85*
	The Value of Time	86
6	**Selecting a Social Network Service**	**87**
	What Am I Looking For?	87
	What Features Do I Need?	88
	Customization	89
	Customer Service Resources	90
	Technical Help	91
	Questions to Ask	92
	Trial Offers	93
	Make the Leap	*93*

Part 3: YOUR Social Network 95

7 Get Your Network Started 97

Choose a Name Carefully 97
    Brainstorming 98
    Availability 100
    Memorability 102
    Length 104
    Spelling 105
    Consider a Trademark 107
    Privacy Settings 107
Customizable Appearance 109
Code of Conduct 109

8 Help Your Members 113

Ease of Joining 113
About Profiles 115
    Organizational vs. Personal 116
    Valid E-Mail 116
    Unique Name 117
    Strong Password 118
    140-Character Biography 119
    Photo, Icon, Logo, or Avatar 120
Adding Further Details to Profiles 123
Relationships 123
    Strangers 124
    Acquaintances 125
    Friends 125
    Groups 126

9 Content Is King 129

Sharing 129
Content 130
    What Is Content? 130
    Types of Content 131
    Copyright 132
Uploading Content 133
Content Moderation 135

10   What to Say 137

Sharing Text 137
- *Reports and Research* *138*
- *Opinions* *139*
- *Dialogue* *139*

Links 140
- *Google Alerts* *141*
- *Bookmarking Accounts* *146*

Sharing Photos 149
- *Digital Camera* *149*
- *Taking Pictures* *150*
- *Photo-Editing Software* *151*
- *Photo-Sharing Accounts* *152*

Sharing Videos 153
- *Video Camera* *153*
- *Taking Videos* *153*
- *Audio-Video Editing Software* *154*
- *Video-Sharing Account* *155*

Part 4: Okay, Now What? 157

11   Cultivating Relationships 159

Define the People You Want to Reach 159
Determine How to Reach Them 160
Make It Easy to Participate 161
Articulate the Benefits of Membership 163
Consider Communication Styles 163
- *Direct Communicator* *164*
- *Spirited Contributor* *164*
- *Peaceful Collaborator* *164*
- *Systematic Methodist* *164*

Overcoming Reluctance 165
- *Determine Common Objections* *165*
- *Develop Responses* *166*

Warmly Welcome Members 167

12 Foster a Vibrant Community 169

Facilitate Dialogue 169
    Ask Questions 170
    Cite Statistics 171
    News of the Day 171
Share Information 172
    Community-Specific Information 172
    Subject Matter Experts 175
Respond to Feedback 175
Invite New Members 176
Interact One on One 177
Moderate Comments 178
Systemwide Messages 180
Get Together in Person 180
Patience 182

13 Enhance with Social Media 183

Make a Social Media Plan 184
Options to Consider 185
    Facebook 186
    Twitter 189
    Foursquare 192
    LinkedIn 193
    Special-Interest Communities 194
Create a Daily Routine 194

14 Making Money 197

But I'm Not Selling Anything 198
What Can I Sell? 199
E-Commerce 199
Advertising Opportunities 201
    Google AdSense 205
    Google AdWords 205
    Sell Your Own Ads 207
Affiliate Marketing 209
Sponsorship 210
Consider Your Competition 211
Understanding the Relationship 211

15 Measures of Success 213
Success Metrics 213
What to Measure 216
How to Measure 220
Data Gathering 220
Assessment 223
Monetary Success 224
Nonmonetary Success 225
  Size of Community 225
  Quality of Interactions 227
What to Do Now 227

16 Develop Network Savvy 229
Anonymity and Obscurity 229
Safety and Security 231
Privacy and Terms of Use 232
Authenticity 233
Quality vs. Quantity 234

17 Keeping It Going 237
Six-Month Check-Up 237
  What Features Are Being Used? 238
  What Do Participants Say? 239
  More, Less, or Stay the Same? 241
Continually Adapt 241
Use Search 241
  Inside Job 241
  Search Engines 242

Part 5: Social Network Service Tutorials 243

18 Ning Tutorial 245
19 Wall.fm Tutorial 253
20 SocialGO Tutorial 263
21 BuddyPress Tutorial 269
22 KickApps Tutorial 287

Appendixes

A	Glossary	297
B	Resources	305
C	Social Network Comparison Chart	315
D	Worksheet for Creating a Social Network	319
	Index	325

Introduction

Social + networking = social networking.

A simple formula for a rich activity.

You've already done social networking in the real world. The social part is easy. Interact with people in any sort of setting and you are being social. Hopefully you're more Kermit the Frog than the Grinch Who Stole Christmas, but either way you're being social.

Networking is easy for some and daunting for others. Even if you have to pluck up your courage, the networking dance is something like this:

Let's say you attend a party or conference. Your clothes are stylish, your business cards are crisp, and you bring out your winningest smile. You take a deep breath, walk into the room, and say hello to an old friend or someone new. Make small talk for a while, exchange business cards, and follow up with a call or coffee. Often you'll find some common interests and share what you know to help one another out. A business relationship may blossom into a friendship, or vice versa. Even without common interests, you still have met a new acquaintance.

Of course, networking has another, very technical, meaning in the context of computers networked together. Clever people who understand products from Novell, Microsoft, and Linux make computers talk to one another and to the Internet. Those threads make up the threads of the World Wide Web.

The term "social networking" has come to mean any online place where people gather and interact. A blog could be a social network, with the blogger and his readers interacting through comments. Discussion boards on services like Yahoo! are also social networks, with like-minded people gathering to talk about everything from parenting to NASCAR. Many social media sites are also social networks, and you've likely tried services like Facebook, Twitter, LinkedIn, or Foursquare.

In fact, Facebook is the largest social network out there. With 500,000,000+ users, that's a whole lot of connecting going on among members of the largest site on the web. That being said, many users are questioning how open social networks like Facebook are protecting their privacy and have concerns about the way their information is being used for marketing purposes. A desire for more control is just one reason why tens of thousands of customized social networks have been created with products like Wall.fm, BuddyPress, and ONEsite.

Please join me for an introduction to the concept of social networks. Together we will frame your particular network with specific objectives for success. We'll also go over some of the common tools available for network hosts and a wide variety of considerations to make your network a positive, effective experience for all.

How This Book Is Organized

The Complete Idiot's Guide to Creating a Social Network is divided into five parts designed to bring you up to speed, and fast. Even if you're a total newbie, we'll cover the basics and help you make the decisions necessary to get your network party started.

Part 1: Figuring Out Social Networks

Here we'll talk about the social aspects of networks, including the connections between real people and some essential etiquette. We'll also clarify how social networks are different from social media and talk in broad terms about the types of social network services. You'll leave Part 1 with a strong understanding of your social network's objectives.

Part 2: Shopping for a Social Network Service

Many services offer the opportunity to create a social network—some for free and others for a fee. We'll explore the options and figure out just what you are looking for in a network. Depending on your objectives, you'll need to spend some time and, maybe, money on your network, and we'll go over your network shopping list and make some buying decisions.

Part 3: YOUR Social Network

Each network requires a few preliminary decisions including a network name, privacy policy, and code of conduct. Once those are in place, you can shift your attention to the core of your community—your members and content. It's the interaction between members that makes a community and you'll want to include lots of great content for them. Don't worry, by the time you've read this part you'll have lots to share.

Part 4: Okay, Now What?

As you create your social network, you may want some advice on what sorts of content to share, how to encourage people to join your network, and how to foster a vibrant community. That community will have its home base on your network's website, but I also recommend having some social media outposts to interact with potential members. We'll also get into some nuts and bolts on how to make money with your network and how to measure your success. Then we'll discuss some general issues like anonymity and authenticity so you can avoid the potential pitfalls surrounding them. You'll finish Part 4 with confidence in your ability to act as host to your social network.

Part 5: Social Network Service Tutorials

Let me guide you through the creation of your first social network. In this part, you'll find step-by-step set-up instructions to help you create your first community on Ning, Wall.fm, SocialGO, BuddyPress, or KickApps. All of these services have user-friendly interfaces, and with the brief instructions in each chapter you'll be able to set up a social network in no time.

Helping You Find Your Way

The Complete Idiot's Guide to Creating a Social Network is jam-packed with details and information. As you read, you'll notice four different sidebars.

DEFINITION

Here we'll elaborate on any tricky words or concepts. Let's all be in agreement about what we're talking about before we move on. You'll also find these definitions in the Glossary for easy reference.

AVOID THE FAIL

Sadly, there are many potential pitfalls in social networking. These tips will help keep you out of the muck.

FLICKERS OF INSIGHT

While I'm not a mystic, I'll share helpful comments, observations, and tips to make your social network better.

CLOUD SURFING

Your directory of weblinks to resources mentioned in the text. If the links are brief, I'll share the original. Those links that are more complicated will be abbreviated using bit.ly to create custom shortened web addresses. Either way you'll navigate to the right resource online.

Acknowledgments

There are many people to whom I owe thanks for the creation of this book.

Thanks to author George Plumley, who saw the potential for me to become a published author myself. Thanks also to Kim Plumley and Peggy Richardson, at TheBookBroads.com for being my cheering squad at all hours.

Thanks to my literary agent, Carole Jelen of Waterside Productions, for becoming champion of Angela-as-author in the publishing world.

Next, I'd like to thank all those at Alpha Books and Penguin Group (USA) who have worked tirelessly behind the scenes to create the pages you're now holding. In particular, thanks to Tom Stevens, my acquisitions editor, for his generosity in helping make this book a triumph. More appreciation goes to my development editor, Jennifer Bowles; my production editor, Janette Lynn; and my copy editor, Amy Borrelli. The nurturing, smarts, and eye for detail of each of these editors helped me tremendously as the book evolved.

To my family, very simply thank you. I am truly grateful for the loving support of my husband, Paul, and our son, Sean, who willingly stepped into this word-filled adventure with me. I'd like to particularly thank my parents, Brian and Yvonne, for jointly instilling in me a lifelong love of books, reading, learning, and tech toys.

Finally, I want to express my deepest appreciation to all those who shared their experiences with social networks with me. Your varied professional and personal experiences have afforded me tremendous insight, and I am grateful for your input.

Special Thanks to the Technical Reviewer

The Complete Idiot's Guide to Creating a Social Network was reviewed by an expert who double-checked the accuracy of what you'll learn here, to help us ensure that this book gives you everything you need to know about creating a social network. Special thanks are extended to Peggy Richardson from WizardofeBooks.com for sharing her impressive knowledge of the technology behind social networking.

Trademarks

All terms mentioned in this book that are known to be or are suspected of being trademarks or service marks have been appropriately capitalized. Alpha Books and Penguin Group (USA) Inc. cannot attest to the accuracy of this information. Use of a term in this book should not be regarded as affecting the validity of any trademark or service mark.

Figuring Out Social Networks

Part 1

Creating a social network is the process of building a community. While there's some online technology needed to house your community, it's really about connecting people with like interests. Those common interests might result in friendships or business alliances. Your objectives in setting up the network will help forge those connections.

To get started, you need to be clear about what social networks are and how they differ from social media. In this part, we'll look at the different categories of social network service providers and get familiar with the varying features and functionality they offer.

Whether it's a labor of love or part of a business strategy, you'll want to nurture your network for the best effect. Let's get started.

What Are Social Networks?

Chapter 1

In This Chapter

- An introduction to social networking
- Rules of engagement, from etiquette to alliances
- The differences and similarities between social networking and social media
- Reasons why Facebook might not be a good option
- Three types of social networks—generic label, white label, and custom label

At its most basic, a social network is any online community where people can connect and interact. You're probably already part of one or more social networks. Services such as Facebook (www.facebook.com) and MySpace (www.myspace.com) are social networks, as are Flickr (www.flickr.com) and YouTube (www.youtube.com). Interest-specific communities such as Etsy (www.etsy.com, for those who buy, sell, and love handcrafted goods) and BlogHer (www.blogher.com, a community for female bloggers) are also social networks. Many big commercial brands, including Heinz, H&R Block, and Kraft, also have communities of their own to engage and service customers.

The function and purpose of each social network varies, as does the scope, which can be from a few people to thousands. It all depends on how many people are interested in the topic and willing to focus some of their online attention to the group.

Part 1: Figuring Out Social Networks

It's a Social Thing

We are sociable beings, whether we're online or in the real world. Social networks are just another way to interact with one another. We can share stories, photos, or links. Opinions can be voiced and information circulated.

Figure 1.1

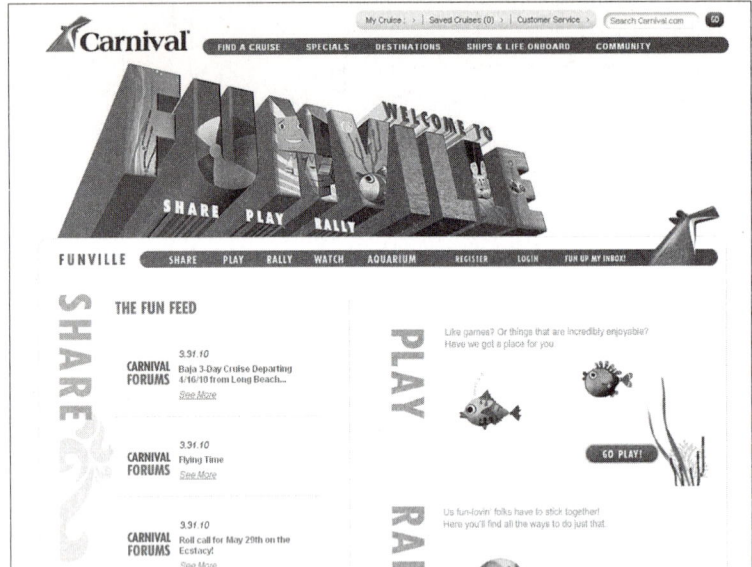

Carnival Cruise Lines passengers connect to share tips and ask the company questions through Carnival's social network Funville, at www.carnival.com/funville.

With the prevalence of computers and smartphones like the iPhone and DROID, it's possible to forget that real people are behind the text on screen. This is a key thing to remember about social networks—you are interacting with real people.

Figure 1.2

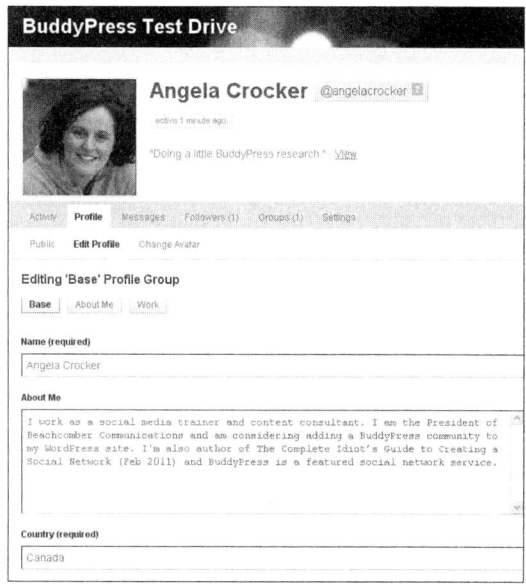

I'm a real person, as you can see from my BuddyPress profile, which includes a photo of me and some personal details.

Meaningful Connections

One of the most wonderful things about social networks is the opportunity to make meaningful connections. You can create links to people and companies that share your interests, values, and priorities—or at least some of them.

Social network connections can start from real-world relationships with friends, family, colleagues, and fellow conference delegates. However, meaningful relationships can also be built solely online. Participating in a particular social network gives you something in common with fellow participants right away, and connections can deepen over time as you interact and get better acquainted with people.

Take, for example, a social network for public art specialists—those people who make our world beautiful with public art installations, as well as more subtle style choices on things like manhole covers. Often these specialists work in their own cities and travel to take on projects further afield. Through a social network, they could share their expertise with others in the field. Over time, they may deepen those relationships to form partnerships for select projects, or at the very least to meet for lunch when convenient in their travels.

Etiquette and Protocol

Common courtesy and social graces are an essential part of any social network. Just as in real life, treating people respectfully and appropriately is essential.

As the host of a social network, it falls to you to set the tone that's appropriate for your network. Say your group focuses on a Christian faith. If so, then "Praise God," "Alleluia," and "Amen" are all going to be common phrases on your network. However, if your social network is for tattoo enthusiasts, it's likely that the tone will be more informal and the tolerance for salty language (and likely cursing) will be high. Then again, if the network is for Christian tattoo enthusiasts, that's another variation on the tone you'll hear from users.

Whatever the standards, there are still common conventions that are worth noting. In most cases, a formal etiquette policy or code of conduct is a good idea, although not a requirement. It's certainly a worthy exercise to think about the rules that will govern your network, even informally.

- Listen courteously.
- Respect other's opinions, even if you don't agree.
- Avoid pointing out other people's faults.
- Use language appropriate to the network.
- Say thank you.
- If in doubt, don't post your message.
- Share your knowledge freely.
- Don't slander anyone. Ever.
- Don't hesitate to apologize if you make a gaffe.
- Be forgiving if someone accidently offends you.

That being said, your particular social network can set other standards as appropriate. In fact, it may be best to let the social conventions of etiquette evolve from the participants themselves.

AVOID THE FAIL

If your network is comfortable with cursing, it is advisable to make a disclaimer to this effect when people sign up to participate. The last thing you need is to manage the reaction of someone offended by a shocking four-letter word.

Whether we call this etiquette, good manners, or common courtesy, following social conventions creates a comfortable environment for all who participate. You want to create a space that makes participants feel at home, giving them the freedom to express themselves naturally and authentically (more on authenticity to come in Chapter 16).

Strategic Alliances

Social networks can create opportunities for strategic alliances. On the one hand there is an opportunity for the host to create supportive alliances. This might mean a cancer patient support network reaching out to professional associations for oncologists and nurses working in the field. This network might also connect with the pharmaceutical companies doing cancer treatment research, as well as to the community organizations doing good work to support cancer patients. In this example, there are a myriad of strategic alliances that support and enhance the network.

Figure 1.3

From the connections made through a social network, three professional women came together to create The Book Broads.

On the other hand, participants themselves can create alliances within the social network for their own benefit. Take, for example, a group of entrepreneurial women in six disparate locations who met through a social network. Each has her own business plan and professional focus—a life coach, a business coach, a personal assistant, a publicist, an editor, and a marketing professional. Through the network, these women become better acquainted on a personal level and better informed of one another's activities on a professional level. In this particular group, it turns out the publicist, editor, and marketing professional all work with books and writers. They then form a strategic alliance to jointly promote their separate businesses.

How Social Networks Differ from Social Media

If you are wondering how social networks differ from social media, you're not alone. In fact, the terms are often used interchangeably, which adds to the confusion, and in some cases how to use them is a matter of opinion. In this book, we will consider social networks to be about community and social media to be about content.

The phrase "social media" is an umbrella term for those online services that allow the sharing of text, audio, photos, and videos. YouTube, Flickr, and Twitter are all sources of social media content. Think of it as a complementary form of media beyond newspapers, magazines, television, and radio. Social media is a way to share content online.

Social networks are those places where communities come together and share common social media experiences. Members of a social network interact through social media. They share content such as business documents, family photos, and other tidbits of interest. By doing so they enhance and engage with their community.

FLICKERS OF INSIGHT

Remember that social networking predates the Internet. People have interacted with one another in groups for centuries. With the technology available today, those networks can now exist both online and offline.

The two concepts are so closely tied that often a website that is a social media service filled with content also includes a community of users—a social network. And, of course, no part of the Internet exists in isolation, so the cross over between social media and social networks happens in many directions and at many places all at the same time. The differences can be subtle and, to be fair, confusing. Much of the advice in this book can be used to enhance your efforts on any social media platform, as well as to build and maintain your social network. Chapter 13 offers information about how to enhance your social network with some specific social media sites.

Why Not Use Facebook?

Facebook is the largest social network today with more than 500 million users. It's a fabulous tool with many uses, from sharing anecdotes and photos with friends and family to reading up on professional news. I use Facebook a lot in my work and see value in being part of this massive social network. I also recommend it as an enhancement to your social network in Chapter 13. However, not everyone is so keen on Facebook.

Figure 1.4

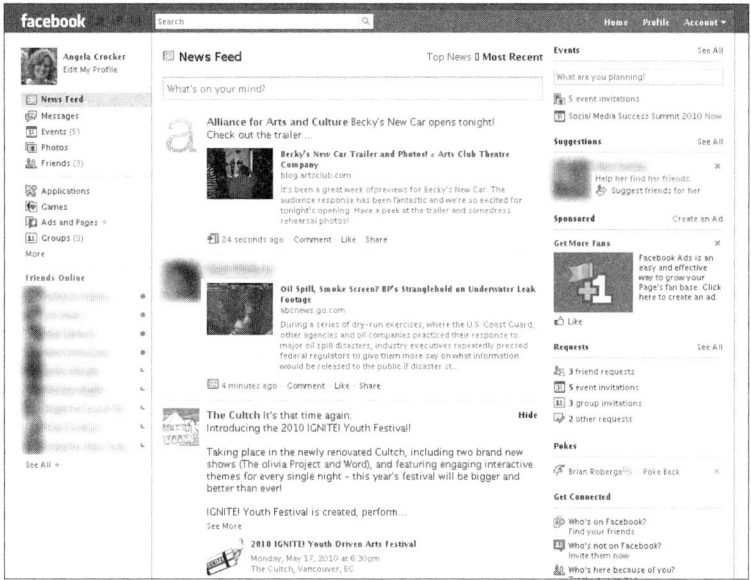

With users spending an average of 55 minutes per day on Facebook, it is one of the most used social networks.

For some, the size of Facebook is too much. They worry that their community will get lost in the mix of millions. This valid concern is similar to those who prefer to live in a rural community rather than a big city. Having control of your social network gives you many opportunities to create the experience your participants want.

Another key reason some aren't keen on Facebook is the way Facebook looks. If you build your community on Facebook you can't change this. It is possible to customize the appearance of Facebook pages to some extent with photos and graphics but you'll always be stuck with their three-column format, the blue navigation bar across the top of the page, and Facebook-controlled content in the right column.

For others, the user data provided by Facebook is insufficient. Facebook provides page administrators with access to data including the total number of fans, the ratio of men to women, geographic and language information, and much more detail. This data, called Insights, can be seen any time administrators log in to their admin panel and high-level data is also sent by e-mail once a week. Although there is a lot of rich content available from Insights, building your own social network can give you more detail and enable you to customize tracking and reports to suit your particular needs.

Figure 1.5

Insights data from a Facebook page. See details for your page at www.facebook.com/insights.

There is also value in the rich data to be gathered regarding the users of your network. Data can be aggregated anonymously to provide statistical information about trends, uses, and demographics. (We'll talk more about data gathering in Chapter 15.) You can protect the privacy and anonymity of your participants and use this data for your own gain—financial or otherwise. What a wonderful resource to enhance your particular brand with up-to-the-minute market research that your competitors don't have. This is something you can't do with Facebook.

There's also the problem of tech support. If you have an issue with your profile account or community page, Facebook is not very responsive to user or administrator questions. When they do respond, there's often a long lag time between your request and that change taking effect. There are Facebook how-to and help resources available in forums and from Facebook experts, but learning to use this complex social network can be too much for some.

CLOUD SURFING

The talented, energetic, and generous Mari Smith (www.marismith.com) is a great resource for information on Facebook. In 2008, Fast Company dubbed her the Pied Piper of Facebook. To me, she's the Queen. Check out her site for amazing how-to's and resource documents on Facebook.

Another issue to consider before making Facebook the home for your social network is advertising revenue. In Facebook's current model, they sell advertising space on your community's page. You have no control over what ads will appear there nor do you benefit from the dollars spent to reach your community. If you'd rather have that advertising revenue in your pocket, not Facebook's, then building your own network is desirable. In Chapter 14, we talk about ways to make money with your network, including advertising.

There's also an opinion factor about Facebook where some grumpy people are just anti-Facebook. If the community you're trying to build includes lots of people opposed to this social network then creating your community will be all the more challenging and may be doomed to failure if those grumpy voices are powerful enough.

Finally, what happens to your network if Facebook disappears? I'm not suggesting this network is going anywhere, but what if it does? The community you so carefully built would have no home and you'd have no means of contacting members. By creating your own social network, you control where and how long your community exists.

If these concerns are unimportant to you, building your community on Facebook is worth considering. Often, short-term projects such as high school reunions that bring a community together briefly are better suited to Facebook.

FLICKERS OF INSIGHT

Even if you do create your community on Facebook, I'd still encourage you to have a website for your community so that you have a presence outside of Facebook that you control.

Three Types of Social Network Services

There are many companies that offer social network services. You may already be familiar with Wall.fm, Ning, ONEsite, BuddyPress, SocialGO, or KickApps. As with everything, they vary in what features they offer, how they can be customized, the cost, and the ease of setting up your network. I think of these services in three broad categories—generic label, white label, and custom label. You'll learn more about specific network services in Chapter 3, but let me introduce you to them here.

> **CLOUD SURFING**
>
> This book focuses on six social network services. For a sneak peak at the kinds of technology we'll be talking about, visit the following websites:
>
> - wall.fm
> - www.ning.com
> - www.onesite.com
> - www.buddypress.org
> - www.socialgo.com
> - www.kickapps.com

Generic Label

Generic label network services provide the means to create your social network and a web address for your community. In this discussion, the key distinction for a generic label network is that the name of the service provider remains part of the *URL*. You control the network but the service's branding remains part of your community. Examples include annerice.ning.com or emlnetwork.wall.fm. These are do-it-yourself services ideal for fan clubs, school groups, and small business associations. These network services are available for free or at minimal cost depending on the service you select.

> **DEFINITION**
>
> **URL** stands for Uniform Resources Locator. More simply, it's a web address that you type into your browser to go to a particular website.

White Label

Network services under the white label umbrella are tools that can be used to build a community into an existing website. In other words, members would find your community as a seamlessly integrated part of your overall website. The white label services featured in this book are SocialGO and BuddyPress; both offer free services with paid enhancements available. White label communities are ideal for professional associations, community groups, and service clubs.

Figure 1.6

Tasty Kitchen (www.thepioneerwoman.com/tasty-kitchen) creates a "happy cooking community" using the BuddyPress social network tool on this website.

Custom Label

Finally we come to custom label networks, which include companies like KickApps and ONEsite that create custom-designed, purpose-built social networks for a fee. Custom label networks are generally used by universities, consumer product brands, or large sporting events to create customized experiences for their communities. As with white label networks, the community becomes part of the organization's website. Often these networks are tied to bigger branding and promotional strategies as part of their overall marketing strategies.

Figure 1.7

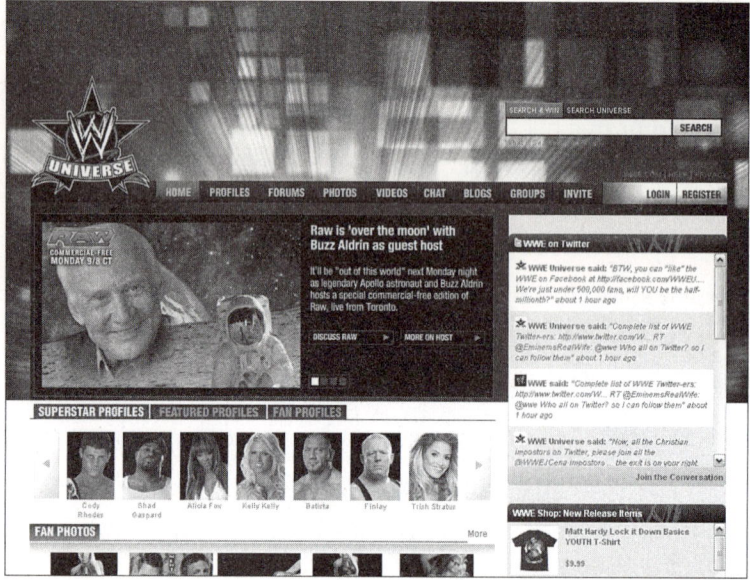

World Wrestling Entertainment (www.fans.wwe.com) used ONEsite (www.onesite.com) to create this customized social network for fans.

The Least You Need to Know

- A social network is any online community where people connect and interact.
- Brands can be given voice by the staff members who represent them on the social network.
- Common practices of etiquette and protocol apply to social networks.
- Social networks are about community while social media is about content.
- The terms "social networks" and "social media" are often used interchangeably.
- There are three types of social network services: generic label, white label, and custom label.

How Social Networks Are Used

Chapter 2

In This Chapter

- Businesses connecting with one another and with their customers
- Individuals connecting over personal interests
- Ten common objectives for social networks
- Focusing your social network efforts to meet your objectives

A social network can be whatever participants want it to be. In this chapter, I'll talk about the types of connections people can make through social networks. Together we'll look at ten specific objectives that may influence how you set up your network to connect people.

As you read this chapter, keep in mind the purpose of the social network you want to create. By clarifying your purpose and the types of connections you seek, you'll help yourself create the network that best serves your needs.

Making Connections

Social networks are about making connections ... meaningful connections. We're talking about linking people with like interests, whether they are personal, professional, or community based.

Business to Business

In the business world, there are many ways that businesses want to connect. Goods and services providers reach out to businesses that need products and services, whether that means Internet access and fleet vehicles or furniture and bathroom cleaning supplies. Other businesses connect as steps in a production line—the plastic pellet manufacturer that supplies the bag-making machine that provides the bakery bread bags, for example. Businesses also reach out to one another for professional services, as every business eventually needs a lawyer or accountant.

Business to Consumer

Meanwhile, many businesses—perhaps most businesses—seek connections with consumers. Businesses can survive only if consumers purchase and use up their offerings and then purchase them again. Through a network businesses can stay in closer contact with their customers.

Let's take an art gallery as an example. The gallery can keep in frequent contact with consumers throughout the year. The customers that join the social network express interest in receiving updates from the company and give their permission for the company to share information with them. This information might include upcoming shows, artwork for sale, event invitations, and critics' comments. The gallery can also invite network members to share their reviews and engage them in dialogue.

Peer to Peer

When I talk about peer-to-peer networks, I'm not talking about the high-tech geek stuff that allows computers to connect. Instead, I'm talking about the professional associations that can be fostered through a social network.

For example, Canadian Women in Communications (CWC) is a national organization made up of women and men in telecommunications, broadcasting, and related fields. Members receive many benefits, including professional development workshops, access to the members' directory, scholarships, mentorships, and other services. Within CWC, the membership has ready access to most services through the organization's social network. This creates an ideal situation for members to make meaningful connections with others in their line of work and related fields.

Figure 2.1

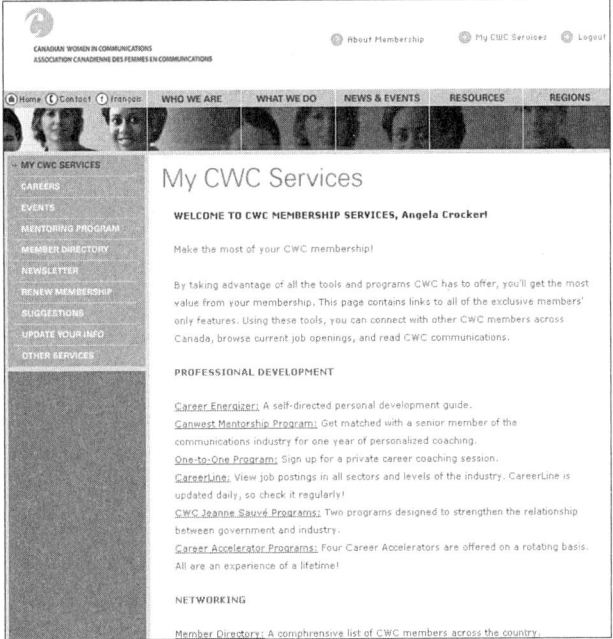

CWC members (www.cwc-afc.com) have access to many materials, from self-directed professional development to one-on-one coaching calls.

Community

Often social networks aren't about connecting for formal business purposes. Instead, connections are made through common leisure interests and activities.

Everyone's personal interests reflect who and what they are. Some folks are all about sports and outdoor activities, while others are about books and spa time. Still others might be focused on volunteering for the arts or coping with chronic illness. Each of us is, in some way, a part of communities that are unique to the things that make up our personal lives, and networks help us connect with or expand those communities.

Figure 2.2

Fans of the Fiskar brand of crafting products can join the Fiskateers club for product news and project ideas at www.fiskateers.com.

When Things Get Fuzzy

One challenge with social networks is when the line blurs between professional and personal connections. For many individuals, social networks are the place where their work and home lives intersect. Finding a way to reconcile the many faces we present to the online world is, perhaps, the biggest challenge.

AVOID THE FAIL

The risk of misinterpretation is a risk in all communications. Just as face-to-face conversations can be perceived very differently by the participants, e-mails can also be misconstrued and judgments may be made based on poor grammar or spelling. This potential for misunderstanding is present in social networks, too.

For some, this balancing act makes them unable or unwilling to participate. For others, they consciously allow their multiple selves to appear online, for better or for worse. And then there is a group of people, probably the largest group, who try to put their best selves forward at all times and isn't concerned with how the online world perceives them.

What Are Your Social Network Objectives?

Creating a carefully planned social network and engaging its community of users is well worth the effort. Step one is to clearly define your network's objectives. Understanding what you are trying to do will go a long way to helping you achieve your goals. Whatever your particular objectives, they will serve as a cross-check for each phase of your social network's existence.

Most communities share certain broad objectives in common. Your community may also have other, more specific objectives, but the following list provides a great starting point:

- Influencing
- Organizing
- Education
- Rallying
- Evangelizing
- Fundraising
- Sales
- Convenience
- Eliminating geographical borders
- Just for fun

It's very likely that more than one of these objectives resonates with you. That's terrific, because the more ways you involve your social network, the more benefit you'll derive from it. As you read on, think about the objectives that fit your situation.

Influencing

All forms of communication are about influencing someone to some degree. Think about the people who have influenced you over the course of your lifetime: family, friends, teachers, coaches, and co-workers. All of these people influence how you speak, your behavior, and even your opinions. But that's not all! You're also influenced by social and cultural experiences, including the books and newspapers you read, the movies you watch, the mall you shop at, and the parks you visit. And that's before we get to the professional influencers—the people who work in marketing.

In some ways, we've gone full circle. One hundred years ago we made decisions based on the people around us. The proprietors of the general store on Main Street knew their customers well and were able to influence their decisions based on that knowledge.

Today, social networks are fostering the century-old way again. We're returning to the model where we know and trust the opinions of those we interact with. The difference is that many of those personal interactions happen digitally rather than in person. For most people today, an endorsement from trusted friends, family, or co-workers is the single biggest influencer.

> **AVOID THE FAIL**
>
> Members of your community will need to decide if off-topic conversations are permitted. Sometimes this occurs when members are trying to influence opinions unrelated to the subject of the community. For example, a women's entrepreneur group might tolerate a sidebar conversation about baby slings and baby wearing. That same conversation might not be well received in a sporting community.

Once again, consider your experience. Would you be more inclined to do something if your best friend suggested it? For most people, the answer is yes, and that demonstrates the power of influence. Harness that power with your social network.

Organizing

We all do too much these days. What with parenting obligations, work commitments, fitness workouts, and household chores, we've all got a lot to accomplish. Wouldn't it be nice to have a means of easily organizing elements of our life in an accessible way?

Several of my friends are soccer parents who head to the playing field six days a week for practices, games, and tournaments. Before social networks, mud-stained handouts were distributed at practices and reinforced by a labor-intensive phone tree. Some clubs had upgraded to a website, but the information was often outdated as updates to the site were cumbersome.

Today, coach, team manager, helpful parents, and even the players themselves can keep everyone up-to-date by simply updating the league's social network. All the details are available including what field to go to, practice times, and which parent is in charge of half-time snacks.

Could your social network help your group get organized? You bet! You might use your network to organize a wide range of tasks, from simple things such as gift exchanges and potluck lunches to more complex puzzles such as special event or conference planning.

Figure 2.3

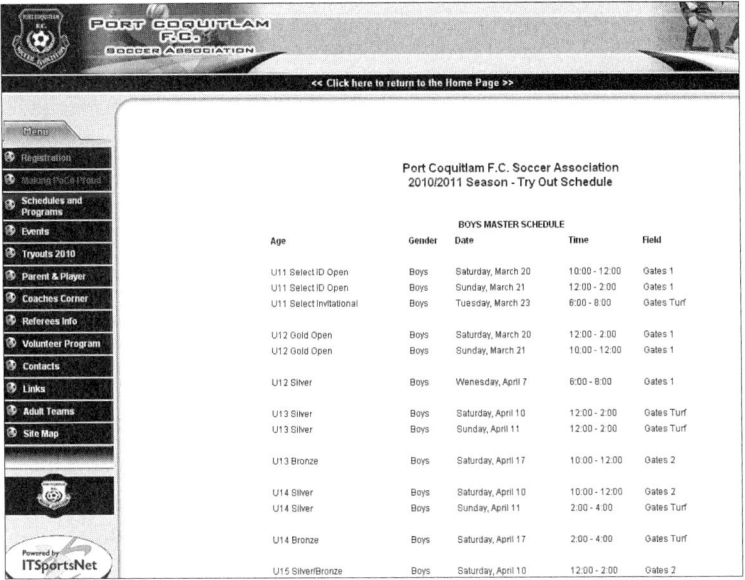

Port Coquitlam Soccer (www.pocosoccer.com) uses a social network to provide detailed information to players and their families to make practices, games, and tournaments easier.

Education

Through social networks all sorts of lessons can be taught, and the information is instantly available to anyone seeking answers. A network may inform the reader on a new topic or provide specific instruction on a new skill. Lessons may come from professional teachers or from laypersons with experience and knowledge to share.

Figure 2.4

The Knitting Network (www.knitting-network.com) includes knitting basics, how-to videos, and patterns for both beginning and experienced knitters.

Rallying

Many networks strive to rally people to causes ranging from local community issues to big-picture philosophical points of view. A cause could be saving the polar bears or supporting cancer research. Through the network, supporters rally to take action in support of their chosen cause.

Lantzville, a small town on Canada's west coast, used social networking to bring out members of the community to clean up a local creek bed that had become an unofficial town dump. Citizens rallied together in their desire to clean up their town and were motivated enough to come out and get their hands dirty.

Figure 2.5

On World Theatre Day (www.worldtheatreday.org), people who are passionate about theatre demonstrate the contributions theatre makes to communities.

Evangelizing

We're going to talk about religion and then politics for a minute. No, wait! Don't turn the page—this will be painless, I promise.

Social networks afford different points of view a platform. They can be used as a forum to discuss points of theology or opposing political views. Any faith can have an online community that supports a particular set of beliefs. Similarly, opposing political views can be expressed, be they Democrat or Republican, Conservative or Liberal.

> **FLICKERS OF INSIGHT**
>
> Please exercise caution when facilitating a social network that encourages strong viewpoints. It's important for members to debate respectfully.

Part 1: Figuring Out Social Networks

Figure 2.6

Members of My Godly Place (www.mygodlyplace.com) share their love of Jesus Christ through discussion groups, games, and other activities on the network.

Figure 2.7

Members of Republicanville (www.republicanville.com) share their views on fiscal conservatism, low taxes, and capitalism.

Consider how a spiritual community with a retreat center on a tropical island, their headquarters in California, and members spread across the globe can share their strong belief through a social network. In this case, the community can share without being physically together in a prayer hall or church. They share spiritual teachings and consider interpretations together. They offer one another support in times of crisis and celebrate in times of joy.

Fundraising

Savvy organizations know that it's important to build relationships with prospective donors before asking them for a contribution in a fundraising campaign. Many fundraisers ditch the term "fundraising" and instead talk about "friend-raising." What better way to do that than through a social network?

> **FLICKERS OF INSIGHT**
>
> There are regional differences in the way things are done. Just as the pace of life in Seattle is very different from that in New York City, the pace of social networks varies depending on the participants. This is an important consideration if a key objective of your network is to build relationships with donors.

Groups seeking support can communicate with current, prospective, and lapsed donors through a social network. Whether you're looking for time, talent, or treasure, the best returns come when donors are engaged regularly and at their convenience. Charities can articulate their mission, share stories of those who have benefited, and articulate what they hope to accomplish. Furthermore, they can use the social network to publicly acknowledge contributors and to thank them for their assistance.

Sales

Some social networks offer products for sale related to the network, while others are networks for those who have purchased or will purchase certain items. Merchandise sales, service sales, and event ticket purchases are all potential sales for businesses of any size. Most social networks have the capacity to handle *e-commerce* transactions.

> **DEFINITION**
>
> **E-commerce** refers to online sales transactions. Shoppers make purchases through an online shopping cart system such as www.1shoppingcart.com and pay with a credit card or through PayPal (www.paypal.com), an online payment transfer system.

26   Part 1: Figuring Out Social Networks

Figure 2.8

Members of the Alli Community (www.myalli.com) support one another in their lifestyle changes to aid weight loss.

Figure 2.9

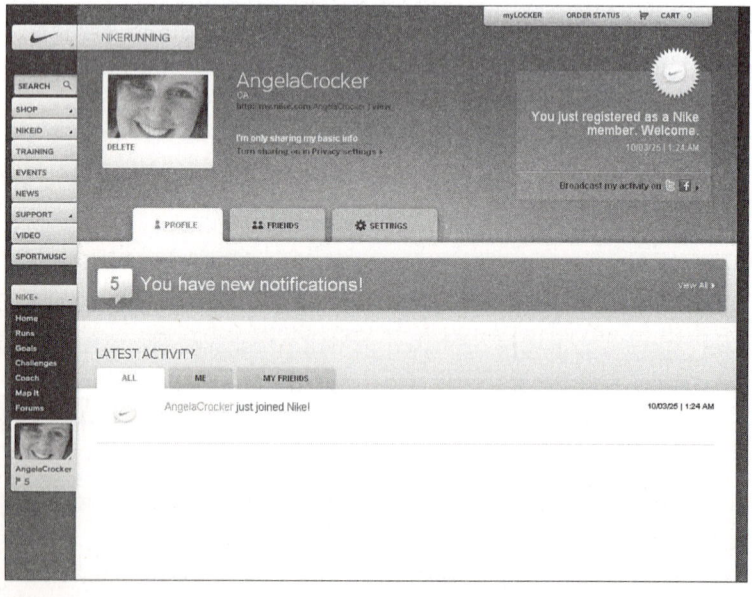

Runners who use the Nike+ technology set goals, share accomplishments, and chart their progress.

Convenience

Social networks can offer tremendous convenience to members. Purchases can be made. Calendars can be checked. Messages can be sent and reviewed. Information is readily available at the user's convenience.

Figure 2.10

Tyze (www.tyze.com) is a social network that allows caregivers and other supporters to conveniently coordinate patient support.

Eliminating Geographic Borders

While borders still exist in the real world, online borders are defined by language and technology to connect to the community. Your ability to speak, write, and comprehend English or any other language opens doors for you all across the world.

Just for Fun

Sometimes it can just be fun to host a social network for leisure. What's your pastime? Do you love classic video games or collect vintage toy soldiers? Maybe you're a NASCAR enthusiast or a champion hula-hooper. Whatever your special interest, it's likely you'll connect with others who share your interest through a network.

The Least You Need to Know

- Connections can include business to business, business to consumer, peer to peer, and community.
- Social network objectives might include influencing, organizing, education, rallying, evangelizing, fundraising, sales, convenience, eliminating geographic borders, and just for fun.
- The more objectives that apply to your situation, the more worthwhile your social network will be.

Shopping for a Social Network Service

Part 2

Fortunately, you don't have to max out your credit card to start a social network. In fact, many services offer free options that will only cost you time and effort. However, there are many options, and we'll talk about some of the most popular, from KickApps, Ning, and BuddyPress to ONEsite, Wall.fm, and SocialGO. We'll also explore the extra costs you might incur for enhanced back office support, mobility, or other specialized features.

No matter which social network service you select, you'll want to sign up armed with a good understanding of the features that are important to your community. From photo sharing and tagging to event planning and blogging, social networks can do lots of different things. Read on to learn the potential of your social network.

Social Network Services

Chapter 3

In This Chapter

- An overview of generic label, white label, and custom label network service types
- A first look at some of the available social network services
- An introduction to generic label social network services like Ning and Wall.fm
- A discussion of white label social network services, particularly BuddyPress and SocialGO
- An overview of custom label social network services such as KickApps and ONEsite
- Thoughts on how to choose the right social network platform for you

With so many social network services to choose from, it's hard to know what service to select for setting up your particular network. Pop the phrase "social network" into a search engine and you get thousands of hits on existing social networks, from Facebook to Second Life. Unfortunately, that search doesn't help you find a social network service—those companies that enable you to build your own network. Further research reveals that there are many companies providing social network services, with more emerging every month. The scope of their offerings and the costs involved vary, but all serve the basic purpose to help you create a social network.

In this chapter, we're going to take a tour of some of the most used and most popular social network services. This will familiarize you with the options available, highlight special features that may be important to you, and get you started setting up your own social network right away. As you read through, you may find the comparison chart of social network services in Appendix C helpful.

Review of Types of Social Network Services

We spoke briefly in Chapter 1 about three general categories for social network services—generic label, white label, and custom label. Now we'll talk about those labels in more detail. If it helps, think of them as three different types of wine—"u-brew," table wine, and collectible wine.

Of course, as with so many things on the Internet these days, the distinction between the generic, white, and custom label categories gets blurred. Many services offer more than one category of service. For example, Ning networks can be either generic or white label. Similarly, KickApps specializes in custom networks, but also has a robust generic option available. This flexibility can be helpful to network hosts who start with a generic label early in their plans, but may want to further enhance a successful, dynamic community some months or years later.

The Six Featured Social Network Services

This book focuses on six specific social network services. They are:

- Ning
- Wall.fm
- SocialGO
- BuddyPress
- KickApps
- ONEsite

These services are considered industry leaders in the field of social networks and most have well-established programs. They represent a wide range of potential platforms, from basic do-it-yourself systems to fully custom networks.

> **FLICKERS OF INSIGHT**
>
> Groupsite, Crowdvine, GoingOn, Haystack, and Google's Orkut are all viable social network services that could have been included in this book. There's also Xitti and Zocku, the social network services for adult content. And then there are the new services that haven't been released yet, particularly dLinked and Diaspora that promise something unique to build social networks.

Beyond these platforms, there are many other worthy platforms to consider and new ones popping up every month. The advice and preparation in this book will serve you well no matter what service you use. Where you choose to build your community is entirely up to you.

> **AVOID THE FAIL**
>
> For every social network service there are numerous opinions about the merits or failures of the service. Some administrators have had a difficult time with a specific technology or received poor customer service from a particular company. In some cases, this has turned into a nasty political maelstrom. The services featured in this book all have merit for various reasons. What service to use is your choice. As with all shopping decisions, you can be swayed by reviews or you can try the product to see if it works for you. I encourage you to form your own opinion.

Generic Labels

Generic label network services are like the u-brew wine stores where you put together the ingredients as provided by the shopkeeper and come up with a batch of wine that you bottle and label yourself. Generic label network services are self-serve, with setup completed in just a few minutes for free or at a minimal cost. Your network name will be something such as "*yourname*.ning.com" or "*yourname*.Wall.fm." These generic networks are not *hosted* with your existing website; rather they are hosted on the social network service's server.

> **DEFINITION**
>
> **Hosting** is the process of making websites, blogs, networks, and any other content available across the Internet by serving content from a dedicated server computer location. Your organization may own and operate this server, or your network might be hosted on the server of your social network service provider or wherever your website is hosted.

Generic label social network services offer a wide range of features, from blogging and photo sharing to chat and music sharing. They are fully functional and work well for many organizations. We'll look at specific features and how you might use them in Chapter 4.

Figure 3.1

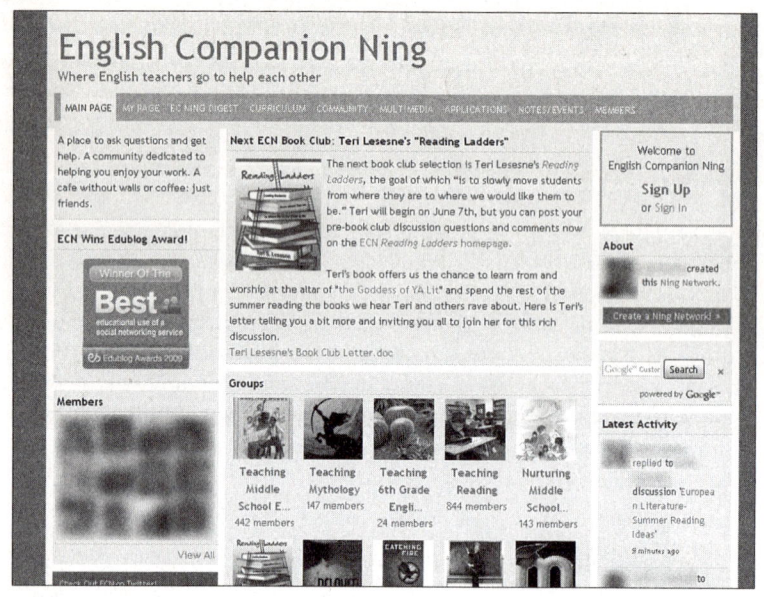

The English Companion community at www.englishcompanion.ning.com was built on the Ning platform.

While very functional, generic label network services offer limited customization, which means your network will always look and function a lot like other networks built on the same platform, just as your u-brew chardonnay is the same as everyone else's. While familiarity is good, it also makes it harder for you to stand out.

Let's begin by getting acquainted with two generic label social network services—Ning and Wall.fm. Both platforms include the name of the network service in your network's URL—for example, "*yourname*.ning.com" or "*yourname*.Wall.fm."

> **FLICKERS OF INSIGHT**
>
> All social networks exist on the web, and every network has a web address in the familiar website domain name format ending in .com, .org, .net, or any other extension. In order to be available across the Internet, all social networks must have a web address.

There are other network services that offer generic label options, too. Both KickApps and SocialGO offer this service. However, in order to be more succinct we will discuss these platforms a bit later in this chapter.

Ning

Ning was launched in early 2007. Today, there are about 45 million registered users and 300,000 active communities connecting through the Ning platform.

Figure 3.2

NING

The distinctive Ning logo is familiar to many web surfers.

> **CLOUD SURFING**
>
> To start building a Ning network visit www.ning.com and follow the prompts. Refer to Chapter 18 for a step-by-step example of how to set up a Ning network.

Social networks built on the Ning platform are easy to navigate and relatively simple to use. With Ning you can create a social network in just a few minutes. Users log in with their *Ning ID*, fill in a few blanks including the desired network name, select the desired *features*, drag and drop the layout, and can instantly publish their network. Ning sends you a confirmation e-mail to verify your Ning ID and a message to confirm each network you create on Ning.

> **DEFINITION**
>
> A **Ning ID** is simply a user name (often an e-mail address) and a password. Users can use a single Ning ID to identify themselves on all Ning.com networks, no matter who has set up the network or in which country they work.
>
> **Features** are the functions that can be included or excluded from a social network. Things like activities, calendars, groups, and videos are all features that can be part of a social network.

Ning's drag-and-drop navigation allows you to choose your desired features and then drop them in the order you want them to appear on your network. Ning also provides more than a dozen predesigned layouts that you can use for the graphic appearance of your community. Once the network has been set up, you can begin to upload your own content. Jump ahead to Chapter 18 for a step-by-step tutorial on creating your Ning ID and Ning network.

You will find Ning networks within many industry sectors including education, business, not-for-profit, and the arts. Ning is well suited to organizations that want to start a social network quickly and affordably with minimal technical know-how.

> **FLICKERS OF INSIGHT**
>
> Up until 2010, Ning offered free social network services. However, a change to its business model phased out no-charge networks and established a fee-for-service model. With pricing packages starting from $2.95 per month, network administrators had to decide whether to continue with Ning for a fee or to migrate their networks to other free services such as Wall.fm or BuddyPress. We'll talk more about the costs associated with network services in Chapter 5.

Wall.fm

Wall.fm is one of several products available from Skalfa eCommerce, an Indiana-based group of young professionals developing a suite of tools for websites and networks. Wall.fm is built on the open source software Oxwall (www.oxwall.org), formerly known as OpenWack (www.openwack.org). As a social networking platform, Wall.fm offers a service similar to Ning. There is currently a free version of Wall.fm as well as paid packages with enhanced functionality available.

Figure 3.3

Wall.fm offers free tools for building a custom social network.

On many levels, getting started on Wall.fm is functionally the same as Ning. To begin, select a network name and network address. From there, you're directed to the basic settings page. On this page, you confirm the network name and network address and you have the opportunity to add a tagline and brief description.

Figure 3.4

With the answers to five simple questions and the creation of a Wall.fm ID, you can instantly create a Wall.fm network.

Once you've entered your basic settings, including your network name, address, tagline, and brief community biography, click **Create** to move to the final step—selecting a network ID and password. If you already have a Wall.fm ID, you can simply sign in. To create one, you'll need a valid e-mail address, a password, and the text from the *captcha*.

> **DEFINITION**
>
> A **captcha** is used to confirm that a human, not a machine, is trying to execute a particular task online. Most often the captcha includes text that is distorted and of variable sizes, making it difficult for an automated computer program to read. The name is an acronym for "**C**ompletely **A**utomated **P**ublic **T**uring test to tell **C**omputers and **H**umans **A**part," a phrased attributed to Luis von Ahn, Manual Blum, and Nicholas J. Hopper of Carnegie Mellon University in 2000.

Figure 3.5

In this example, the captcha reads "available forader." Note the variable text size.

Wall.fm sends a confirmation e-mail to verify the e-mail address used to set up the account. Once verified, expect to receive a welcome e-mail containing a summary of your Wall.fm account, including your password and your network address. This e-mail will also provide links to suggested next steps for building your network, including the appearance and features of your network.

> **FLICKERS OF INSIGHT**
>
> Wall.fm publishes your network right away with a default appearance that can then be customized by administrators at any time. By contrast, Ning requires you to select an appearance prior to publishing your network, although you can also alter the appearance of your Ning network later.

Within Wall.fm, both administrators and users look for the word *dashboard* or the house icon to take you to the main control screen, often called a dashboard, for your interactions with the network.

> **DEFINITION**
>
> Network administrators have access to social network administrative functions that are not available to general members of the community. These admin functions are presented in a control panel, commonly referred to as a **dashboard.** Some social networks, including Wall.fm, give all users a dashboard to view their activity, profile, and other interactions with the network.

Wall.fm's feature list is comprehensive, with the capability to include all sorts of content including blogs, photos, and videos, as well as sophisticated connecting tools to link users through the membership directory and groups. You'll also see links for admin access, custom text/HTML, and RSS features in the center of your dashboard. We'll talk in detail about these features in Chapter 4.

As you can see, generic label–based social networks are quick and easy to set up and offer a robust menu of common features.

Figure 3.6

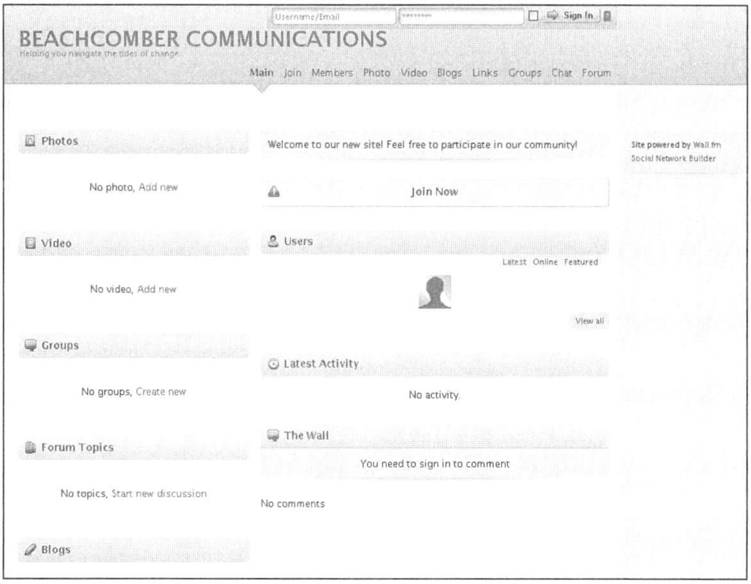

The Wall.fm dashboard gives administrators an at-a-glance view of the network and its various features.

Their limitations include limited options for the way your network will look and the inconvenience for users to have to click through from your website to the community or having to remember the network's location. Depending on the needs of your community and your objectives in creating the community, services like Ning and Wall.fm can be a great choice for you.

> **AVOID THE FAIL**
>
> Both Wall.fm and SocialGO specifically forbid adult content within their social networks. The creators of Wall.fm are currently developing a parallel social network tool called Xitti (xitti.com) and the folks at SocialGO are offering Zocku (my.zocku.com) to allow for adult users to engage in networks focused on adults-only topics.

White Labels

White label network services are comparable to the everyday table wines you pick up at your local grocery store or wine merchant. They are inexpensive and thoroughly enjoyable, but aren't the kinds of wines you're going to put in your cellar as investments.

White label networks take a bit longer to set up, as the network features are more robust and the network itself must be embedded in an existing domain name. This means that the community becomes part of your website. With many social network services, including Ning, Wall.fm, SocialGO, and KickApps, you can build a generic label network and then upgrade to a white label service at a later date, if desired.

Utilizing a white label network service is desirable because you direct your community to a single location rather than divide their attention with invitations to visit your website in one place and your community in another. There can also be advantages to self-hosting the community in terms of ensuring server redundancy, timely backups, and network security. However, I would caution that self-hosting comes with many potentially costly risks, and most organizations outsource to companies that specialize in hosting. We'll talk more about these technical considerations when we discuss back office costs in Chapter 5.

White label social networking services allow for some feature customization and can be incorporated into the look, feel, and domain name of an existing website. For many businesses and organizations, this is the most common type of social network. Here, we will briefly explore two common white label platforms—BuddyPress and SocialGO.

> **FLICKERS OF INSIGHT**
>
> Ning and Wall.fm can both be incorporated into an existing domain name, given a customized appearance, and have custom features added, making them both potentially white label network services. Although the six selected services in this book are presented under one of our three labels, they are all chameleons that can perform at different levels as required.

SocialGO

SocialGO (www.socialgo.com) is a sleek platform that offers a generous suite of network features to all customers. Its Free service includes SocialGO branding, advertising, and references, but is a functional and affordable option. SocialGO's higher-level services charge monthly fees to access more features and more support, and remove the SocialGO branding.

> **CLOUD SURFING**
>
> Visit www.socialgo.com/blog/socialgo-tour to watch an introductory video for a three-minute overview of SocialGO's capabilities.

SocialGO has created many useful *widgets* that serve the needs of different networks. Administrators can elect to use particular features at their discretion—for example, if Facebook and WordPress integration are important to the community. Some widgets are available for free, while others are available for a one-time user fee.

> **DEFINITION**
>
> **Widgets** are the bits of add-on software found in all sorts of computer technology. Within a social network you might add a widget for an online shopping cart system or to tie in your Twitter feed.

Figure 3.7

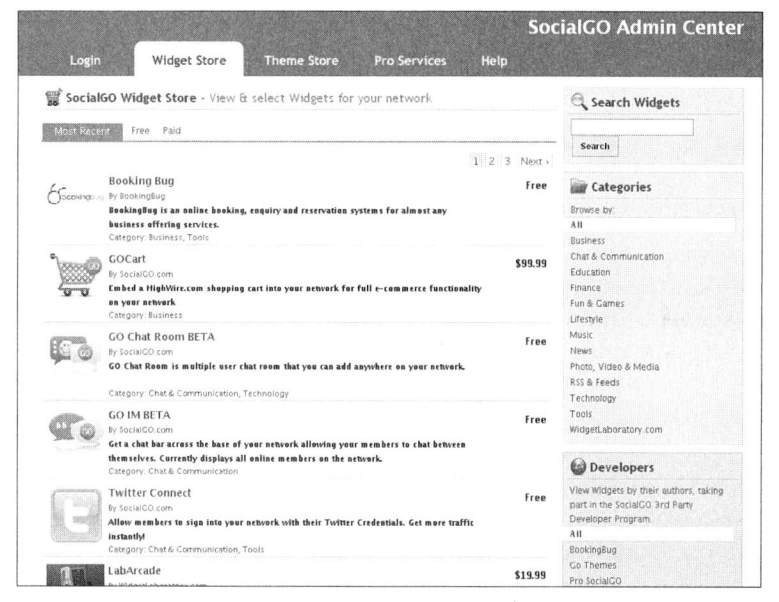

The SocialGO Widget Store.

SocialGO's Widget Store offers an assortment of additional features that can be added to a SocialGO network. Some features are free, such as the BookBug or Twitter Connect options, while others have a one-time cost attached, such as the $99.99 cost to add the shopping cart function.

One of the advantages of SocialGO networks is that they can grow over time. When necessary, a seamless upgrade to the next level of service is possible for any SocialGO community. SocialGO offers three tiers of service—Free, Premium, and Concierge.

BuddyPress

BuddyPress (buddypress.org) uses the open source code of the popular blogging platform *WordPress*. BuddyPress and WordPress are independent organizations whose products complement one another. As of 2010, WordPress was reporting about 27 million active WordPress websites. Only those websites driven by WordPress can use BuddyPress, a *plug-in*. This *open source*, community-driven platform allows users to build a BuddyPress-based social network within their existing WordPress site.

> **DEFINITION**
>
> **Plug-ins** extend the capabilities of a piece of software. Just as BuddyPress is a plug-in that makes WordPress more useful, there are many plug-ins available to extend the use of BuddyPress.
>
> **WordPress** is a free blogging platform that can be hosted either within WordPress.com or on your own domain. If you don't currently have a WordPress site, you can create one in minutes for free at www.wordpress.com. If you want to add one to your website, then download the free software available at wordpress.org and install it on your web server. Either way this blogging platform is free. You can also hire a WordPress theme designer to create a design for you with the functionality and appearance you desire.
>
> **open source** software is a community-built code, usually a software product, where anyone with programming knowledge can access, adapt, and use the code to create new software, plug-ins, or designs.

BuddyPress allows for the quick and free creation of a social network. As with Ning and Wall.fm, different WordPress design themes can be applied to customize the look of the network. However, be sure to select a WordPress that is compatible with BuddyPress.

Custom Labels

Custom label network services are like collectible wines that have been carefully crafted in vineyards around the world. These wines are showcased at festivals and eagerly sought out by collectors. Custom label network services offer all of that cache and special status. They are similar to white label networks in that your network is part of your overall domain name and they incorporate many features. However, custom label solutions are, as the name implies, custom made.

While custom labels offer a suite of common features similar to those available in generic label and white label platforms, the custom level offers the most flexibility, personalized design, and the potential to develop and add proprietary features.

To create a custom label network, your company or organization would work with a social network service provider like KickApps or ONEsite to define your needs, articulate the network activity you desire, and then build and brand your network.

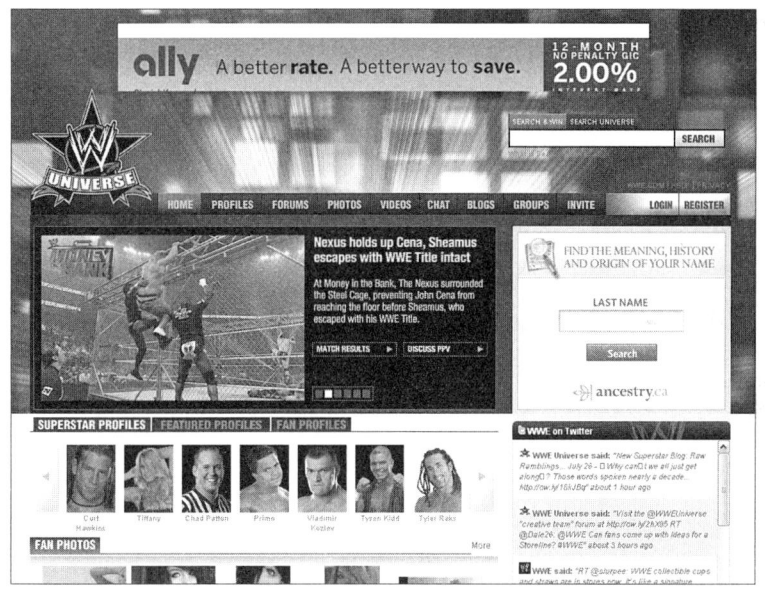

Figure 3.8

World Wrestling Entertainment (WWE) has built a custom fan community with the assistance of ONEsite.

From a cost perspective, custom label networks are the biggest investment of both time and money. However, they can be very rewarding, with a fully customized and seamless interface with other aspects of your website and marketing efforts. You can also build features and functions that address particular unique goals for your network. Perhaps your weight loss community needs a target weight-o-meter. Or perhaps you want to showcase a particular partnership with a branded online game.

In this book, we focus on KickApps and ONEsite for custom label networks. While not the only social network services offering custom networks, their portfolios are impressive as they demonstrate what they have accomplished for other brands. With rosters including everything from the Food Network to the WWE Universe, these companies are working with big brands to deliver big social network value.

KickApps

The KickApps (www.kickapps.com) team offers services to create a social network, implement the social network, and then manage that community over time. With a comprehensive suite of standard features available, KickApps distinguishes itself with tools such as a custom video player that can be built into a social network.

The following images show some examples of KickApps social networks.

Figure 3.9

KickApps developed Food2 (www.food2.com), the social network for fans and friends of the Food Network.

Chapter 3: Social Network Services   **45**

Figure 3.10

In cooperation with KickApps, the Harlem Globetrotters created a social network for its fans. Check out the custom basketball navigation feature at www.harlemglobetrotters.com.

Figure 3.11

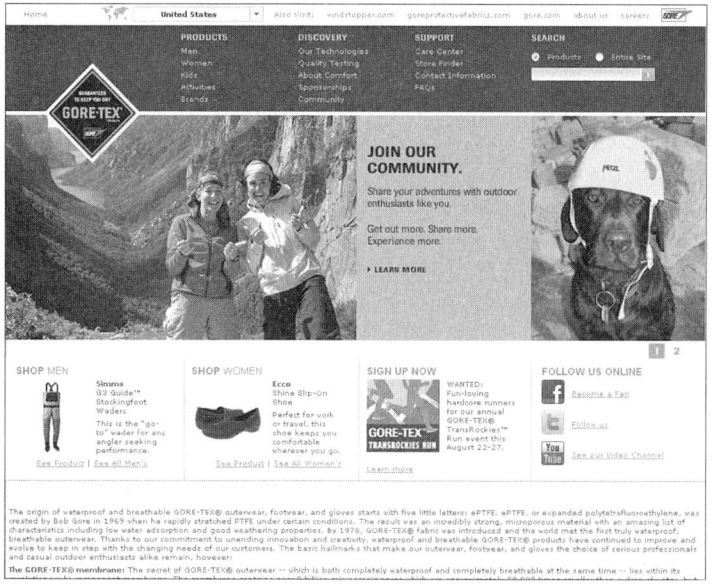

Outdoor gear icon Gore-Tex worked with KickApps to create a community for outdoor-activity enthusiasts at www.gore-tex.com.

ONEsite

ONEsite (www.onesite.com) is a leading service provider for *enterprise*-scale social networks. Founded in 2005, ONEsite's team has implemented over 3,000 communities for some of the world's most familiar brands. ONEsite boasts over six million users to date. Social networks built with ONEsite have access to their team's substantial experience in community building, and sophisticated features such as *microsites* and e-commerce.

> **DEFINITION**
>
> **Enterprise** refers to large, corporate-scale computing systems that have many types of computers, operating systems, and user needs, and are managed by an IT department.
>
> A web page or cluster of web pages created for a particular purpose is called a **microsite**. Microsites are often used to complement existing web pages or social networks for short-term promotions, events, or other activities.

As every network created by ONEsite is a customized community, highlighting ONEsite's work is the best way to illustrate the potential of using their service. The communities illustrated in Figures 3.12, 3.13, and 3.14 were built by ONEsite.

Figure 3.12

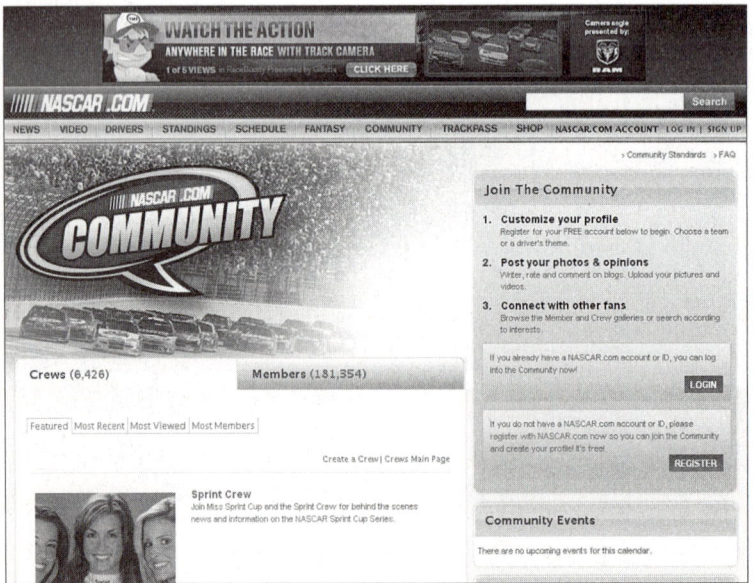

ONEsite and NASCAR worked together to create the community at www.community.nascar.com for tens of thousands of active members.

Figure 3.13

Panasonic worked with ONEsite to create a community for those embracing high-definition (HD) technology at www.livinginhd.com.

Figure 3.14

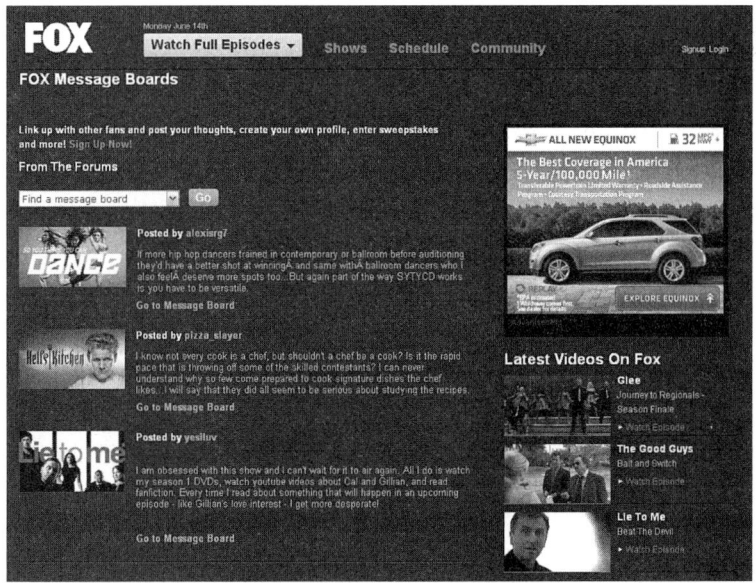

Fox Television engages viewers at community.fox.com with busy discussion forums, live video replays, and other rich content on its social network, developed by ONEsite.

While best known for its enterprise-level work, ONEsite also offers some do-it-yourself packages for smaller-scale organizations. Essentially, this package provides administrators with access to ONEsite's social networking platform without access to the expertise and customized features available at the enterprise level. It is recommended that a highly skilled person familiar with ONEsite in particular work with you to create a social network this way.

Comparing Network Services

Now that you've had a brief introduction to a handful of social networking platforms, pick one that looks like it will suit your style and needs and try it out. All of the network services offer case studies to show how their platforms have been used. Many also allow you to test the service without commitment, so try out one or more services before you settle on the best one for you—get in there and experiment!

> **FLICKERS OF INSIGHT**
>
> There are many other reputable social network services that offer a plethora of great network solutions. Feel free to check out Groupsite, Crowdvine, or any one of dozens of other service providers. One way to find both new and existing services is to plug the words "social", "network", "build", and "community" into a search engine.

Making a final decision on what platform to use can be overwhelming. The comparison chart in Appendix C lists features and functionality across all six featured platforms, and the advice in Chapters 5 and 6 will also help you make a selection.

No matter what type of social network service you choose, all of these network tools can be optimized to look polished and professional. Your goal is to connect with your community for one or more of the reasons we talked about in Chapter 2. Focus on meeting your community's needs and you won't go wrong.

The Least You Need to Know

- Generic label networks are available on Ning and Wall.fm.
- White label networks are available on SocialGO and BuddyPress.
- Custom label networks are available from KickApps and ONEsite.
- All social network services offer a variety of levels of service such that a generic label network could also be white label or custom label and vice versa.

Social Network Features

Chapter 4

In This Chapter

- An overview of social network features to consider when creating your social network
- Communication features such as activities, blogs, chat, and forums to help members connect
- Relationship management features including members, groups, and events
- Features for sharing rich content including music, photos, and videos
- RSS feature used to syndicate content
- Additional features including tagging, badges, ratings, and polls

Social networks can do many things. Each action, from photo sharing to event planning, is accomplished by utilizing a tool, called a feature, of the social network service you've selected. In this chapter, we'll review the most common features included on social networks and how they are used. This will help you determine what features your network needs to function the way you want it to.

Features

Features are simply the functions that can be included or excluded from a social network. Each feature offers opportunities to connect and engage members of the network. Some features may be required in order to meet certain network objectives, while others are functions that may be expected by the community. Not all features will be part of every network; rather, features should be deliberately chosen to meet the needs of each network.

Let's explore the specific features available from Ning. You'll find all of these features available in other social network services, but in some cases—for example, SocialGO and KickApps—you'll need to pay for a widget or service upgrade to access the feature.

Figure 4.1

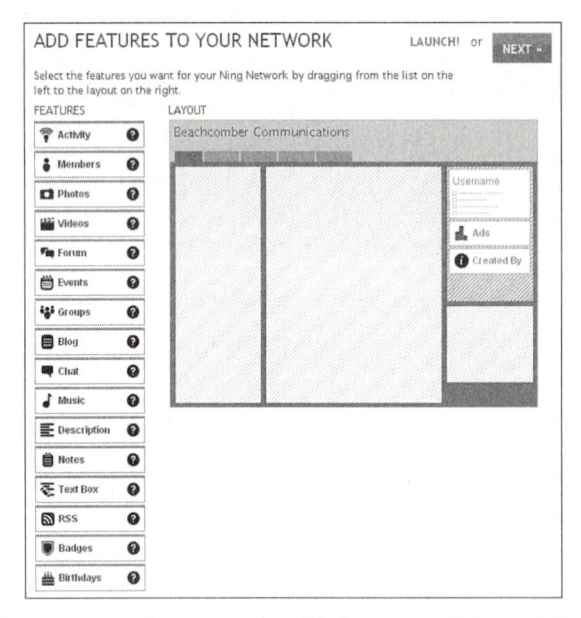

Ning's 16 core network features can be added or removed from a Ning network layout through a drag-and-drop interface.

The following descriptions articulate what the features do and how they are commonly used within a network. If a particular feature is essential to your network, be sure to note that on your social network service worksheet in Appendix D. This worksheet is a quick reference document that you will use each time you make plans to create a social network. You may also want to refer to the social network service comparison chart in Appendix C to ensure your selected platform supports the features you desire.

These features are discussed in the following sections:

- The Activity Feature
- The Members Feature
- The Photos and Videos Features
- The Tagging Feature
- The Forums Feature
- The Events Feature
- The Groups Feature

- The Polling Feature
- The Ratings Feature
- The Blog Feature
- The Chat Feature
- The Music Feature
- The Description Feature
- The Notes Feature
- The Text Box
- The RSS Feature
- The Badges Feature
- The Birthdays Feature

The Activity Feature

The activity feature, or activity feed, is the water cooler or newspaper of your social network. This is where the news of the day is broadcast to all members of the community. This feature provides details on the most recent actions in any area of your network, usually in reverse chronological order. Activities allow members to see what's going on and who has been online recently. The activity feed provides hosts with a record of activity that can be useful for assessment and evaluation of how members are using the network. You'll find more information about assessing and evaluating a network in Chapter 15.

Figure 4.2

Fans of WD-40 share tips and tricks at www.mywd40.com. Note the activity feed called WD-40 Buzz on this network developed by ONEsite.

On some networks, the activity feed is information from all members of a network. On other networks, members see only the activity of people they are connected with as friends. Often, members can select which activity feed they want to review and can, in some cases, organize more refined lists of their friends. By using lists, the members can then organize news in ways that suit them.

Let's say that Sally Smith is a member of your network who is focused on her home community in rural Idaho. Other members of her family are also members of your network. Perhaps her first priority is family news, then hockey team news, and finally community news overall. She can create lists of members who provide the news relevant to each of these categories. The default on all network services is to provide each user with one list that includes everything. Users who choose to filter the content they see create one, two, or many lists based on the way they want to be able to view information. For example, the hockey coach or team manager could go on the hockey news list. So when Sally logs in to see what's happening, she can decide which information is of most interest if she hasn't got the time to read everything.

Remember that most people don't have enough time to keep up with every single item posted in the activity feed. Instead, members will see a snapshot of the recent posts when they decide to log in. In this way, their experience of the network and their access to the news depends on when they can log on and for how long. There's a river of information and a member only gets wet with a small amount of the available info on any given day.

The Members Feature

The members feature is the address book or membership directory for those that have joined the network. In some networks, the directory is open and everyone can see every other member. In other networks, only limited information is available to all members—usually a person's name, location, and brief description—and full information is available to those members who have confirmed their acquaintance through a friend connection. This membership roster can help show members of the network that they are part of a community. This feature is helpful for both administrators and users to connect with members of the network.

The "everyone-knows-everyone" model works best for smaller communities where members are more likely to know each other. The friend confirmation model is desirable for larger communities so that members aren't overwhelmed with information of little interest or forced to share their details with strangers. There are also some personal safety advantages to the friend confirmation method. We'll talk more about safety in Chapter 16.

Figure 4.3

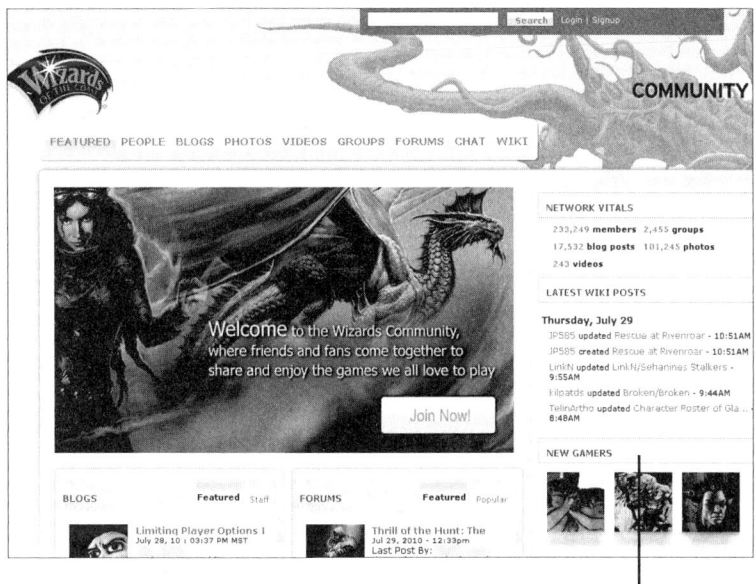

The Wizards of the Coast community, built by ONEsite at www.community. wizards.com, offers a directory of new gamers.

The Photos and Videos Features

The photos feature allows members to upload photos for sharing both within the social network and across the Internet. Often the feature allows users to upload a single photo, upload a group of photos, or take a photo with their webcam to share with the community. Within the photo feature, pictures can usually be organized into albums with captions. The photo feature is a wonderful way to connect members. It helps them get better acquainted and puts faces and names together.

Figure 4.4

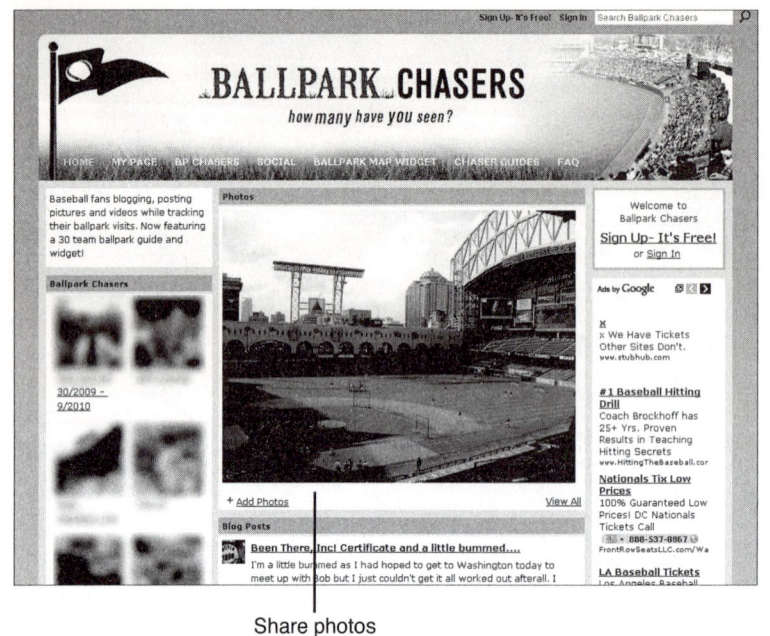

Ballpark Chasers (www.ballparkchasers.com), a Ning community for fans of Major League Baseball venues, includes fan photos.

As with the photos feature, the videos feature allows members to upload videos for sharing both within the network and across the Internet. On most platforms there is a limit on the size and length of the video clips that can be shared. Sometimes the videos can be uploaded directly to the community, and other times an embedded video link can be shared to lead members to a video uploaded to an external video service such as YouTube.com. Again, videos make for rich content and meaningful sharing amongst members.

Figure 4.5

Experience a video feature, built by KickApps, on the VitaMix community home page (www.community.vitamix.com).

The Tagging Feature

Tagging is the process of identifying web content with short descriptive words that describe a blog post, photo, or video. All sorts of things can be *tagged*, including people, places, and products. The tags then become a searchable index of sorts to help people explore the content. Tags are helpful as they are usually links to a search results page showing all content tagged with that word or phrase. This can be useful if you are interested in more information on a topic.

> **DEFINITION**
>
> **Tagging** is the process of putting an electronic bookmark of sorts on an image, video, or text that indicates who or what's in the content. The tags make it easy to record the who, what, and where for any content and can alert people and brands that they have been featured.

Figure 4.6

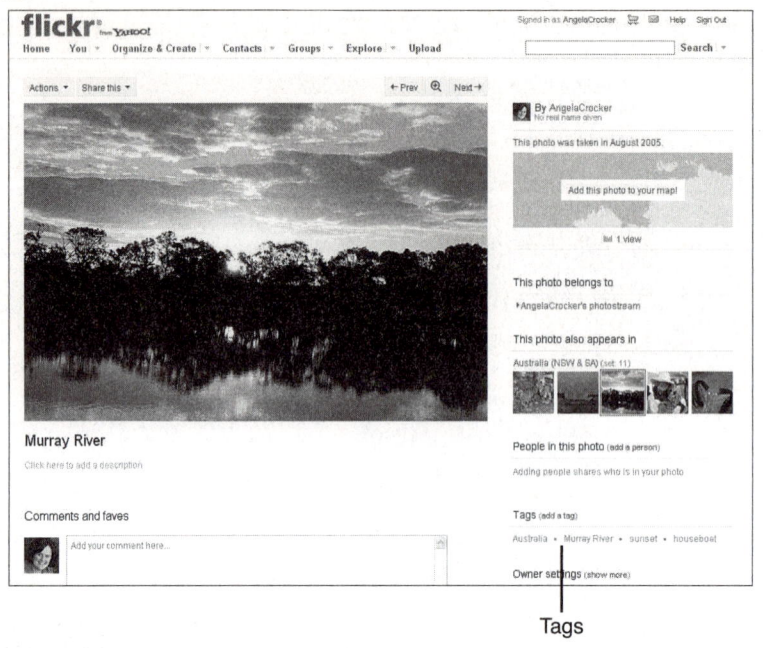

Tags on this photograph include Australia, Murray River, sunset, and houseboat. (See bit.ly/MurrayRiver.)

Tags are a great organizational tool that brings order to the potential chaos of thousands of pieces of information within a network and, indeed, across the web.

> **FLICKERS OF INSIGHT**
>
> Often tags relate to keywords that describe the network. For more information about keywords, refer to Chapter 14.

Tags can also be used to inform people and brands that they have been associated with particular content. Most networks allow members to remove self-identifying tags upon request.

The Forums Feature

The forums feature allows network members to interact in conversations about topics related to the network. In some networks, discussion topics are posted by administrators and there can be standing conversations about ongoing topics. In addition, user-initiated discussions engage members in dialogues on topics of interest. The discussions can be playful or heated. Whatever the tone, the power of dialogue is wonderful.

Figure 4.7

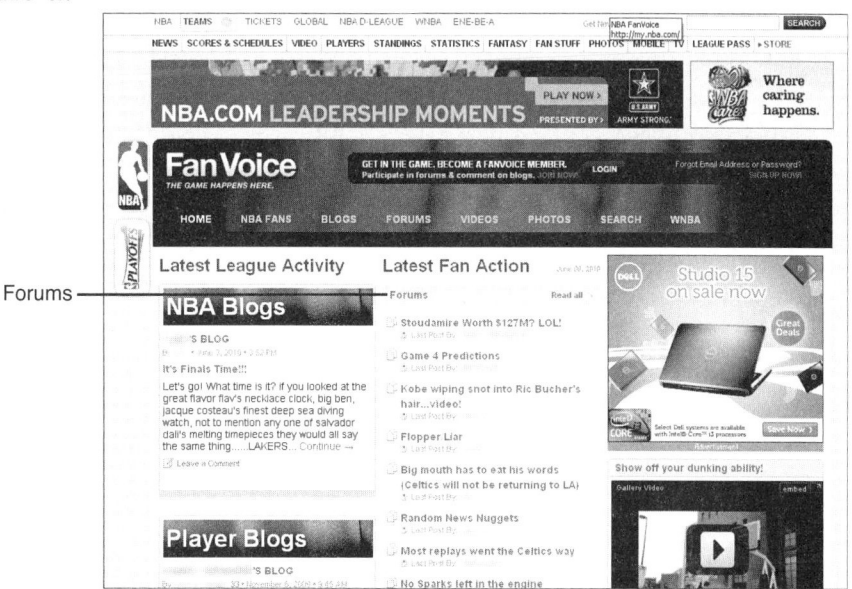

FanVoice (my.nba.com), the social network of the NBA built by ONEsite, highlights the most recent forum discussions.

Someone who wants to start a new forum discussion can pose a question or can post a link to a thought-provoking blog post as the opening content of the discussion. Whatever the source, group members can then reply to the initial message with their opinions, additional information, or further questions.

Forums can be a great place for lively debate and for silly amusement. They are whatever the members want them to be. Often administrators lay out ground rules for forum discussions to ensure that everyone's contributions are within the code of conduct for the network overall. We'll talk about this code in Chapter 7.

The Events Feature

As the name suggests, the events feature acts as a social secretary for the network by disseminating event information. Events proposed can be real-world meetings such as a cocktail party, or virtual events such as a webinar where members gather at a particular time to interact with one another in real time. Both administrators and members can be authorized to create events.

For social networks filled with social butterflies, an event-planning tool will be well used. An event-planning tool can help members make collective decisions about key aspects of any event. Where will it be held? When? Who's bringing the wine?

Often, this feature also has an RSVP feature, which can track those who have confirmed, declined, or are on the maybe list. Also, the RSVP feature can be more robust than simply who's attending or not; it can be used to note things like how many children are coming or how many vegetarian meals should be ordered.

Figure 4.8

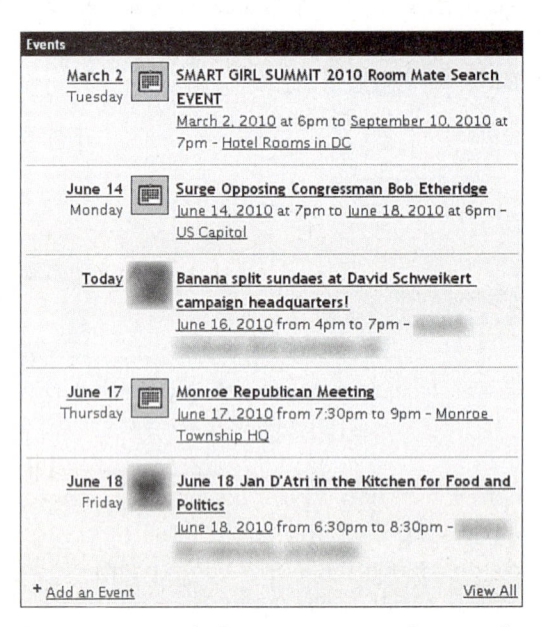

The savvy politicos at smartgirlpolitics.ning.com use the event function to plan meetings, rallies, and events.

The RSVP function also allows guests to get acquainted prior to the event and helps them connect after the fact. In addition, the RSVP function creates a list that can be accessed to issue invitations for future events.

The Groups Feature

The groups feature allows members to connect in meaningful ways through niche topics or relationships related to the network. For example, a parent network may have groups for parents of different ages—babies, toddlers, preschoolers, school age, tweens, and teens. Another network might have groups to connect members living in close geographic proximity to one another. This feature can aid administrators with setting up real-world events to promote their product, cause, or activity. Or they can simply foster community. (You'll find more information about in-person get-togethers in Chapter 12.)

Figure 4.9

Posting Up (postingup.2dogs.com), the official social network of the Detroit Pistons, features both new groups and popular groups.

The Polling Feature

Whether you want to conduct a quick lunch menu poll or poll for political opinions, the function of a survey can be very useful. Some polls are instant polls taking the pulse of a group during a moment in time. Other polls are conducted over a period of time.

Figure 4.10

The Connected Peace Corps community surveys members on their plans to help Haiti at npca-social.ning.com.

Generally speaking, polls within social networks are not academic surveys with checks and balances and ethical review. Rather, they are another way for members of the community to connect and contribute information.

> **CLOUD SURFING**
>
> Two popular poll tools are Doodle (doodle.com) and Polldaddy (polldaddy.com).

The Ratings Feature

Ratings allow users to share an opinion about some form of content within the community. They might cast a vote in favor or against a particular blog post, photograph, or video.

Most networks have a ratings system of some sort. It could be a polar scale where things are good or bad. You may be familiar with Digg's thumbs-up or thumbs-down system.

Other ratings systems are based on a quality scale, where one is the worst rating and the top number is the best rating. Things could be voted on with five stars or five cars, or whatever other icon makes sense for that particular network. You're likely familiar with this from reading movie and restaurant reviews in your local paper.

Figure 4.11

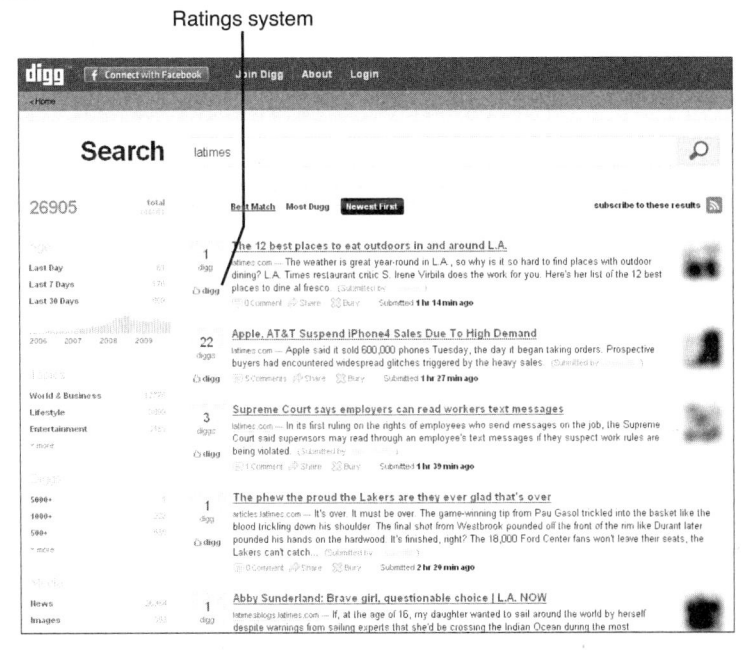

A search for the L.A. Times *on Digg brings up numerous articles. Note the thumbs-up icon ratings system.*

The Blog Feature

Very literally, blogging is any form of writing on the web, whether that's text on the screen, video, photos, or other types of content. The word is a mainstream abbreviation of "web log," a phrase used to refer to a space on the Internet where content creators (not necessarily professionals) share news and opinions on a regular basis or at random when inspiration strikes. Your social network can include a feature to allow members to blog directly on your network or to share the blog they maintain elsewhere on the Internet.

For many users, a blog is a type of online diary that chronicles their personal life in whatever way they choose. Other blogs are more business oriented and are written with an organizational objective in mind. These objectives might include sharing recent research, announcing new products, or marketing new services.

Part 2: Shopping for a Social Network Service

> **CLOUD SURFING**
>
> Writers can create a blog in minutes on Blogger (www.blogger.com), TypePad (www.typepad.com), or WordPress (www.wordpress.com). Blogger and WordPress are for the most part free platforms, while TypePad charges a monthly fee after a free trial period.

The blog feature on your social network can work in a few ways. Some networks have a built-in blog where members can post their thoughts in a longer format than provided in the status updates. These might be individual blogs for each member of a network or they might collaborate on a communal blog. Alternatively, some networks provide facility for the external blogs of members to be re-published or simply linked to from within the network for easy reading by network members.

Figure 4.12

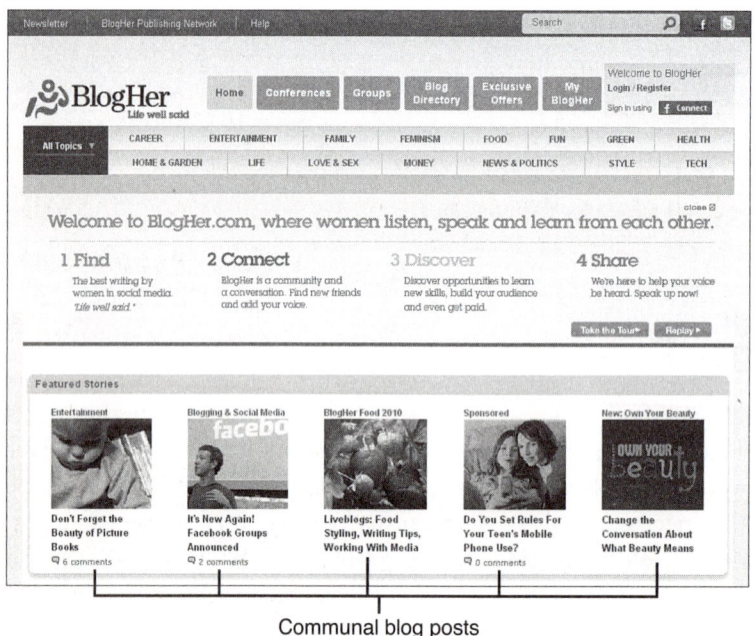

The BlogHer community features selected contributions to its communal blog at the top of www.blogher.com.

If you decide to have a communal blog, review the content moderation discussion in Chapter 9. You must consider who uploads and moderates the posts as well as any technical support your users might need. If you offer individual blogs, plan for sufficient storage and disaster recovery. Think about any limits on size, content, or other use of the blog. The discussion about back office costs in Chapter 5 will orient you to these technical considerations.

Blog sharing can be a great tool for generating dynamic content and for fostering relationships within the network. There is no right or wrong format here. Short or long, communal or personal, internal or external—blogs are all equally valid contributions to your overall network.

The Chat Feature

The chat feature allows closed one-on-one or group conversations between members who are online at the same time. (Remember that group conversations can happen within the forums feature.) Often generated in a sidebar or pop-up window, members can send and respond to short text messages. Chat conversations are not often documented for future reference or publication.

Networks often provide some sort of indicator about who's online as part of the chat feature. Ask your network service if this functionality is available for your network.

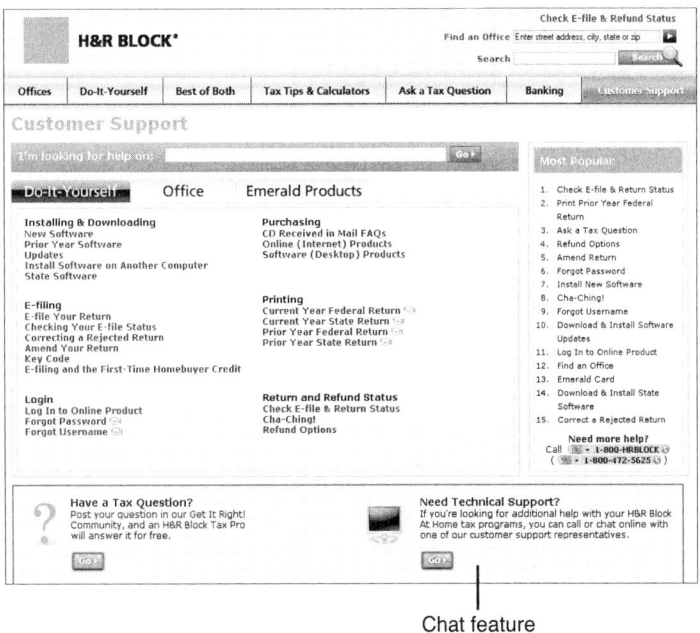

Figure 4.13

H&R Block offers online customers technical support by phone or online chat within its KickApps-powered community at www.hrblock.com.

Chat is a great opportunity for administrators to engage with members, thank them for participating, or acknowledge a contribution they've made to the community.

The Music Feature

Just as the name suggests, the music feature allows members to upload and share music both within the network and across the Internet. Music clips, complete songs, and entire albums can be shared and enjoyed by all.

> **AVOID THE FAIL**
>
> Music sharing leads to the tricky topic of copyright infringement. The laws on copyright vary around the world, but in general it is an infraction of copyright law to distribute a copyrighted work without compensating the original author. As a general rule, independent artists are flexible enough to be able to grant permission when requested. However, artists represented by the big music companies must defer to their representatives. Of course, even the music moguls understand the value of a fan endorsement in spreading the word about a particular band. You can read more about this tricky topic at en.wikipedia.org/wiki/File_sharing.

The Description Feature

The description feature allows administrators to share an explanation of the purpose and content of the network. The information can be brief or long winded, but should always be informative. For members, the description aids them in understanding the topic, focus, and purpose of the network. For the administrators, it is a space to promote the network and also an opportunity to keep current members up-to-date with the latest news and information. Often administrators also use this description space to introduce and humanize the people behind the network.

The Notes Feature

The notes feature provides the opportunity to add additional pages of information to the network. Administrators find this feature useful for sharing material, such as an "About Us" page or answers to commonly asked questions. Notes pages can enrich and enhance the *static content* of the website.

> **DEFINITION**
>
> **Static content** is content on a website that does not change. It is constant (until it is edited for current content).

The Text Box

The text box feature is very useful for adding additional information to your social network. Text boxes can be used to publish plain text information and also to publish HTML web code with more complex information. The simple version can be used to create a box of text that includes contact details, an inspiring quote, or a mission statement. The HTML version can be used to add things such as a Facebook or Twitter widget to your community. Sites like Facebook and Twitter provide the HTML that can be copied and pasted into a text box.

This feature is useful to members wanting to share content from outside the network with fellow members. It is also helpful to administrators who can share content from the network's outposts within the network. (There's more about outposts in Chapter 13 when we talk about enhancing your network with social media.) More than one text box can be placed in the network layout.

Figure 4.14

Twitter provides users with the HTML code that can be used in a text box feature of any social network.

The RSS Feature

Spend any time at all surfing the web and you've probably seen an invitation to subscribe to the RSS (Really Simple Syndication) feed for a website or blog. You may even be familiar with the RSS icon that has been adopted by many sites.

Figure 4.15

The orange square and concentric semicircles are familiar to web browsers looking for an RSS feed.

The RSS feature allows administrators to feed in network-related news from websites, blogs, and other social networks. The RSS feature can also be set up to allow members to export content from the network to share in other websites and blogs. In a sense, RSS is a content streaming tool that pushes content to the reader.

At its simplest, RSS is a way of syndicating content. Think of it as you would syndicated TV programs like *Star Trek* or *Friends*, where the program is created in one location and transmitted for viewing in multiple alternate locations. RSS works the same way on the web by taking content created in one location and making it available in infinite other locations on the Internet. Sometimes it turns up as referenced content on another site (your network, for example) or it appears in an RSS reader, such as Google Reader (reader.google.com) for reading much like an unformatted magazine or giant ticker tape.

> **FLICKERS OF INSIGHT**
>
> While RSS is commonly understood to stand for Really Simple Syndication, it also refers to Rich Site Summary, but both refer to the same thing.

The benefit of RSS to your social network is twofold. You can automatically flow content of interest to your community with RSS feeds while simultaneously making your content available elsewhere on the web with a feed of your site's content going out. Because the web is constantly changing, RSS makes it easy to ensure that you are referencing the most recent version of the content available.

For users, RSS is a time-saver. Instead of manually checking each of your bookmarked websites for new information, RSS shows you at a glance when there is new content. Another benefit is that unlike subscribing to a newsletter, subscribing to an RSS feed is an anonymous activity, which helps ensure privacy. For content providers (that's your social network), the further advantage is that readers control their subscription to your content, thus avoiding the risks of failed unsubscribe requests via e-mail.

While the specific RSS subscriber details are for the most part anonymous, website owners (that includes you as owner of a network with a web address) can check the number of RSS readers referencing their content. Google Feedburner (www.feedburner.com) provides summary data and sophisticated analytic tools for free.

Figure 4.16

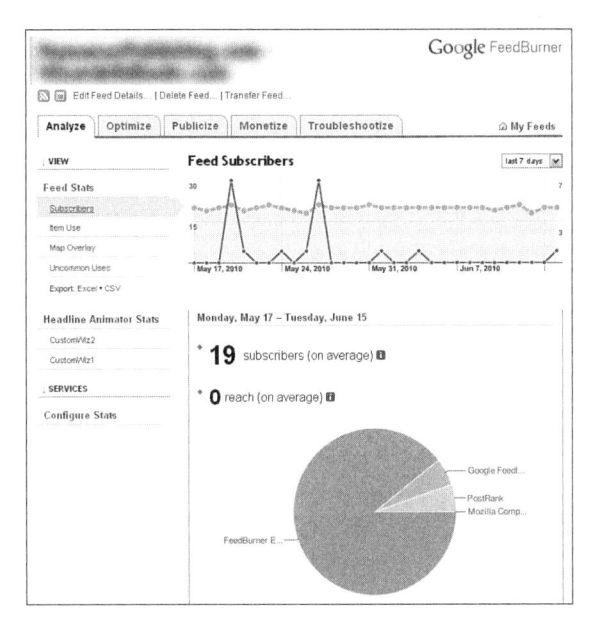

In this example, the data at www.feedburner.com reveals that this blog has an average of 19 RSS readers during a particular week.

CLOUD SURFING

For a more technical explanation of RSS, visit www.whatisrss.com for a one-page overview and links to further reading.

Import

So you've found some RSS feeds that would be of interest to your community. You now must decide whether or not to make the entire feed available to your membership. By bringing content from outside sources to your community automatically you have frequent fresh content for community members.

> **AVOID THE FAIL**
>
> You must decide whether to allow only RSS feeds selected by your administrators or whether to allow feeds from all users. If you do, look for a widget suitable for your social network service to facilitate this.

Sometimes, it makes more sense to review the content and only post links to the most relevant, informative, and entertaining posts. Reviewing relevant items that appear in your RSS subscriptions should take only a few minutes each day (assuming you're not subscribed to hundreds of sources!). Items of interest can then be flagged or forwarded to appear in your stream automatically.

Export

If you want to export the content from your social network so it's easily available to others outside your community, set up an RSS feed for others to subscribe to. Your web design guru can aid with this bit of code and the appropriate icon (remember the little orange square?). By creating content of interest to others and making it easily available, you inexpensively spread the word about your community.

The Badges Feature

Through the badges feature, the network can be easily promoted across the Internet. Websites, blogs, and other networks allied with the featured network can display the badge to promote their support of the network quickly and easily. This is a very valuable promotional tool for administrators and offers members an easy way to exercise their bragging rights.

Badges are the digital equivalent of those nifty bits of fabric that Scouts earn for learning new skills and doing good deeds. Badges are typically an attractive graphic that you can display anywhere that HTML can be inserted. The graphic typically contains a clickable link back to a site or location of interest. On the Internet, users proudly display digital badges to celebrate who they are and what they do.

Figure 4.17

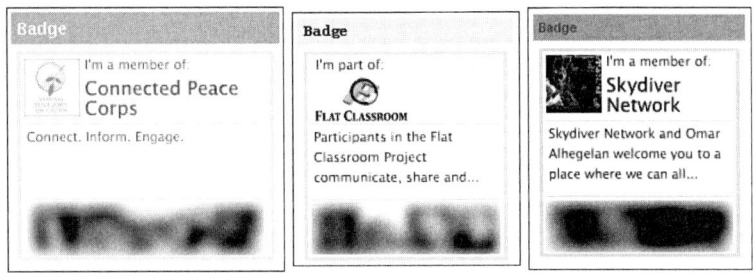

These are badges on Ning networks. The badges look very similar, making them familiar to users.

Membership badges are common, as are badges for events—both virtual events and those in the real world. You'll also see badges related to suppliers who are valued by the blogger. You might also see money-related badges requesting donations or suggesting payment through PayPal.

Figure 4.18

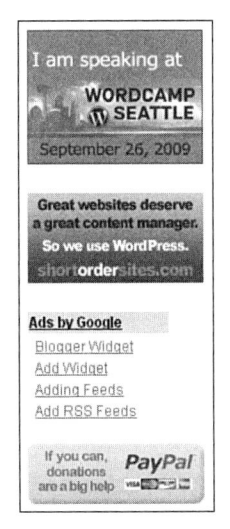

In this example from seehowtwo.com, visitors see an event badge, a supplier badge, and a PayPal donation badge in the lower-right corner.

Location-based services like Foursquare, Gowalla, and Miso are leading the way with a trend toward badges for activities. With each *check-in* on the service, users come closer to unlocking the related badge. For example, check-ins at five different Starbucks locations will unlock the barista badge on Foursquare.

> **DEFINITION**
>
> A **check-in** happens when a user announces his presence at a particular location. This is usually done with a smartphone or, occasionally, through a web browser on a computer at that location. Check-in services access global positioning satellites (GPS) to determine the person's approximate location.

For many users, collecting digital badges is just a bit of fun. For others, it's a way to showcase the needs of the site and make a discreet plea for support. Consider how you can make badges work for your community.

> **CLOUD SURFING**
>
> Digital badges are such a hit that users can now purchase real-world versions, which are cotton-stitched, Velcro badges from Nerd Merit Badges at www.nerdmeritbadges.com. Kitsch or trend? It's hard to say, but fun nonetheless.

The Birthdays Feature

Finally, if appropriate, the birthdays feature highlights members' birthdays to the rest of the membership for purposes of celebrating, honoring or, perhaps, good-natured old-age teasing of fellow members. Only those members who enter their birth date and set their privacy controls to share it publicly are listed in the birthday announcements.

Overall, there are many, many features that can be part of a network. Some platforms, like Ning and Wall.fm, offer a limited set of available features similar to those just described. Other services, like BuddyPress, have many developers creating and sharing new features for the platform. And then there is the limitless potential of features developed for custom networks through platforms like SocialGO and ONEsite.

Remember that your social network will always be made up of people with a wide variety of computer skills. Many will be comfortable with the simple features like the activity feed and forums, and that's all they'll ever use. More advanced users will expect and utilize a greater number of features.

Features provide many opportunities to customize a network. Select features for your network wisely to provide a rich experience for your network members, while avoiding an overcluttered and confusing page.

The Least You Need to Know

- There are many features for you to choose from when creating your social network.
- Common features include: activities, members, photos, videos, tagging, forums, events, groups, polling, ratings, blog, chat, music, description, notes, text box, RSS, badges, and birthdays.
- Community members will be looking for advanced features.
- Your network is not an isolated part of the Internet; users will want to share both internal and external information using sharing and RSS features.
- Practical tools like a calendar, event planner, and RSVP feature are desirable.
- Informational and organizational tools such as tagging, polls, ratings, and badges may be needed in your network.

What's This Going to Cost?

Chapter 5

In This Chapter

- Confirmation that you can create a network by spending little or no cash
- The range of potential costs from the social network service provider to create and maintain your network
- Additional costs considerations including back office expenses for hosting, storage, bandwidth, and backups
- Understanding the value of time invested in social networking

To create a social network, you will incur some costs. These costs could be expressed as money, time, or a combination of both. How much of each you spend depends on the choices you make. The features you choose to include, the size of your network, and technical decisions such as hosting and data backup can all cost something.

In this chapter, we'll talk about the various costs you might encounter. In particular, we'll focus on the technical issues that may result in expenses for your social network. We will discuss these issues in general terms; I recommend that you consult your network provider, social network service, and your go-to tech for more detailed technical information specific to your network.

It's not unusual for the initial purchase of the social network service or software to be the only financial outlay. Once a social network is set up, the costs can shift from cash investment to time investment.

We live in an information economy at a time when thought, opinion, research, and words are of tremendous value. The old adage "time is money" rings true in a new way—think of your time as an important investment in your social network. (And sometimes a few dollars help, too.)

What Will You Pay For?

Almost all of the social network platforms offer a free or inexpensive service, but you can spend lots more money making it exactly what you want. This is the moment where you have to decide which is more important—an enhancement to your network or cash in your wallet. Some of those paid enhancements are cosmetic, while others are related to the technology behind the scenes. Let's walk through the things to consider.

Many businesses and organizations don't want to spend anything to get their social network up and keep it running. That's fine. In fact, that's very common and there are tens of thousands of networks built on free platforms without any paid enhancements.

Even if you plan to spend nothing, I encourage you to read on as this chapter may prompt you to plan for potential expenditures in the future. This will be especially necessary if your network draws a large membership and turns into a hub for your business.

Spending Money

Shopping for anything means keeping a budget in mind. You might be working with a modest budget of a few hundred dollars, or perhaps be lucky enough to have several thousand dollars at your disposal. Let's start by considering the cost of the network service itself.

	Free Trial $0	Free $0	$ <$100/year	$$ <$500/year	$$$ $500+/year
Ning	Yes	No	Yes	Yes	Yes
Wall.fm	Yes	Yes	No (only free service at this price level)	Yes	Yes
SocialGO	Yes	Yes	No (only free service at this price level)	Yes	Yes
BuddyPress	Yes	Yes	No	No	No
KickApps	Yes	No	No	Yes	Yes
ONEsite	Yes	No	No	No	Yes

Free

Free social network services are available from Wall.fm, SocialGO, and BuddyPress. Wall.fm and SocialGO both have paid options that offer enhanced features or functions. All three free network services work well for community groups and other volunteer-driven organizations. Family groups and educators working with a group of students also use these networks to great effect.

> **CLOUD SURFING**
>
> You can download and install BuddyPress for free or you can visit testbp.org to explore a sample installation with all the default settings intact. Visitors are encouraged to play with features and modifications, as all items return to the default setting at the end of your session.

As BuddyPress is based on open source software, it's reasonable to assume a free version will be available in perpetuity. However, SocialGO is the only service that makes the promise "free forever" right on their pricing grid.

Bare-Bones Budget

Let's define a bare-bones budget as one that allots less than $100 per year for paid social network services. Ning is the only paid service that meets this criteria, with its Ning Mini option. The fees are currently $2.95 per month, or $19.95 a year, prepaid. Ning requires you to set up billing and payment information at the launch of your network, but if you cancel your service within 30 days there's no charge. If you forget to cancel, Ning offers a grace period of up to 60 days during which you can request a refund.

Ning offers an affordable option ideal for community groups, classrooms, and families.

Spend Some

Our "spend some" category is for network services that cost less than $500 per year. This level of service is available from Ning, Wall.fm, SocialGO, and KickApps. Common reasons for spending some money on your network include the following:

- Removal of the social network service's branding
- Increased bandwidth

- Increased storage
- Unlimited membership
- Enhanced technical support
- Your own domain name
- Control over advertising

With costs such as Wall.fm's $25 to $30 per month, small businesses, professional associations, and others seeking a branded social network might invest at this level.

Sky's the Limit

Some organizations have more money to spend on their social network—whether it's $2,000, $200,000, or more. For our purposes, let's discuss these larger budgets as ones that allot over $500 per year for social network costs. Ning, Wall.fm, SocialGO, KickApps, and ONEsite all offer services at this level, which can include the following:

- Monetization options, such as membership fees and a shopping cart
- Dedicated or priority technical support
- Network setup service
- Custom design service

Other Costs

You may end up spending money on other network-related expenses. For example, you might hire a WordPress expert to set up your WordPress website and the BuddyPress plug-in. This can cost anywhere from $50 to $2,000 or more. Once your social network is set up, you could then take over managing it. You might also pay for graphic design elements, content, or credit card merchant fees.

Back Office Costs

So far, we've only evaluated the options based on the fees of the social network service providers. To make your network work the way you want it to, you must also consider costs related to technical things that most people won't see or know about—the *back office* functions. These costs cover a number of technical issues that are considerations for any website.

> **DEFINITION**
>
> The **back office** is all of the structure behind your social network, including the computers it runs on, the services that it uses to connect one part to another, and how it functions within the broader scope of the Internet.

Hosting

Your network has to live somewhere on the Internet, as do all websites. You'll need a computer, more specifically a *server*, to host your network. Your organization may choose to host your network on the server of your social network service provider, or you can use an in-house server or a hosting company to house your network instead.

> **DEFINITION**
>
> A **server** is a computer whose operating system and hardware have been designed to provide information to a large audience at high speed with a minimum of potential issues due to failure.

Anyone interested in your network will find it by visiting its web address—something like the familiar format of www.webaddress.com. This web address is sometimes referred to as a *domain name*. The World Wide Web is composed of the connections between millions of these domains. In order for users to find your social network, it must be part of a domain, so it has to be hosted somewhere.

> **DEFINITION**
>
> A **domain name** is the technical term for a web address normally belonging to one company. For example, www.google.com is a familiar domain name.

As mentioned earlier in this section, you have three options for hosting:

- Option 1: Using hosting provided by your social network service
- Option 2: Hosting on your organization's server
- Option 3: Hiring a hosting company

Let's talk about each type so that you can make an informed decision for your network.

The simplest option, Option 1, is the free or inexpensive hosting included in your social network service package. By setting up your network on Ning, Wall.fm, SocialGO, or KickApps, your network is hosted on the service's respective server. If what they offer fulfills your needs, then you don't need to worry about hosting.

Many organizations prefer to have the web address of their social network match the domain name of their overall website. (You'll recall we talked about this in Chapter 3.) For this reason, many organizations choose to move the hosting of their community to a paid server—either Option 2 or Option 3.

If you plan to host on your own server (Option 2), your organization will either purchase or lease a computer that can support your network and make it available on the Internet. The purchase and maintenance of a server is a significant cost of anywhere from a few hundred dollars to $10,000 or more. This option gives your organization the greatest degree of flexibility and control over the content and operation of your network, including the domain name issue.

However, hosting your own server comes with great responsibility and tremendous risk. I would recommend this option only for companies that already have a dedicated IT staff with the experience to manage the machinery and provide ongoing maintenance and support. Many organizations perceive this as a cost-saving measure when quite the opposite is true when you weigh the potential costs of back office failures. We'll talk about these later in this chapter.

If you do not have the infrastructure to support an in-house server or you decide to host your network somewhere other than with your social network service, there are many services that offer hosting (Option 3). Some charge a monthly or annual fee, and a few offer free service.

Some free options include:

- 0000free.com
- www.000webhost.com
- www.x10hosting.com

Paid hosting is available from:

- www.1and1.com
- www.rackspace.com
- www.godaddy.com

The following sections introduce considerations related to hosting, including fault tolerance, volume of storage, bandwidth, backups, and restoration. Read these sections before making any hosting decision, as each company offers slightly different hosting packages. This will help you decide which hosting option to use and which hosting service is best for your network.

Volume of Storage

Volume of storage is an important consideration, as many hosting packages have a base amount of storage and then charge for storage over and above that amount. For example, your hosting package might include 5GB of storage, but once your network's membership and content grows to a certain point you will need 6GB or more. Consider the fees for that increased storage and plan for them. This is a good problem to have, as it's an indicator that your community is growing.

Each hosting arrangement has some restrictions on usage depending on the package available. For example, if you host with a network service like Wall.fm you'll get 5GB of storage for free, whereas SocialGO offers 1GB of storage for free. The size required will vary based on the number of users, the type and volume of content shared, and the number of features included in your network. How you and your members use that capacity can be somewhat controlled by administrators. All platforms sell more capacity.

There are tools available to aid administrators in limiting use of the network. This prevents any single user from swallowing up the capacity of the network for his or her own purposes. For example, BuddyPress plug-ins allow administrators to limit the number of blogs per user and groups per user. Meanwhile, KickApps has a 20-user limit for sending messages, so each member can only send messages to 20 friends at a time. You might also limit the number of photos that a user can upload each month or restrict the size of video files that can be shared. These rich media are of much greater concern than e-mail type messages, as each photo or video uses up many megabytes, or even gigabytes, of storage at once.

As with everything, there are pros and cons to limits within a social network. Establishing limits can help ensure fair access for all members. It can also reduce the risk of unwanted or excessive content from a small group of users overwhelming the system. However, some users may perceive limits negatively and as an impediment to their full enjoyment of the community. Once again, this is an area where you need to do what's best for your network.

Many social networks seem to echo the limits set by Facebook. Individual profiles are limited to 5,000 friend connections. Event organizers are restricted to messaging not more than 5,000 attendees. And members are limited to 200 photos per album. For many users these limits are very generous and more than the average user would ever leverage.

More Bandwidth

Bandwidth determines how quickly people can access your network. If the connection is too slow, they may become frustrated and less likely to interact with your network. Think of bandwidth as a pipe filled with strands of yarn (representing your active users) moving through it. If someone logs on, a strand is added; when a user logs off, a strand is removed. At first, it might seem there is lots of room, but as more users access the network at the same time there is less room in the pipe. Too many users at once can clog the pipe so that it's difficult to add new strands of yarn or to move any of the existing strands. When the pipe is full, service slows down for everyone.

> **DEFINITION**
>
> **Bandwidth** is the technical term for the size of the pipe moving your information to and from your network. A bigger pipe generally moves more data at the same time than a smaller pipe. Bandwidth can range from dial-up connections of 50kb to dedicated fiber lines that move megabytes per second. Data moves only as quickly as the narrowest part of the pipe can handle.

Most hosting services provide a medium-fast solution in their regular packages. This is the equivalent of cable or DSL service into your home. If your community is very active with as many as 100 simultaneous users or you have substantial amounts of content, as in hundreds of photos or dozens of videos being uploaded or viewed simultaneously, then you'll want to consider paying for more bandwidth.

For example, SocialGO offers three levels of service: Free, Premium, and Concierge. The Free level includes 10GB of bandwidth, while the Premium service offers 50GB, and the Concierge service includes 100GB. Your costs increase depending on the level of service. There is no charge for the Free service, the Premium service costs $24.99 per month, and the Concierge service costs $149.99 per month. Now, keep in mind that the charges are not only for bandwidth, as the services and features also increase at the higher levels.

Figure 5.1

	Concierge WE BUILD IT FOR YOU	Premium ALL THE FEATURES	Free BASIC + ADVERTS
Monthly subscription	$149.99/mo.	$24.99/mo.	–
Free trial period	7 DAYS FREE	1 MONTH FREE	FREE FOREVER
Included storage	UNLIMITED	UNLIMITED	1 GB Storage
Included bandwidth	UNLIMITED	UNLIMITED	10 GB Bandwidth
Standard features	✔	✔	✔
No SocialGO advertising	✔	✔	✘
Run your own advertising	✔	✔	✘
Widget store	✔	✔	✘
Use your own URL	✔	✔	✘
Live audio/video chat	✔	✔	✘
Advanced layout manager	✔	✔	✘
Advanced developer access	✔	✔	✘
Priority Support	✔	✘	✘
White Label	✔	Add $19.99/mo.	✘
Member Billing	✔	Add $19.99/mo.	✘
GO IM Premium	Add $9.99/mo.	Add $9.99/mo.	✘
Setup and Design Service	✔	Add $349.99/once.	✘

SocialGO publishes a simple three-tiered fee structure for easy reference.

There are no firm guidelines for determining how much bandwidth you'll need. The size of your community, its rate of growth, and the amount of content they share will all influence bandwidth. For most networks, it's a matter of launching the network with a plan for expansion, if needed, and monitoring the use of bandwidth so you can implement a bandwidth upgrade if/when it's needed. One of the advantages of using a site like SocialGO is that you can seamlessly upgrade to more bandwidth.

Backups and Restoration

Just as with your computer at home, you want to ensure that you back up your network—both the infrastructure as well as the content. An automated *backup* system copies your files daily or weekly, or whatever time interval works for your network. The consequences of losing all your network settings, member profiles, and related data are immense.

> **DEFINITION**
>
> **Backup** refers to the process of making a copy of your software, files, and settings that can be used to restore a computer if it should break.

Original material used to create a network is backed up on your computer. However, this backup does not include comments or other content uploaded by members. Rather, you need to back up what's changed online. Some hosting companies will do a backup, but most won't unless you pay for the service. If you host your network with the social network service, then there are backups made on most platforms but the frequency and accessibility of those backups may be inconvenient.

You need to check that your backup is sufficient for your community. A backup system involves regularly making a copy of your network to be used if something bad happens to your data, the software, or the physical machines where it is hosted. When you decide where to host your network, review what backup procedures are included with your package. You want to avoid a single backup copy that is overwritten each time your network is backed up. A more robust and useful backup routine should include:

- A daily backup of what changed today.
- A complete backup of the entire network weekly.
- A library of several weeks of backup so you have older versions to restore, if necessary.

In order to have the more robust backup system described above, you may have to pay for the additional service from your hosting company.

A backup solution is complete only if the network can be successfully restored from the stored data. It is advisable to have your network host conduct a test restore in a virtualized environment. This means they would create a copy of your network on a test machine, deliberately break it, and then work to restore it from the backup. By doing a test restore you can ensure that the correct information is being archived at every backup. In this way, if the network should fail in earnest, a restoration can be completed with confidence.

Of course, all this backup and restoration costs money.

Fault Tolerance

Another consideration when making hosting decisions is *fault tolerance*. Faults are things that happen to equipment and software. Equipment can fail for any number of reasons (age, heat, shock, etc.). A fault tolerant server will keep operating even if a failure occurs. Similarly, the software aspect of your network can be made fault tolerant with a redundant copy of your software and data on another server. It's important to note that a redundant copy is not the same thing as a backup copy.

> **DEFINITION**
>
> **Fault tolerance** is the concept of making a computer system resilient enough to withstand a failure of one or more physical components. This concept can be extended to include a duplicate copy of software and data. A fault tolerant system will continue to operate even if there is a hardware or software failure.

If there is a fault of either software or hardware, administrators for your host server will be notified automatically, usually by e-mail or pager. The administrator can then arrange for the failed equipment or data to be repaired or replaced and returned to normal operation.

How well will your network tolerate a failure? The social network services may already have a fault tolerant system. However, if you have elected to host your network elsewhere, then be sure to consider fault tolerance. I suggest you make inquiries with your hosting company to determine what their procedures are on this topic.

Other Costs

Beyond the network service fees and the back office costs, there are a few other potential expenses to consider. In this section, we'll review two potential expenses—functionality and mobility.

Additional Functionality

As we've discussed, there are numerous features readily available from all social network services. To make use of all the available features, you may need to upgrade to a more expensive level of service. There may also be things you want to do that will require the creation of specialized tools that bring your vision to life. This kind of enhancement and innovation can add to the vibrancy and cache of your network, especially if you come up with something no one else has done before.

Dreaming of enhanced features is wonderful, but the development and testing of those new features will have costs. Programmers or web developers need to be hired to make the back end of the technology work. In addition, it is advisable to test these new features in a parallel or beta version of the network before going live. The last thing you want to do is break your existing network while testing a new feature. Nor do you want to frustrate users with a lame-duck version of the feature if it doesn't roll out the way you'd planned.

Figure 5.2

	MINI For Small Groups	PLUS Advanced Features	PRO Built for Scale
	The simplest and fastest way to set up a social network for your classroom, community group, small non-profit or family	The tools and features you need to customize your Ning Network with greater design flexibility and control over your members' experience	The ideal solution for building a custom social experience with premium add-ons, integration options, and more bandwidth and storage
	SIGN UP	SIGN UP	SIGN UP
Price	$2.95 Monthly or $19.95/year* (save 44%)	$19.95 Monthly or $199.95/year* (save 16%)	$49.95 Monthly or $499.95/year* (save 17%)
Ning Sponsored Networks	Education		
Members	Up to 150	Unlimited	Unlimited
Storage	1 GB	10 GB	20 GB + upgrade
Bandwidth	10 GB	100 GB	200 GB + upgrade
FEATURES			
Blog	✓	✓	✓
Photos	✓	✓	✓
Forum	✓	✓	✓
Birthdays	✓	✓	✓
Video embeds	✓	✓	✓
Video uploads with branded players		Continued access to current videos	✓

Ning service begins with a $2.95 per month Mini account, but many hosts will want to upgrade to Ning Plus or Ning Pro to access enhanced features.

Enhancing functionality with a custom-created feature for your network can come with a big price tag including the potential expense of moving your network to a social network service provider who can support the enhancement. (Ning and Wall.fm are less able to provide these enhancements.) Of course, everyone has a different perception of money—for some, a $150 investment is too much while others are overwhelmed only at the five figure mark. Whatever your financial perspective, custom features require some cold hard cash. Often the investment is well worth it. Check out these sites built by KickApps to experience some custom features:

- The band Stone Temple Pilots' (www.stonetemplepilots.com) community includes a music video player where the viewer can select one of four videos to accompany the featured song.

- Try out H&R Block's Ask a Tax Question feature at getitright.hrblock.com for an example of a custom interactive form.
- Even Microsoft has a unique feature; check out their three-part sliding banner promotion at www.microsoft.com.

Before you create something awesome like these examples for your community, you'll need to find someone to create it for you. I suggest you start by consulting your social network service provider—either directly or through the relevant help community (listed in Appendix B). As with hiring any contractor, do your homework by checking out some of their other projects, getting a quote in writing, and checking references.

Mobility

Is your network a community on the go? If so, you may want to develop a *mobile* version that can travel with members on their smartphones. This can be as simple as generating a mobile-friendly version of the appearance of your network that can be easily read and navigated on a cell phone screen. Or you could go as far as creating a mobile application that echoes the functionality of your network.

> **DEFINITION**
>
> **Mobile** technology is any computer, device, or system that allows users to connect to the Internet and each other while away from traditional wired computers and phones.

Think of your community as having two guises—one for computer use and one for mobile device use. The content is the same but the way it is represented varies. Compare your experience on Facebook with the same experience on the iPhone or Android app for Facebook. You'll see differences in how much information is displayed and how it can be used. The information from your community is the same, but the web versus mobile experience varies.

Developing a mobile solution involves hiring a programmer or web developer who can work with you to create a streamlined version of your platform and content. A programmer can create a mobile version of your network in HTML that will work on all web browser–enabled mobile devices. I know one organization that did this recently for about $400, but your costs might be more or less. You may want to go one step further and create software for the most popular platforms—iPhone, DROID, and BlackBerry—but the cost is higher. The cost to develop an application, or app, can vary widely depending on what you want the app to do and how complex it is. I've heard of projects like this starting at $2,500 for a simple app and of more complex apps costing $10,000 and up. Usually there is also an annual license fee to the app developer for the app, which can vary widely.

Users in Europe and the United States are most fully engaged in mobile use at present. Mobile use of the Internet is definitely on the rise worldwide, and more and more users will come to expect this kind of adaptation.

The Value of Time

What is your time (or that of your employees, contractors, or volunteers) worth? You could think of the time in terms of an hourly salary, be that $10 or $100 per hour. However, I encourage you to think about the value of time as the value of the results from that time spent.

What is it worth to you to increase your number of qualified prospects? What kind of a price tag do you put on customer satisfaction? What's the value of reputation management? All of these things can be a boon or a bust for your business. Investing time can increase your sales and reduce your risks.

The Least You Need to Know

- Social network services are available at various price points from free to expensive.
- Even if you decide to use a free service, it's a good idea to be aware of potential costs your network may encounter as it grows.
- Hard costs can include back office costs such as hosting, storage, bandwidth, and backups.
- Additional costs may be incurred if you elect to create custom features or a mobile option for your community.
- You will need to invest time in your social network.

Selecting a Social Network Service

Chapter 6

In This Chapter

- A review of your primary and secondary network objectives
- Features you need versus features you want
- Fulfilling your customer service and technical support requirements
- Questions to ask yourself when choosing a network service
- Trial offers to experience the network services before committing

Once you have a handle on the social network services available and the features they offer, you need to decide which service you'll use. This chapter explores some common considerations to keep in mind as you make your decision.

Establishing a social network has so many variables—what platform to use, the most useful features to include, and the customization required are just a few of the things to consider. After all the thinking done so far, it's now time to make a choice.

What Am I Looking For?

Chapter 3 offered a quick introduction to six common social networking platforms. With so many possible service providers, deciding which one to use can be overwhelming. To make your decision, consider your network objectives as defined in Chapter 2.

- Influencing
- Organizing
- Education
- Rallying
- Evangelizing
- Fundraising
- Sales
- Convenience
- Eliminating geographic borders
- Just for fun

What did you select as your primary and secondary objectives? It's important to keep this top of mind with every network decision, including what service to use.

> **FLICKERS OF INSIGHT**
>
> There are many social network service providers beyond the six featured in this book. Appendix B includes a list with website addresses for further exploration.

What Features Do I Need?

So often we have to choose between what we want and what we need. As you narrow down your selection for social network service, decide on the features that are vital to your network as they address your needs. Then, list those features that are on your wish list—you know, the features that would be nice to have but aren't essential. (Revisit Chapter 4 for an overview of common features.)

In the following table, you can make note of the features you need, those on your wish list, and those that don't matter to you at all. If you're at all intimidated by the process, start small. Pick five key features and get started with those. You can always add more features later, just as you can remove any features that are not working for you and your community.

Features	Need	Wish For	Don't Need
Activity			
Members			
Photos and Videos			
Tagging			
Forums			
Events			
Groups			
Polling			
Ratings			
Blog			
Chat			
Music			
Description			
Notes			
Text Box			
RSS			
Badges			
Birthdays			

Customization

For some social network services, filling in your information for the default features and appearance are all that's required to get your network going. However, all networks can be customized. For many networks only minor changes can be made, such as a new color scheme or adding a logo. For other networks, more complex changes are required. These changes can further modify the appearance of the network or add custom features.

Customization happens on the largest scale when you must integrate a brand with an established appearance with your social network. Integrating logos, color schemes, mailing lists, and customer databases are all examples of the kinds of customization that can happen. Beyond appearance, custom features that accomplish specific objectives and engage members in unique ways are desirable but often expensive. Deciding what those features might do and then developing the technology to make that feature happen is key.

Customer Service Resources

When shopping for a social network service, customer service resources to aid your efforts to build and maintain your social network will be vitally important. Different platforms offer different types and levels of support resources, be they forums, phone assistance, or e-mail assistance. Ask yourself these questions:

- Are you a do-it-yourself type who's willing to get in there and experiment?
- Are you comfortable doing Google searches for answers and asking for help from strangers in discussion forums?
- Do you prefer to document your questions and the official replies with e-mail correspondence?
- Do you learn best by speaking with someone on the phone?

Your preferred communication style may influence the service you select. Customer service contact is currently provided by the featured network services as follows:

Service	Web	E-Mail/Chat	Phone
Ning	Yes	No	No
Wall.fm	Yes	Yes	No
SocialGO	Yes	Yes	Yes
BuddyPress	Yes	No	No
KickApps	Yes	Yes	Yes
ONEsite	No	Yes	Yes

Your degree of patience will also influence what kind of help you want. Instant answers aren't going to come from a discussion forum. You must post your query and wait for a reply. Even with phone support you might have to leave a message and wait for a call back, or worse, spend time on hold waiting for someone to answer your call. Only the most custom services offer dedicated support where a staff member is assigned to respond to your needs right away. Of course, this speedy, responsive service comes with a price tag.

Technical Help

When undertaking anything technological, it is reassuring to have a help line available to assist you when you get stuck or, even more important, when things go wrong.

Most network platforms have free community resources available to help solve a given problem. Some of these help resources are run by the companies offering the service while others are created by a community of users. The social network services featured in this book have the following resources:

- help.ning.com
- Wall.fm/help.php
- wpmu.org (for BuddyPress)
- owners.socialgo.com and socialgo.com/help
- kickdeveloper.com (for KickApps)
- ONEsite supports with in-house resources

Online forums both within the service and on tech websites like ZDNet are available. If in doubt, search through Google or Bing; essentially, you pose the question to your browser and hope that someone else has already had your challenge and found a solution by asking the community. If you are unable to find an answer in the search results, then pose the question on an appropriate newsgroup and ask for help. You may have to wait a few hours or a few days for a reply, but generally someone's there and willing to share his or her knowledge. Of course, if your question is extremely specialized or obscure then you might wait a long time for an answer. Be sure to check back for any replies promptly, as busy forums will bury your question and any replies in less than a day.

> **CLOUD SURFING**
>
> ZDNet (www.zdnet.com) is a social network for technology professionals. It includes an extensive archived forum of technology-related questions and answers.

Some services, including Wall.fm and SocialGO, offer on-call support where you can send your question to the team by e-mail or voice-mail and get a response within a few hours or days. Sometimes this support is free; other times, depending on your service package, you are allowed a certain number of questions and above that limit you are charged per call. Get your credit card ready in that case!

> **FLICKERS OF INSIGHT**
>
> If seeking an answer to resolve an error message, be sure to have the error message on hand when you call for help. You can also look for a solution through a search engine by copying the error message into the search box. Be sure to contain it in quotation marks to limit search results to the specific error you are experiencing.

KickApps, ONEsite, and other services offer dedicated support. This is by far the most expensive type, as you're essentially paying for a qualified expert to be on call to answer your questions immediately at any hour of the day. While this is a cost, the cost of downtime on your network may outweigh this expense.

You know where your technical skills lie, and everyone needs help sometimes. Beyond the help forums and hot lines, the solution is often to have a go-to tech—maybe more than one. Whether the list is in your mental Rolodex or on your iPhone, know where to reach the specialists who can help you when you need assistance. The help can come from your husband or best friend, or it can come from paid professionals who bill hourly. Regardless, make sure you're tapped into people who truly know their stuff, as things will go wrong that you can't fix and it's a lot less stressful if you know who you're going to call.

Questions to Ask

If you're still struggling to make a choice, ask yourself these key questions for each network service provider you are considering.

- How can I make my community attractive to visitors? What do they want?
- How do I want to represent my brand online?
- How much money do I have to spend now?
- What level of customer service works for me?
- What technical support do I need?

Work your way through these core questions. It may take some time to find all your answers, and that's okay. Investing the time to prepare will mean you are clear about what you need for your social network. That preparation will help you make an informed choice about your social network service.

> **FLICKERS OF INSIGHT**
>
> Selecting a network service with an interface familiar to users can help you establish your network. If community members are already familiar with the tools, their learning curve won't be as steep and they will be more willing to engage in the content and community of your network. To determine which, if any, social network service is familiar to your audience, evaluate existing networks on similar or related topics and don't forget to ask those likely to join your community.

Trial Offers

I suggest you take advantage of the free trial offers available on Ning, SocialGO, and KickApps. You can also try out BuddyPress and Wall.fm for free. If you're just test driving these services, you may want to use a temporary project name to explore the service as all of the free trial communities will be visible online at the time they are created. Once you've settled on a platform, invest time and energy in branding the network to meet your needs.

Most of the networks can be set up in a few minutes and you can then play with the service to see if it works for you. Experiment with all the features available in your trial offer. Invite a trusted group of those close to your business or project to join as members and experiment with you. In part, your decision will be based on the features and level of service, but you should also consider which service you find easiest to use. The best way to judge this is with hands-on experience.

Maybe one platform is too labor intensive for your purposes or it doesn't have the one feature that really matters to your community. Whatever your judgment of the platform, you'll feel more confident in accepting or rejecting it based on your own experience.

Make the Leap

Don't dither anymore. Truly, this isn't rocket science or brain surgery. If you want to create a social network, get on with it. You can always make changes at a later date, whether that means shifting to a different platform or adding more features. If you're ready, read ahead to Part 5 and its tutorials on several different network services.

While this is an important decision, remember that you can change your mind. If one social network service isn't working for you, then switch to another. Similarly, if a particular service level isn't right, then upgrade or downgrade, as needed.

Having read this far, you know the sorts of issues that you must consider and the time has come to make the leap. Good luck!

The Least You Need to Know

- Be clear on your primary and secondary objectives for your network.
- Decide which features you need and which are only wants.
- Figure out the communication style that works best for you in terms of customer service and technical support.
- Take advantage of the free trial offers available from social network services before you commit.

Part 3

YOUR Social Network

Let's get your network started! In this part, we'll get into practical advice for establishing your network. Naming considerations, the appearance of your network, and a code of conduct to guide your members are all discussed.

We'll also focus our attention on the all-important fuel to keep your network running—content! We'll explore the types of content and how to gather contributions of interest to your members. In a sense, you're driving a digital bus. Take the wheel!

Get Your Network Started

Chapter 7

In This Chapter

- Methods for brainstorming and selecting a network name
- Important name variables to keep in mind: memorability, length, and spelling
- Considering a trademark
- Secure an address and domain name
- Privacy concerns
- Selecting an appearance for your network

Creating a network takes thought and planning. You've already begun the process with what you've read so far and selected a social network service provider. In this chapter, we'll walk through specific considerations, like naming your network and securing your network's domain name. Each of these steps will take you closer to having your network up and running.

Choose a Name Carefully

Deciding on a name for your social network is worth careful thought and consideration. In many cases, the logical name will be the name of your company, organization, or product—you've already chosen that so it's ready to use.

However, there are instances where a network name will be different than the company or product name. For some organizations, the existing name is unrelated to their social network project. For example, Carnival Cruise Lines calls its social network Funville and the band Lynyrd Skynyrd calls their's Skynyrd Nation.

There may also be practical considerations, such as a name that is too long, too hard to spell, or difficult to remember. In other cases, the network name links to the marketing strategy of a particular product, not the company as a whole. In this case, a network built around a product needs to be named for the product. Companies with many products might have multiple social networks. For example, an outdoor outfitters retail chain might have different networks for its fishing, hiking, biking, and kayaking customers. To avoid confusion each network needs its own name.

If you decide to select a unique name for your network, choose it carefully. The name should reflect the feel of the organization, be it formal or informal, humorous or serious. Naming a network is a bit like naming a baby. It requires much discussion and research, a short list of options, market research to test the name with your customers, and, finally, a commitment to the name because the network can't be called "Hey, you!" forever.

Brainstorming

Start by brainstorming a list of possibilities. Don't rule anything out at first, just jot down each idea as it comes up. Bringing together a group of people who are familiar with the organization or project is often a good way to bring out lots of possibilities. This also serves the dual purpose of team building among those who will be advocates for the network once launched.

There are many ways to conduct brainstorm exercises; one that works well for this purpose is to use a mind map. Start with a central idea—in this case the cause, product, or service to be the center of the network—and from there note each idea in thought bubbles. Keep adding until the concept is fully fleshed out and the useful brainstorms are exhausted. (You'll know this is the case when your team starts to toss out goofy or absurd names. When this happens it's definitely time to call it a day.) Through this exercise, key phrases or ideas will repeat and the group can come to a consensus about the ideal network name, or at least a short list of good candidates.

> **CLOUD SURFING**
>
> Mind Meister (www.mindmeister.com) is a free online tool for creating mind maps. The service allows for multiple users to collaborate on the content, as well as paid accounts that offer mobile and offline options.

Figure 7.1

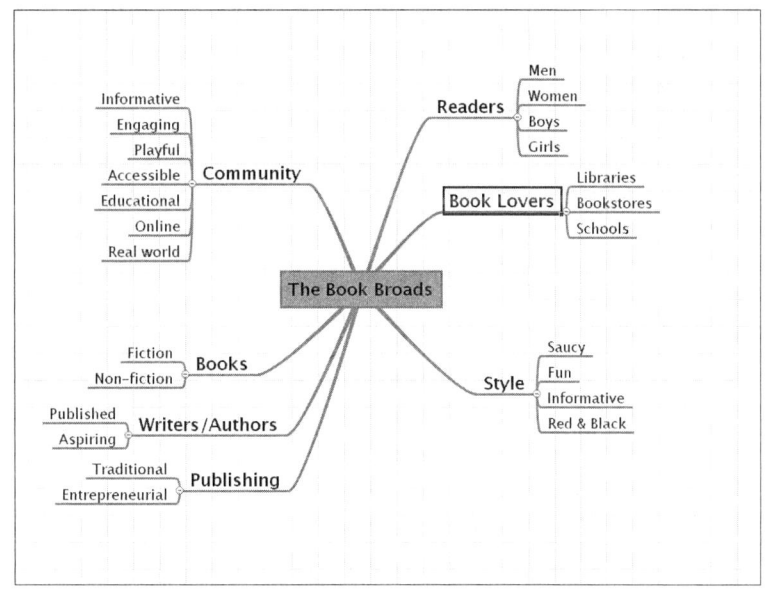

Using Mind Meister, The Book Broads documented a brainstorming session.

Another approach is to use existing text documents that talk about the project to build a word cloud. Simply copy and paste those documents into a word cloud creator such as Wordle and allow the software to generate a word cloud for you.

> **CLOUD SURFING**
>
> Wordle (www.wordle.net) is an online tool for taking text and creating word clouds—images where words are scaled according to their importance in the text provided. Wordle clouds are created under a Creative Commons License so that users can export and distribute, sell, or otherwise share their word clouds for free.

Within word clouds, the most repeated words are made bigger in the illustration drawing your attention to common words and themes used to talk about the project. Scramble the word cloud a couple of times to try different layouts and change your point of view on the words that pop out at you.

Figure 7.2

I built this word cloud at Wordle.net by copying and pasting the manuscript for this chapter.

Of course, brainstorming doesn't have to be high tech. A notepad or flip chart and some coffee can fuel an equally valuable brainstorming session.

After using your preferred brainstorming strategy, identify a short list of potential names for your network and evaluate them based on the following:

- Availability
- Memorability
- Length
- Spelling

Availability

Before committing to any particular name, you should research it. The last thing you want to do is devote a lot of time, energy, and money only to discover that you must abandon the name and start over. Here are some questions to ask yourself:

- Is the name available on my selected social network service? Visit the service's website to check.

- Can I purchase the domain name? Services such as whois.domaintools.com will let you check availability.

- Is someone else already using the name? Look for the name in a search engine like Google or Bing. Use quotation marks to search for an exact match.

- Is the name available on key social media tools like Facebook and Twitter? Log in to www.facebook.com and use the search box, and check search.twitter.com.

- Can I secure a supporting channel on AudioBoo, BlogTalkRadio, Flickr, and YouTube? Visit each site to search for availability. Refer to Chapter 13 for information on why these are important. Links are listed in Appendix B.

- Has the name been trademarked or restricted under license? Visit the United States Patent and Trademark Office's website at www.uspto.gov to do a search.

- Does the name closely resemble an existing name? These may pop up as alternate suggestions in your earlier searches.

- Am I at risk of infringing on someone else's intellectual property?

- Is there anything about the name that might create confusion?

If you are satisfied with the answers you find and are confident that your chosen name is still viable, then proceed. If there is any risk that you are infringing on an existing name, change your plans. The confusion with similar names and the potential legal hassle and expense far outweigh the inconvenience of selecting and checking another name.

AVOID THE FAIL

Do not proceed with a given name if you cannot secure the .com address. Odds are if the .com is unavailable someone else is developing a commercial activity related to the same name. I also recommend buying the .net, .org, .edu, or any other extension available even if you have no immediate plans to use them. The cost to license each domain is only about $8 per year, a modest price to control the use of your brand name. Why proceed with the hassle and heartache of confused brands if you don't have to?

Think of your custom domain name as the lot your house is built on, except this is a digital piece of real estate where you build your community.

If your network is hosted on a domain name you control, then you must ensure you have registered your domain name for an appropriate amount of time. Some administrators choose to renew the domain name on an annual basis, while others purchase five years or more at one time. Either way is correct as long as you remember to renew. Services like www.networkedsolutions.com, www.godaddy.com, and other domain name registration services walk you through the process of these registrations.

> **AVOID THE FAIL**
>
> Ensure you know who will be notified when it's time to renew your domain name. Most service providers send an e-mail reminder, but that reminder is useless if the e-mail address becomes invalid. The last thing you want to have happen is to spend five years building a community, only to lose it when you fail to renew your domain name.
>
> If you forget to renew, your network will be homeless for a time. Sometimes you get lucky and no else will have purchased your original name and you can register it again. But why rely on fate to keep your domain name? Register and renew regularly.

To aid the success of your network, you want to prevent confusion with similar names or potentially losing control of your name on selected platforms. By securing your chosen name across the major social network services, social media tools, and anywhere else you deem necessary, you can ensure that you control your brand. You want to prevent a situation where someone else secures your name and attempts to represent you. While they may represent you in good faith, they may also set out to malign your reputation. By controlling the relevant accounts, you can prevent this. You are building a brand or enhancing an existing brand. Whatever you do in the best interests of that brand will only help your organization in the long run.

Memorability

Using the existing name of your company, organization, or product will help make your network name memorable and easily recognizable. You are already investing in the promotion of your company, so adding a social network to your efforts under the same name will benefit from your current efforts.

Making your name memorable is key to helping users avoid confusion. You want something both descriptive and catchy—a name that will stick in people's memories. There's no real formula for building a memorable name; you'll just have to work to find the artful answer that suits your community.

The descriptive aspect of the name should make it clear what your community is about. Are you a gaming community, a singles group, or a network of wanna-be chefs? You've already defined your target audience, so describe them succinctly in your name.

Figure 7.3

The Mom Central community (www.momcentral.com), built by ONEsite, is instantly recognized as a hub for parents.

The catchy aspect of your name is the piece that sets it apart. What word or phrase elaborates on the style, feel, and camaraderie typical of your community? More importantly, what distinguishing feature sets your community apart? Take Skidazzle (skidazzle.com) for example—what a great name for a snow sports community. Or consider Tudiabetes.org, whose name is a delightful play on the Spanish "tu" meaning "your" as in "your diabetes." Be creative with your name to help people remember your community and not confuse it with others.

If you are building a network for an already familiar brand, then you're well on your way. If your network name is different (and many are, so that's okay) then carefully consider how to make it memorable. If the name of your network is different, it should enhance your brand name. By picking something complementary, you may be able to establish a community with ties to the brand without being so overt with your advertising.

Length

The length of a social network's name is an often-debated topic. Some like to keep names short so that they can be quickly referenced, while others like to use a longer, more descriptive name. Think about Goldilocks and the Three Bears when determining if your potential social network name is too short, too long, or just right.

Too short and you may not be able to secure the network name, domain name, and supporting social media accounts as desired. Often, someone else has already thought of and secured the accounts for brief names. A short name also limits your ability to explain who you are and what you are about. Although sometimes a short name can work just fine, as it does for GetUrGoodOn (geturgoodon.org), a community organized by Youth Service America and endorsed by Miley Cyrus. The lack of spaces and deliberate misspelling help shorten this community name. Using short forms that are acronyms can create confusion, as this "insider" name is known only to a select few. Of course, there are also well-known acronyms like SPCA (Society for the Prevention of Cruelty to Animals) and you'd want to include SPCA in your name if you are creating a network for a branch of the SPCA.

Conversely, a name that is too long can lead to other kinds of problems, such as the challenge of typesetting a name onto a business card. A long name also lends itself to typos when users point their browser at the network. After all the effort you put into enticing someone to join your network, the last thing you want to do is alienate or frustrate them as they try to find your community. Many users will see this as an insurmountable annoyance and give up.

No one can tell you exactly the right length for your network name, but do keep length in mind as you make your final decision.

Figure 7.4

U2's community (u2.com/community), built by KickApps, is called Zootopia, a unique, brief, and memorable name.

Spelling

To avoid confusion, select a name that can be spelled easily. This means avoiding words that are commonly misspelled or those that are difficult to spell in the first place.

It's a good idea to avoid words that sound the same but have multiple spellings, each with a different meaning. Some examples of homonyms include:

- there/they're/their
- two/to/too
- road/rowed/rode
- raise/rays
- one/won
- your/you're

As your network has the potential to reach a global audience, you'll also want to carefully consider words that are spelled differently in various parts of the English-speaking world. Here are some examples:

- humor/humour
- mold/mould
- caliber/calibre
- dialog/dialogue
- jewelry/jewellry
- alumni/alumnae

> **CLOUD SURFING**
>
> Visit Karen's Linguistic Issues at bit.ly/BondWords, where Karen Bond has created a directory highlighting the variations in American, Canadian, and British English words.

Although you may not use the acronym of your network, please do take a moment to check your name for any inappropriate potential acronyms that its initials could spell. It would be most unfortunate if an organization damaged its brand with a risqué acronym. You'll also want to check that the acronym doesn't already represent another brand (e.g., NPR). Let me suggest a fictional network called Indigenous Rights Applicants. At first glance, IRA seems like a harmless reference. However, IRA also stands for the International Reading Association and the Provisional Irish Republican Army, making it a potentially confusing selection.

> **AVOID THE FAIL**
>
> Give your name the telephone game test. You know, that childhood game where you whisper in someone's ear, and they whisper to someone else, and so on, and the message usually comes out all garbled at the end. Say your name quickly in a loud voice and a hushed voice and ask people to write it down. Do they hear the name you are saying, or do they muddle the word(s) up?

All in all, naming your network takes careful thought. Consider all the options and cautions, and then do your best to select a name that will work throughout its life.

Consider a Trademark

You may want to explore securing a trademark for your network name. Most often this is done to protect a name or logo for an overall organization, not just their social network. Your network name may be your brand name, so a quick discussion is warranted.

Trademark is a form of intellectual property protection. This mark is used to distinguish goods or services from those of an organization's competitors. A trademark can be a word, a phrase, a logo, a combination of words and logo, or a distinguishing guise (for example, a unique shape for a perfume bottle).

The process of securing a trademark takes about two years and requires some spending on legal fees and registration costs. Expect to spend $2,000 or more per country on the trademark process. Trademarks must be registered in different countries separately, so a trademark protected in the United States isn't protected across North America without registration in Canada and Mexico. Once secured, the trademark lasts 15 years with an option to renew for an additional 15 years.

> **FLICKERS OF INSIGHT**
>
> A domain name cannot be registered as a trademark, so your network address cannot be protected but your network name can.

If you decide to register your trademark, I recommend that you consult a law firm that specializes in this type of intellectual property protection. There are many steps to the process, and having a professional with experience guide your efforts will make for a stronger trademark in the end.

Privacy Settings

Privacy is a constant hot topic on anything to do with the Internet. As we share more and more of our lives online, we open ourselves to potential privacy concerns. As a network administrator, you need to take privacy very seriously.

Every network should be up-front about how members' information is being stored and used. Members need to be confident that their personal details are kept private, save for essential network functions. This can involve a privacy statement, which we talk more about in Chapter 16.

Privacy controls allow users to manipulate how much of their information is available to the public, to other members, or just to their friend connections. Administrators can choose whether to offer privacy controls and select the degrees of control available.

Figure 7.5

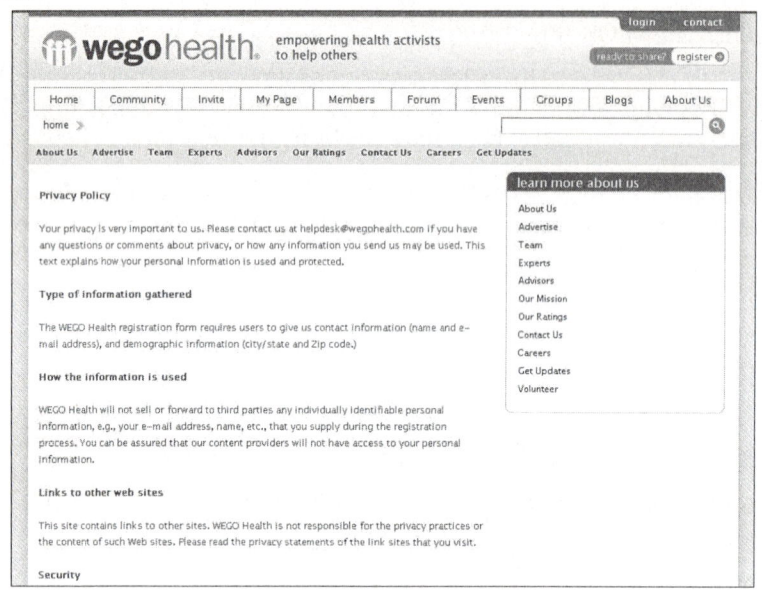

The privacy policy of WEGO Health (www.wegohealth.com/privacy-policy.html), a Ning network.

It also falls to the admin team to educate members about the issue of privacy. A privacy policy circulated to all members, usually at sign-up, is the most common way to publish the network's stand on privacy. Administrators can be further trained with procedural manuals, team meetings, and professional development seminars or webinars. If members are sharing personal information such as where they live, when they will be away, or banking details, they are at risk no matter how good the privacy controls might seem. There is an element of personal responsibility necessary to protect people's privacy.

Customizable Appearance

Social networks built on the same platforms all look the same from the administrative side. The dashboard of any BuddyPress network is identical to all other BuddyPress networks. The same holds true for other platforms. However, the outward appearance of the community can be customized.

Sites built on Ning and Wall.fm have limited options available. The process of selecting features changes the appearance and there are options to vary the header at the top of the page. Ning and Wall.fm administrators can also manipulate the color palette, font selections, and other minor tweaks to create a unique look—although the options are sufficiently limited that it's often easy to spot a Ning or Wall.fm site at first glance.

Other platforms offer more robust visual options. BuddyPress, for example, can utilize a variety of WordPress themes, provided the theme is compatible with BuddyPress. Think of this as a wardrobe for BuddyPress networks. As administrator, you can browse through the wardrobe and choose the outfit that suits you best. New themes are constantly being developed and made available. There is also the option to hire a designer to create a custom BuddyPress theme.

Whatever your platform, administrators have control over the network's appearance.

Code of Conduct

Drafting a code of conduct when you create your network is a good idea. Such a code becomes the road map for the ways members use the community and the ways they should not use it. It also affords the administrators some way to adjudicate behavior. This is especially important as what one person sees as offensive might be considered creative expression by another.

> **CLOUD SURFING**
>
> There are as many potential code of conduct policies as there are social networks. Some are simple like Wells Fargo's (bit.ly/WellsCom), while others are more complex like the 31-page policy from the U.S. Air Force (bit.ly/AirFMedia). Visit Social Media Governance for free access to a policy database (bit.ly/SocGov).

The code is the place where you can articulate what's allowed and what's expected of members. This could include:

- The types of content that can be shared.
- Cautions for or against adult-only or mature content.
- Instruction to treat all members politely.
- Firm rules against personal attacks, spam, and anything illegal.
- Rules about whether or not you permit off-topic subjects.
- A statement that the network holds no responsibility for the validity of external links.

Some policies also include recommendations about how to protect members' privacy, although this important topic is often covered in a separate Internet safety document. In addition, you can state that the administrator reserves the right to remove content at its sole discretion so that you can act quickly if something offensive appears. Be sure to include a way for members to contact the administrator with code of conduct–related questions.

Figure 7.6

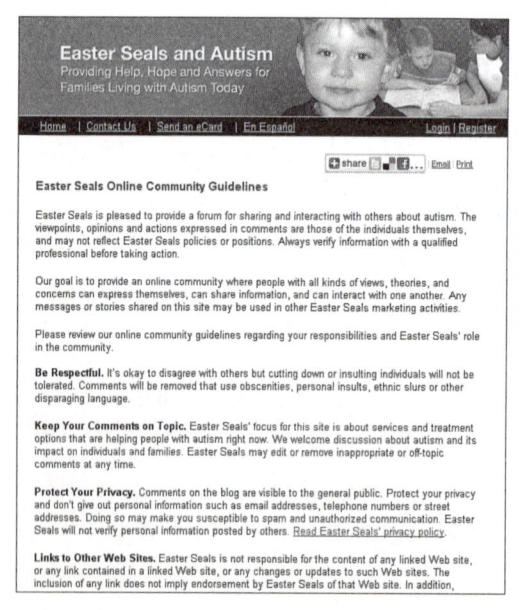

The Easter Seals Online Community Guidelines clearly spell out what is permitted and what is not at bit.ly/ESeals.

The Least You Need to Know

- Naming your network is like naming a baby. Choose wisely.
- Assess your selected network name in terms of availability, length, spelling, and memorability.
- Consult with a lawyer to secure trademark protection for your intellectual property.
- You can select the appearance of your network from available options or pay for a custom look.
- A code of conduct for your network is a good idea.

Help Your Members

Chapter 8

In This Chapter

- Elements of an easy sign-up process
- Balancing personal and professional identities within a network
- Techniques to help your members create a strong login password
- Suggestions on short biographies to help network members get acquainted
- The importance of a profile image such as a photo or logo
- Tips for members when selecting a unique user name
- Different types of relationships among network members

All of your effort to build your social network is fruitless unless someone signs up to be part of the community. In this chapter, we explore ways for administrators to make it easier for members to join and start participating.

Ease of Joining

A community member's first experience with your social network is the process of signing up. A good network places the sign-up area in an easy-to-spot place on the home page, and keeps the process quick and simple. A big button that says Join Now goes a long way to helping turn a visitor into a member. Hiding the sign-up link in an obscure spot will only frustrate the visitor, who may give up trying to join.

When creating a sign-up process, don't waste the time your new members could be investing in your community with needlessly complex procedures. In general, users are accustomed to providing a name, e-mail, password, and birthday. This is definitely one of those moments to KISS (Keep It Simple, Stupid). Tap into people's enthusiasm and let them join the community as quickly as possible. Further information can be added when they complete their member profiles.

Let's look at a great example from Fairfield University, an online extension of this school's community. Visitors to www.fairfield.edu/fairfieldlive instantly see the invitation to join by clicking the Join Now link.

Figure 8.1

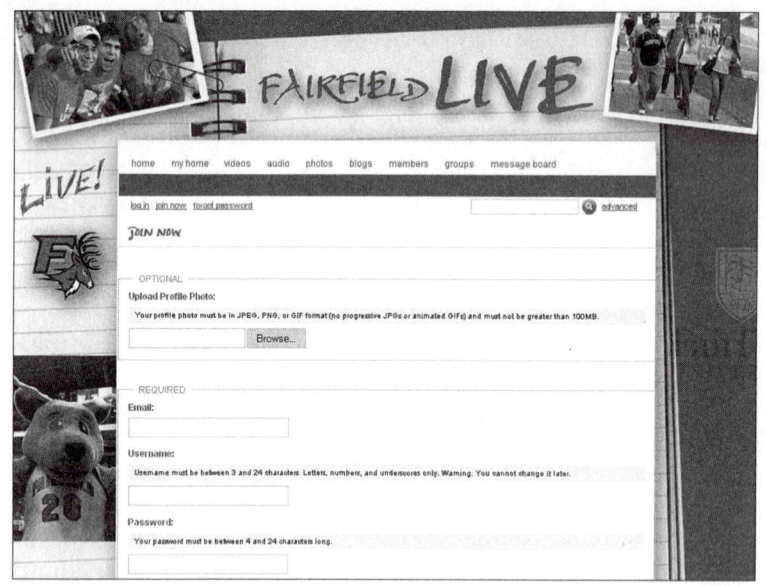

The sign-up page for Fairfield Live, a community built on the KickApps platform.

Visitors fill in a brief form with their profile image, e-mail, user name, password, and a few other details. From start to finish, it takes less than a minute to become a member of the Fairfield Live community.

The vast majority of social networks are free for users—at least there is a basic account with basic functions available for anyone's use without charge. If you plan to charge for membership or for premium membership services within the network, be up-front about it at the sign-up stage. (Paid memberships can be set up with an appropriate plug-in or service upgrade on most network services.) This will avoid disappointment and confusion among your members when they hit the threshold for "paid" services.

FLICKERS OF INSIGHT

Some folks are a bit shy about sharing their birthday on the Internet. There are a wide variety of reasons, from concerns about appearing too old or too young to fears of identity theft. If you decide your network needs to ask for a birthday, be sure you understand exactly why you are asking the question. Often, this is used as a security measure to verify identity if they need to reset a password or resolve some other problem with their membership. Birthdates are also used to confirm that members are old enough to participate in the content of your network. Obviously, members need to be the age of majority—be that 18 or 21—to access mature content that includes things like violence or sex. Other networks might consider age 13 old enough to interact with the content. Those 12 and under need a parent's consent to participate, as young children haven't yet learned to be socially savvy about their personal safety and security.

About Profiles

User profiles are where the social part of social networking comes into play. User profiles allow members to share some information about themselves. This might include a photo, a preferred nickname, a list of favorite books and movies, and, sometimes, contact details like a web address or Twitter name. A complete profile not only lends credibility but also creates instant introductions and memory joggers, and thus a richer experience for all users. Hosts should lead by example with a strong profile.

The brief introduction in a profile helps define users in the context of the network. Think of it as an elevator speech—members have 45 seconds between floors to explain to fellow riders who they are, what they do, and why they are interesting. Within social networks, this introduction will vary depending on the network. For example, a member of a business community site might not announce his dog's name, at least not in his profile's lead sentence. However, that same pet owner might proudly boast in his profile about all of his fuzzy, scaled, and feathered friends in a pet lovers' community. Completed profiles help community members get acquainted and find common interests as starting points for dialogue.

AVOID THE FAIL

One of the challenges in social networking is deciding how much personal information to share. If members share too little, their profiles appear impersonal, cold, and unapproachable. At the same time, members who share too much information can become just as hard to engage as they may appear needy, overwhelming, and smothering. Network administrators can set the standard for their community by asking relevant questions in the user profile form.

All social network services have a user or member profile form. There are default questions or fill-in-the-blank forms to complete. Customized or more comprehensive profiles can be added to most networks.

Organizational vs. Personal

The company or community group that creates a social network should create a profile for the organization to share with community members. Individual participants, whether they're called members or users, should also have personal profiles.

Typically, an organizational profile uses a logo or other icon instead of a photograph. (We'll talk more about appropriate profile images later in this chapter.) There is still one or more real people behind the organizational profile, and that person should be comfortable speaking in the *voice* of that organization.

> **DEFINITION**
>
> **Voice** is a theatrical term that refers to the character and feel of a particular way of speaking. By changing the voice, companies can change the way their brands are perceived.

Personal profiles should authentically reflect the person—remember my profile in Chapter 1? (More on authenticity in Chapter 16.) The social network's profile should reflect the values and vibe of the company that created the community, and should be polished and professional. Members should be encouraged to have a strong profile, but they can represent themselves as they wish.

Valid E-Mail

It may seem obvious, but each individual participating in the network should include a valid e-mail address in his or her profile. This is essential for communicating with members for auto-reply functions like resetting a forgotten password, as well as sharing important news about events or other activities through *opt-in* updates.

> **DEFINITION**
>
> **Opt-ins** gives participants choices about whether or not to receive certain kinds of information. Within a social network, they can usually opt in or opt out of various notifications. For example, a member can choose to receive a notification when she is tagged in a post, photo, or video. She may also receive notification of a private message from another member.

Unique Name

A unique name for each profile is desirable to avoid confusion between members. However, some networks allow several people to use the same name while others limit each name to a single user. As you work with your community, you'll be able to determine which method to use. Most start out allowing multiple accounts with the same name. They are distinguished by unique login name and password.

Even if the name can be repeated, a unique login name is required. In some cases, this is an e-mail address while other sites require a unique name. You'll use whatever the convention is for your selected social network service.

> **FLICKERS OF INSIGHT**
>
> Participants in your network may have two names associated with their accounts. The first is their login name, which can be an e-mail address or a unique name. The second is their display name, which can be their proper name (such as Betty Smith) or a pseudonym (such as Painter Peter). More than one person can use the same display name on the same network.

If you are advising members to create unique display names, suggest a variation of a person's proper name as the best choice. Depending on the culture in your network some may prefer to use something quirky, like "MommaBear" or "BeerPig." If using proper names, only the first person with a particular name will be able to use that name. If your network grows and you have two Jane Smiths or John Henrys, then they will need to use variations. People with common names are used to the presence of their doppelgangers and have to stake out a variation for their online identities. For example, if MarieNunn was unavailable, then alternatives might include:

- Marie.Nunn
- Marie.G.Nunn
- MNunn
- MarieN
- MarNunn
- Marie2719
- Nunnery

> **AVOID THE FAIL**
>
> Discourage members from using hyphens or underscores in their network names. These types of punctuation can be easily confused with spaces if the line of text is underlined and can be hard to distinguish against some background images. They are also more complicated to communicate verbally.

Strong Password

Network administrators should encourage all participants to use a strong password to reduce the risk of their account being compromised.

A weak password is something easily guessed or discovered by trial and error. Things like "1234" or "ABC" or the person's first name are all poor choices.

A strong password should combine several of the following elements:

- Minimum of eight characters
- Both letters and numbers
- One or more capital letters
- Should not spell a known word
- Used only on this network
- Known only to the user

There are tools available online to help autogenerate strong passwords. Both PC Tools (bit.ly/PCPass) and Tech Zoom (bit.ly/TZPass) have free password generators that help you create passwords that meet these criteria.

> **FLICKERS OF INSIGHT**
>
> If you feel that your memory isn't up to the challenge of retaining all your passwords, try some pneumonic tricks. For example, make a silly sentence that relates to your password—something like "Tigger bounces three times for Piglet" for the password "TB3T4P."

Figure 8.2

With a quick click at bit.ly/PCPass, PC Tools' password generator provides a strong password to use anywhere online.

140-Character Biography

A short biography of just 140 characters is your Internet calling card. This very brief summary must include all the letters, numbers, punctuation, and spaces within the 140-character limit. Typically, social networks display this brief bio on members' profile page.

Figure 8.3

Here's my 140-character biography from www.twitter.com/AngelaCrocker.

The 140-character limit stems from text messaging on cellular phones and other mobile devices. The SMS (which stands for Short Message Service) technology that makes these brief messages possible has created a convention to use 140 characters on social networks and social media sites.

While you often have 160 characters available, I suggest creating a 140-character bio instead. Why create a situation where you have to edit your biography over and over? Please be sure to note that it's 140 characters, not 140 words.

Network hosts should encourage biographies that reflect the person and his or her interests in the context of the site. A person's biography on a professional association network will certainly include different information than the same person's bio on a dog lovers' website.

Let's look at three examples. Meet Peter, a young dog owner, entrepreneur, and homeowner who loves soccer.

Informal:

Director SkillSpark eLearning with 8 years+ int'l experience in instructional design & learning management systems. Dog lover, avid traveler.

Professional:

Director of SkillSpark eLearning, with over 8 years of international experience in instructional design and learning management systems.

Casual:

Happy Dad to four-leggers Hailey (German Shepherd, age 2) & Moira (Sheltie, age 8). Loves road trips, hikes, picnics, and agility classes.

However members describe themselves, they should make all 140 characters count.

Photo, Icon, Logo, or Avatar

An image of some sort is essential to any profile. It literally adds a face to the name. It becomes a quick visual reference as people interact within the social network. As a member takes action on the network—for example, leaves a comment on a discussion forum—his name and image appears next to what he's written.

For individuals, I recommend using a photograph. All network services include the opportunity for members to upload a photo of themselves. A quick snapshot will do for some informal networks, but it is definitely worth investing in a good head shot with a professional photographer if social network activity has a professional component.

Chapter 8: Help Your Members   121

Figure 8.4

Peggy Richardson's informal snapshot.

Figure 8.5

Peggy Richardson's professional head shot.
(Photo credit www.WendyD.ca)

Of course, a photo isn't always possible or practical, and it may make more sense to use a logo or other icon. If you're participating in a social network to represent your company or charity, then it may be more appropriate to use your logo, as you build your brand by participating in the community. If you don't have something readily available, there are many services that will create an avatar for you.

Figure 8.6

Renee Shupe, owner of Redhead Business Management, kindly shared some fun variations on her image. Created at www.photofunia.com.

> **CLOUD SURFING**
>
> If your network is informal your members can have some fun with their profile pictures. Suggest they make a billboard advertisement or a pencil sketch at www.photofunia.com. Photos can also be turned into magazine covers and major league game photos on this site. There are even some options that will create an animated profile picture.

You can create your own fun images using the tools in photo-editing software packages, or use one of many great online tools. If you've got time to try only one, visit Photofunia.

Adding Further Details to Profiles

A more in-depth profile can provide valuable information to round out our perception of a person. Invite your members to share simple lists of favorite books and movies as well as more personal notations on marital status, political persuasion, and religious views. These extra bits of background give a more complete sense of a person and his or her values and interests.

If desired, you can create a custom list of questions relevant to your network. For example, a pet-oriented group might offer space to list the types, breeds, and names of the participants' pets. Have a look at the BuddyPress tutorial in Chapter 21 for an example.

You might also consider asking members to share how to reach them elsewhere on the Internet. This might mean their Twitter name, Facebook account, LinkedIn reference, or website or blog address. Don't restrict your list to these common few—select those that make sense for your network.

Relationships

Social networks are about relationships. Real people are the voices behind the avatars and status updates. Over time, genuine relationships can form between some members, while others will continue to be total strangers. As with all relationships, these connections can grow, or sour, over time.

As a network administrator, you'll need to decide what kinds of relationships your network will facilitate. Do you have a structure where everyone knows everyone else? Or do you have a large community where members will interact with the group at large and have some more meaningful relationships with a few fellow members? Let's consider the following types of social network relationships:

- Strangers
- Acquaintances
- Friends
- Groups

Different networks use different terminology for the same thing. Your acquaintances might be followers, while your friends might be fans. Don't fuss too much about the specific language; rather, decide what types of relationships your members require or want.

Strangers

Unless someone has been invited to join by an existing friend, everyone within a social network is a stranger at first. However, having joined a particular community, users have a common interest in the focus of the community, be it sports, crafts, business, or any other topic.

Many new users will observe for a while before taking any action. They want to get used to the surroundings, listen in on some conversations, and generally get the vibe of the place before jumping in. They might look for familiar names and faces or take note of other members who are particularly interesting to them.

> **AVOID THE FAIL**
>
> Don't assume that only the talkative members are reading or listening to a particular conversation. It has been suggested that the vast majority, perhaps as much as 99 percent, of members simply observe and listen rather than become active participants. This group is sometimes referred to as lurkers. Lurkers are great, as they are still members of the community and may eventually be drawn out to participate in what's happening. Often, they are more likely to use information learned and participate in activities in the real world rather than online.

Acquaintances

Superusers who are very familiar with the community and, sometimes, gregarious members who are naturally outgoing often greet a new member and strike up an acquaintance. If the network is large, they might also approach a not-so-new member. This is not a deep relationship, but the users are on speaking terms and learning about one another.

This preliminary acquaintance dialogue often happens in the context of a forum discussion or through comments on a public status update or blog post. Over time, certain members may become familiar to one another and strike up friendships.

AVOID THE FAIL

One of the reasons that acquaintances are reluctant to deepen their relationships to friend, fan, or follower status is that they run the risk of being spammed by those connections. The worst kind of friends to have are those looking for people to sign up for a particular tool, game, or other service so that they can get something. Facebook games like Mafia Wars and Farmville are classic examples.

Within the network, there is no formal link between users who are getting acquainted. Rather, the only record of their interactions is through the dialogues they have had publicly.

Friends

For many networks, the core of relationships is "Friend" status. This reciprocal relationship is confirmed by both members and generally affords them access to more detailed profile information and adds the ability to send private messages. Your network service may include a friend feature in the default set-up, or you may have to go looking for a plug-in or add-on service to achieve this functionality.

For some users, "friending" is only acceptable with people they know in the real world. For others, they will befriend fellow members with whom they have a passing acquaintance. In general, it's not advisable to encourage members to become friends with strangers. Just as in the real world, there can be some "stranger danger" issues within online communities. We'll talk about safety and security in Chapter 16. Your job as an administrator is to decide if you want to offer the functionality for members to establish friend relationships.

> **AVOID THE FAIL**
>
> On occasion, relationships can go sour, just as they do in the real world. When this happens within a social network, the best-case scenario is for the affected members to simply stop interacting with one another. The worst-case scenario is one in which the members continue to antagonize and bait one another in a nasty public display. This is another area where a code of conduct policy can be helpful to administrators. (Remember we talked about that in Chapter 7?) The guidelines can help mediate any issues that are negatively influencing the specific users and the experience of the community overall.

Some networks come with a cap on the number of friends a user can have. Facebook, for example, allows only 5,000 friends per profile. At the same time, research suggests that the human brain can only retain and process about 150 genuine relationships. How many friends a user is allowed in a particular network is up to the administrator and the technical limits (if any) of the selected network service. I recommend permitting as many connections as technically possible so that your users are not hampered in their use of the community.

> **FLICKERS OF INSIGHT**
>
> Ning's least expensive service, Ning Mini, limits the community to 150 users, whereas their Ning Plus and Ning Pro packages allow for unlimited numbers of users.

Groups

Groups are the clubs within a social network. Members of a network can join any number of groups as suits their interests and their desired level of participation. Groups can include discussion forums, photo sharing, event planning, or pretty much anything else the members want to connect over. You'll need to decide whether groups can be created by the administrator only or if users can create groups, too. I recommend the latter so that members can manage their own interactions, thus reducing the administrative load.

For social networks that cover broad geographic areas, it is not unusual to see regional groups pop up so that members in particular cities can connect with one another. There may also be groups for those attending particular conferences, reading certain genres, or participating in an allied activity such as a choral singers group within a music network.

Figure 8.7

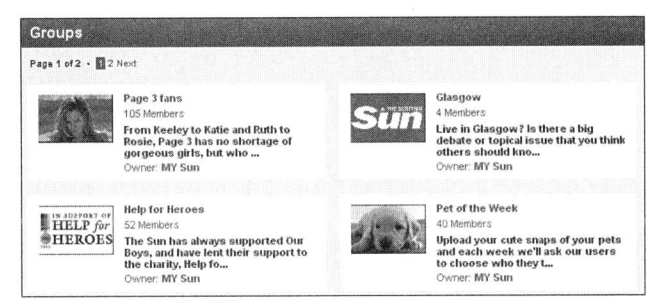

Readers of The Sun *newspaper who join the My Sun community (powered by ONEsite) can join groups to connect with fellow readers.*

Groups also morph over time, either broadening or narrowing their focus. Occasionally, groups run their course and are disbanded. Groups are one of the most fluid parts of a social network adjusting to meet the needs of the community.

The Least You Need to Know

- Make it easy for members to join your network.
- Both organizations and individuals need profiles.
- All participants require a valid e-mail address.
- Create a strong password. Use a generator to help.
- Encourage members to present themselves professionally with a 140-character bio, smart photo, and appropriate in-depth profile.
- Members of your network can be strangers, acquaintances, or friends. They can also interact in groups.

Chapter 9

Content Is King

In This Chapter

- A discussion of why content sharing is the integral part of a social network
- Who contributes content to a social network
- The different types of content you can share on a social network
- An overview of copyrights and how they affect the content on your network
- The importance of referenced and original content

As the chapter title states, content is king. Whether you think of King Tut or Elvis, remember that content is as central to your community as the king or any other ruler is vital to his or her community.

Sharing

The Internet is all about sharing. Individuals and businesses post content and want others to see it. Some post lots of content, while others don't post much at all. Either way there is a market for information and entertainment. Making content available online is the act of sharing that feeds this appetite. This culture of sharing is integral to the experience of every Internet citizen.

Within a social network, community members are seeking experience, knowledge, or some type of interaction with information. The content shared within the community becomes the connecting tissue of that community. Only by sharing does the community thrive. Otherwise, it's just a static website.

Bear in mind that no social network is isolated on the web. Your members will visit other communities and other resources will matter to them. For most communities, users will expect to be able to share content with outside communities. Similarly, they'll expect to be able to share content from outside communities with their fellow community members.

Content

Without content, a social network is really just a fancy website. If the information on your network is going to stay the same from day to day or week to week, why go to the trouble of creating an online community? Content is the substance that keeps the network going and keeps members coming back time and time again.

Members expect content. They look for the latest news, product updates, opinions from other members, and many other sorts of content to amuse, enlighten, and influence their lives.

In some networks the content is solely user generated, but in many networks, especially those associated with a business, a large amount of content is contributed by administrators. In some ways the administrators act as editorial curators for news and entertainment of interest to network members.

What Is Content?

Content is anything that is added to the social network beyond the members' names and biographies. Content can be made up of words, pictures, movies, ideas, op-ed pieces, cartoons, drawings, artwork, research papers, industry reports, and so much more. Whatever is of interest to the community is the content that should appear on that community. Even occasional seasonal or amusing tangents are acceptable on most networks.

> **AVOID THE FAIL**
>
> When sharing content, consider your tone of voice (even if you're typing). How does it translate? Are you using academic words that sound snobby, or crass words that sound lowbrow? It's okay to use the sort of words that are appropriate to your community, but be conscious of the impact of your words on others perception of you and your topic.

Types of Content

There are many ways to think about types of content. In broad terms, think of content as text, links, photos, and videos. Before we get into specific content, it's important to know where content comes from. What's the source of inspiration? Sources are either referenced content or original content.

Referenced content comes from external sources. Other people's websites, committee reports, photographs, and videos can all be fodder for sharing within a social network. Odds are you've already shared referenced content in a Facebook status update or through a tweet on Twitter. Sharing referenced content in your social network works in much the same way.

> **FLICKERS OF INSIGHT**
>
> Referenced content can take two forms—linked or embedded. Linked content involves typing a link into the network that will take members outside the network to see the content. Conversely, embedded content happens when the text, photo, or video is included within the network. Services like YouTube provide an option to get the HTML to embed content in the social network itself.

Referenced content can come from anywhere. Let's consider an example. Suppose your network is for parents of school-age children. Your content could draw from a myriad of sources:

- Parenting magazines and newspaper articles
- Psychology websites that deal with child development
- Education sites with content from teachers
- Current affairs discussions
- Photographs from family-friendly events
- Corporate content about kid-related products
- Eco-content about reducing a family's environmental impact
- Menus and recipes to feed busy families from food-related sites
- Bookseller information on parenting titles and books for kids

All of these sources and many others will add rich content to inform, educate, and entertain the parent members of this network. The content gives the membership a shared experience through which to connect with one another.

Pulling content from other sources is a great way to get started, but all successful networks also generate at least some original content. Original content is the news, opinions, photos, videos, and research created by the network's administrators and members. Original content is a key reason why members keep coming back. They will experience this content within your network and likely share it with other communities they participate in.

> **AVOID THE FAIL**
>
> One of the worst offenders in social networks is the person who contributes content only when he or she wants something. In some cases, administrators are the worst offenders. Be sure to take time to participate in the community you have developed so that members are familiar with you throughout the year—not just when you have something to announce or sell. Mike Stelzner from SocialMediaExaminer.com is a great example. He is consistently present on the site's various platforms—blog, Twitter feed, Facebook page, and so on. As such, his community feels they have a relationship with him before he offers any products or services for sale.

Copyright

Content creators own the copyright for the materials they produce. Copyright is the legal term that protects the intellectual property of creators. The words in this book are protected under copyright, as is the music you downloaded from iTunes last week. To hold the copyright gives you the legal right to control how your work is used and how it is monetized. For some copyright holders, the ethical use of their work is paramount. For others, the potential lost income is the top concern. There is much to know and learn about copyright. A good place to find information is the U.S. Copyright Office at www.copyright.gov.

> **FLICKERS OF INSIGHT**
>
> Copyright law varies in different countries, with some countries protecting creators' rights to the fullest and others offering no protection whatsoever and everything in between. Although your network may be grounded in one country, members may be in other countries with different understandings on copyright law. The copyright law of the country where the network is headquartered is the reigning law.

Network creators run the risk that members will share content and infringe on someone's copyright. In other words, they may take someone else's words, images, or other content and present them as though they were created by the person sharing the content. As administrator, you should have a clear policy that copyright infringement will not be tolerated in your social network.

> **AVOID THE FAIL**
>
> When sharing content, failure to link to the source of information or inspiration is considered bad form. Online communities are about open sharing, but it is important to give a nod to the source that sparked a particular train of thought.
>
> Similarly, plagiarism is not acceptable. Ever. Copying content from a blog or website and presenting it as your own is a breach of copyright and against the law.

Uploading Content

Planning to share content isn't enough—you actually have to gather it and upload the content to the network. We'll talk in detail about gathering different types of content in Chapter 10.

It is important to decide who's responsible for uploading content for the organization. Is it just one person or a team? To avoid putting too much responsibility on any one person, it's better to have a team of people share the responsibility. In this way, sick days are covered, vacations aren't a problem, and if someone's abducted by aliens there's no worry (about the content, I mean).

Of course, having a team uploading content means they need to be in regular communication with one another. Who's uploading what? When? How often? Careful planning and clear communication will prevent duplicate uploads and lost content.

Another issue that arises is how to get the content to the people who will upload it. Sometimes the content is gathered by a team member, but often it's someone else who's taken the time to write the blog post, take the pictures, or capture some video. Text content can usually be sent through e-mail or a Skype chat without any trouble. In theory, sharing photos and videos is just as easy, but some e-mail systems have size limits—a 10-minute, 1 gigabyte video will never arrive on the other end.

As with all things geeky, there are lots of alternatives. Perhaps your network needs an *FTP* site for file sharing among team members, or you could use a tool like DropBox, Google Docs, or a Sharepoint site. Both the person creating the content and the person needing the content would have access to the same file location and be able to share all types of files without being in the same office. Whatever your needs, there is a way to get that digital content moving between team members and ultimately uploaded to your community.

> **DEFINITION**
>
> **FTP** stands for File Transfer Protocol and is a means of sharing files between computers on a network or across the Internet. All types of files can be shared, from text documents and spreadsheets to photos and videos.

Before your team gets carried away uploading content, please take some time to consider a schedule. You should roll that information out over a few hours, days, or even a couple of weeks. When making scheduling decisions, think about how often your members want to hear from you. Don't forget that members are also uploading content each day so there's (I hope) lots of activity. The pace for administrator-generated content may be a matter of trial and error. Only you know your community and you will likely experiment to determine the best pace. This pace may change over time, so be fluid in what you do.

There are tools available to help with content scheduling. You might use a simple spreadsheet to identify content, when it's going up, and who's responsible. You can also use project management tools to assign jobs to particular team members with escalating reminders to keep them on track. Supporting social media content can be scheduled in programs like HootSuite and TweetDeck.

Figure 9.1

Twitter tweets, Facebook updates, and other social media activities can be scheduled using HootSuite through its web interface at hootsuite.com or through its mobile application.

If you're still struggling, you may also want to assign a staff member or retain an assistant to help manage content and the upload schedule. This person doesn't have to do all the uploading, although he or she could, but rather will have an umbrella view of all the content and when it's intended to be shared on the network.

Content Moderation

For content contributed by members, administrators must decide whether to allow all users to upload any content at any time or whether to temporarily hold content for review before it's posted. In the administrator panel for your network, you'll have the option to have content publish immediately or be held for review.

> **AVOID THE FAIL**
>
> Set ground rules for your social network on what can be shared. Refer back to Chapter 7 for information on a code of conduct to assess community members' behavior. Consider an escalating set of consequences to censure unwanted behavior.

Open content makes for a richer community, with content instantly being published as members share it. This makes for timely sharing of information. However, it also opens the community to the risk of undesirable, offensive, or illegal content. For instance, if the community is at risk of spam from dubious users, or certain types of content could be offensive, then a moderated environment might be best. For example, a network for artists might be open to nude images but a user who doesn't understand the artistic intent of the community might share images that are considered pornographic. In this case, the moderator (usually an administrator) would hold and review the content for abusive language, spam, offensive photos, or whatever else is not appropriate for the community. The choice is yours, and it's not always an easy one.

> **AVOID THE FAIL**
>
> Depending on the laws in your jurisdiction, many network administrators are required to block or remove comments that are libelous, derogatory, or illegal. Be sure to understand the relevant legislation in your area and take appropriate action.
>
> The Legal Information Institute is a not-for-profit group at Cornell University Law School (www.law.cornell.edu) that makes U.S. laws available to all for free, including federal codes and state statutes.

Content held for moderation requires the administrator to be available consistently to accept or reject content. Even though it's the matter of a single click to approve content or to reject it as spam, the volume of content can be daunting. This can be a time-intensive activity if you have a busy community. To ease the time crunch, an administrator might choose to moderate only selected types of content or perhaps to only moderate members' first few contributions to confirm that they understand what is appropriate.

The Least You Need to Know

- Sharing is a big part of what makes social networks social.
- All networks must be fueled with content.
- Content can be text, links, photos, or videos.
- Content can be referenced from another source or be original content created specifically for the network.
- Copyright must be respected on both legal and moral grounds.
- A team is recommended to schedule and upload content.
- Administrators must decide whether to hold content for moderation or allow all user-generated content to appear on the site live.

What to Say

Chapter 10

In This Chapter

- In-depth discussions about the types of content that can be shared
- Suggestions for text-based content, including reports, opinions, and dialogue
- Tools you can use, such as Google Alerts and social bookmarking, to find relevant links to include on your network
- Tips for successful content created with digital photographs and videos

Once a social network is set up, hosts can find themselves stumped on what to say. Some are simply tongue-tied, while others can't seem to recognize the interesting stories within their own organizations. Consider this chapter your friendly neighborhood content consultant.

Sharing Text

Words are the easiest thing to share on a social network. Type something up, post to the network, and the text is instantly available to network members. This may sound technically easy and straightforward, but what words do you share?

> **FLICKERS OF INSIGHT**
>
> Word use sets the tone within the social network. Is your group casual or formal? Is it an academic or technical circle where industry lingo is accepted, or is the network's tone casual and quick? Do you want to be accessible to all with common language? Are you informal with street slang; is cursing the norm? As the host, it's up to you to set the tone and lead by example.

Reports and Research

Reports are a great source of information for social networks. Perhaps your company or organization generates regular reports, newsletters, or other research papers. Use that content and share it through the network.

Don't simply post an entire report all in one go, though. Instead, break it down into logical chunks or roll it out as a series. Similarly, you could post each article in a newsletter over the course of a couple of weeks. So if your eight-page newsletter includes 20 articles, that's 20 posts ready to go.

If your organization does original research, don't hesitate to include your network in the process. Polls, focus groups, and questionnaires can all engage participants. By offering an opportunity to have a say, you innately express value in that person's contribution to the network.

For example, many social media marketing professionals participated in a poll for Social Media Examiner (SME) on the uses and trends in social media. Poll participants were randomly selected through SME's social media outlets, including Twitter and Facebook, during a five-day window when the survey was open for responses. Members of SME's network were later provided with a copy of the final report, which you can read at bit.ly/SMEreport.

> **AVOID THE FAIL**
>
> Members of any given network have a certain attention span. Keep this in mind in terms of the length of your posts. Maybe your audience will read two sentences. Others may read an entire essay. Give participants what they want—don't overwhelm those who prefer shorter posts and don't dumb things down for readers looking for more depth. At first, test a variety of lengths and determine the right length for your network. You'll know you've got it right when your content engages members in dialogue through comments or other interactions.

Many organizations don't conduct original research, nor do they publish research papers or even a newsletter. If your company doesn't do research, that's okay. Odds are you use research and reference work that has been done by allied companies and professional organizations. If something in their work is particularly relevant to your network, then quote that report—just be sure to give credit to the source. For example, a community for health-care professionals might reference research papers on breakthroughs in medicine. The original research and writing are often done by medical schools and pharmaceutical companies.

> **AVOID THE FAIL**
>
> If you want to quote a brief excerpt from someone else's research paper, you can confidently quote up to two paragraphs, as long as credit is given along with a link to find the original document. For longer quotes, full chapter excerpts, or reproductions of the entire work, it's a good idea to contact the author and ask for permission. Get the permission in writing to avoid potential legal hassles in the future.

Opinions

Another great source of word content for your network is opinion. Comments on events, politics, community affairs, and the like are wonderful content for a network.

The beauty of opinion is that everybody has one. Expressing one opinion can prompt agreement, questions, or opposition from members, often cultivating further responses from members.

For example, a music teacher was fired from her job at a Catholic school allegedly on the grounds that she had spoken about her joy as a new parent with her lesbian partner in front of the students. This single news report prompted all sorts of opinions—about how much students should know about teachers' lives, about the Catholic Church's views on same-sex partnerships, and about the parenting that baby would receive. Supportive or provocative, everyone had an opinion on some aspect of this story.

Of course, not all opinions are polarized and antagonistic. In fact, many communities have a built-in harmony amongst members with a common interest. Members of less opinionated communities still have differing points of view, but they are more the same than different. In addition, there are networks where the differences of opinion are strongly held and hotly debated, but the topic is not life or death important. For example, a cooking community will have the occasional heated debate regarding the use of boxed cake mixes versus homemade. There are also instances where strong opinions are not the culture of the community, and members may simply bite their tongues and politely say nothing rather than start a debate.

Dialogue

Sparking dialogue is an art, both in the real world and online. It involves bringing together the right people at the right time and introducing a topic. You've already brought together like-minded people in your network; now, get that conversation started.

Here are some terrific conversation starters:

- What was your favorite moment this weekend?
- Tell us about your most challenging running route.
- Looking for suggestions on great music for cocktail parties.
- How are you using the material from last week's conference?
- What topics should be covered in the next webinar series?
- What was your top takeaway from today's team meeting?

Don't be tempted to fall back on lousy conversation starters like these ones:

- Are you having a nice day?
- Have you got socks on?
- Are you there?

In general, avoid questions that can provoke a dead-end one-word answer. The goal is to ask open-ended questions that will result in meaningful responses. As host, it's up to you to keep the dialogue moving along. Ask for clarification. Prompt with follow-up questions. Probe for more details. You get the idea.

With a text conversation, you have the option to start the conversation at your convenience and watch it evolve over a few hours or even a few days. However, you could also schedule a live chat at a particular time, inviting members to interact in real time. A record of the conversation would still be available to members after the live session and further comments can be added. Sometimes galvanizing people to be part of a live session is easy because they feel part of the community and get immediate responses to their contributions.

Links

Sharing links to web resources of interest to your network can be a real boon to your group. By providing these links, the host becomes a go-to expert on all things related to the topic. By example, the host also encourages members to share relevant information they discover online.

Google Alerts

One of my favorite tools is Google Alerts. You can configure this free service to send you a notification, usually by e-mail, anytime a particular topic or name is *indexed* by Google's search engine algorithm. Usually, this indexing happens quickly when new content is posted online. However, on occasion, links to older data that had not previously been indexed will appear in search results. The appearance of a search phrase in a Google Alert is not a ranking or endorsement by Google, nor is it an indication that someone has been looking for this material. However, it can be a useful tool for monitoring your brand and finding relevant content to share.

> **DEFINITION**
>
> Think of Google as a giant index for all the content on the Internet, similar to the index at the back of this book. Google web crawlers, called Googlebots, constantly survey the web cataloguing the content found. Once the Googlebot has reviewed a particular web page, it's said to have been **indexed.**

To create an alert, go to alerts.google.com. To manage your alerts, log in to your Google account. If you don't already have a Google account, all you need is an e-mail address and password to get started.

To start, type the search term you want to be alerted about in the Search Terms box. Your search terms might include the following:

- The name of your company
- The name of your network, if different
- The names of public figures within your organization, such as the CEO
- Keyword phrases that relate to your topic

When setting up a Google alert, use quotation marks to narrow your search. Type "Marketplace Grocery" in the Search Terms box rather than Marketplace Grocery. This will make the search results more exact. Without the quotation marks, the search results will return mentions of Marketplace Grocery, Grocery Marketplace, and any instances when the two words appear on the same web page but not side by side.

I also suggest entering search terms using common misspellings, such as "Market Place Grocery." Some members may not know how to spell your brand or may mistype it, so monitoring misspellings can also return relevant search results.

For example, the proprietor of a company called Pink Star Events that provides catering and event planning services for nontraditional weddings might run a social network for brides and grooms. The network's alerts might include the following search terms:

- Pink Star Events
- Bridal madness
- Nontraditional weddings
- Unique weddings
- Elvis weddings
- Catering weddings

After entering each search term, Google asks you additional questions to make the alert work for you.

Figure 10.1

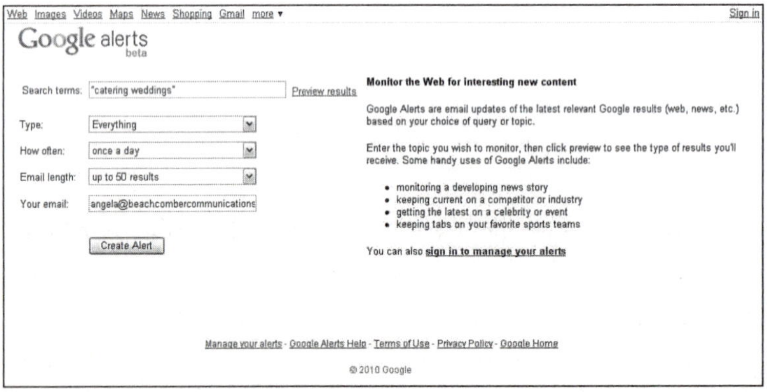

In this example, we create an alert for the search term "catering weddings" with all types of results, delivered daily by e-mail, with up to 50 results included.

In Figure 10.1, you can see the five questions you must answer to set up your alert. We've already talked about the top box called Search Terms, so let's turn our attention to the drop-down menu selections in the next three questions.

The second box allows you to select the type of content you receive. You can choose from the following options in the Type drop-down menu:

- **Everything:** The default setting, it returns search results from all types of content. I suggest you use this option to receive a broad spectrum of content.
- **News:** Returns results from news websites
- **Blogs:** Returns results from blogs
- **Video:** Returns only video results
- **Updates:** Returns real-time results from social sites such as Twitter, Facebook, and YouTube
- **Discussion:** Returns results from forums and other discussion groups

The third box allows you to decide how often you receive your alerts. The choices include the following:

- As-it-happens
- Once a day
- Once a week

Make your "How often" selection based on the sensitivity of you finding this information and how often you can deal with the influx of e-mail. I recommend selecting once a day. Also, recall that the results are based on content that has been indexed by Google's search algorithm, and thus the alerts are delivered relative to when the content is indexed, not when it is published.

In the fourth box you choose the number of results that will be included in your alert e-mail. There are two options for "Email length":

- Up to 20 results
- Up to 50 results

There is no hierarchy to the search results included in an alert, so the alert that matters most to you might be in the first 20 or the next 30. I suggest you start with 50 results—you can always change to 20 results later if you need to see fewer.

The fifth and final box is to fill in the "Deliver to" address. Make sure you enter a valid e-mail address, as Google will send you a verification e-mail. When you receive this e-mail, click on the "Verify" link to confirm that you want to receive the alert or click on "Cancel" to discard the alert. You must verify your request before Google will start to send you alerts. Once you've done that, your alert has been created.

Figure 10.2

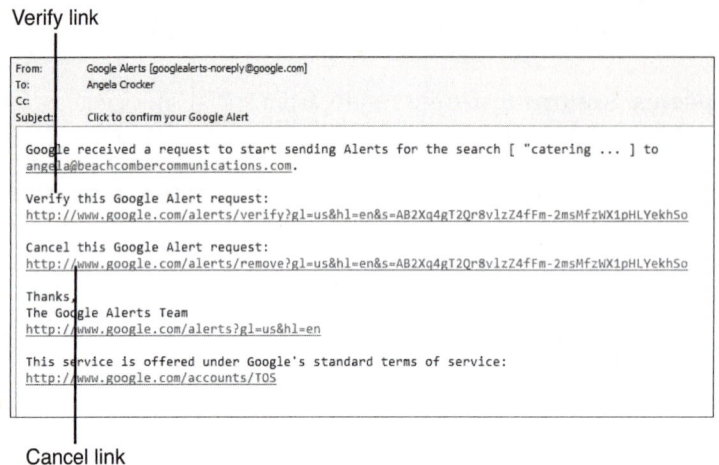

```
From:     Google Alerts [googlealerts-noreply@google.com]
To:       Angela Crocker
Cc:
Subject:  Click to confirm your Google Alert

Google received a request to start sending Alerts for the search [ "catering ... ] to
angela@beachcombercommunications.com.

Verify this Google Alert request:
http://www.google.com/alerts/verify?gl=us&hl=en&s=AB2Xq4gT2Qr8vlzZ4fFm-2msMfzWX1pHLYekhSo

Cancel this Google Alert request:
http://www.google.com/alerts/remove?gl=us&hl=en&s=AB2Xq4gT2Qr8vlzZ4fFm-2msMfzWX1pHLYekhSo

Thanks,
The Google Alerts Team
http://www.google.com/alerts?gl=us&hl=en

This service is offered under Google's standard terms of service:
http://www.google.com/accounts/TOS
```

Verify link

Cancel link

Here is the confirmation e-mail for our search terms "catering weddings." Note the "Verify" and "Cancel" links.

> **FLICKERS OF INSIGHT**
>
> To make setting up a Google alert even faster, use the default answers to the three questions. Then all you have to do is enter the search words and e-mail address, and click **Create Alert**.

Each e-mail from Google Alerts will include a list similar to the one in Figure 10.3. Depending on how many instances your search term has been indexed, some notifications may include only one or two links, while others will list the full 20 or 50, depending on your search criteria. Note that on days when no search results are indexed, you will not receive a Google Alert e-mail.

Chapter 10: What to Say 145

Figure 10.3

Once you've set up one or more alerts, you'll find a list like this one in your Google account at alerts.google.com.

Figure 10.4

A sample Google Alert e-mail for the search term "catering weddings."

Over time you'll discover which alerts bring you the most valuable information. Every Google alert e-mail includes three links at the bottom of the page to make it convenient to add, delete, or modify your alerts, as needed. These options are:

- Remove this alert
- Create another alert
- Manage your alerts

If an alert is of no value to you and you want to cancel it, click **Remove**. If you want to add a new alert, click **Create**. Both of these functions can be done without logging in to your Google account. If you want to edit the search terms or adjust the length or frequency of your alerts, you'll need to log in to your Google account. Click **Manage** in the alert e-mail to go to a login screen.

> **FLICKERS OF INSIGHT**
>
> Managing the Google Alerts you receive can be a daunting task. Give yourself permission to prioritize the alerts you read thoroughly and, on occasion, delete some alerts unread. Also, get in the habit of skimming the short introduction that appears, and click through to only the most relevant links.

Once you've set up some Google Alerts, you'll have a steady stream of potential links to share as content on your social network.

Bookmarking Accounts

Another way to find links for sharing is to use one or more social bookmarking tools. These tools are similar to the bookmark feature in your web browser. However, social bookmarks are shared publicly and can be searched by topic. Many social bookmarking sites also offer a way to rate content.

For social network hosts, social bookmarking can be a valuable way to share resources—but more importantly, it can be a tremendous source of links to share within the social network.

For example, a visit to StumbleUpon (www.stumbleupon.com) reveals dozens of top topics. To get started, you have to sign up for a free account. Once that's done, you can log in and start browsing around. The easiest way to do that is to click on the yellow, rectangular **Stumble** button.

Figure 10.5

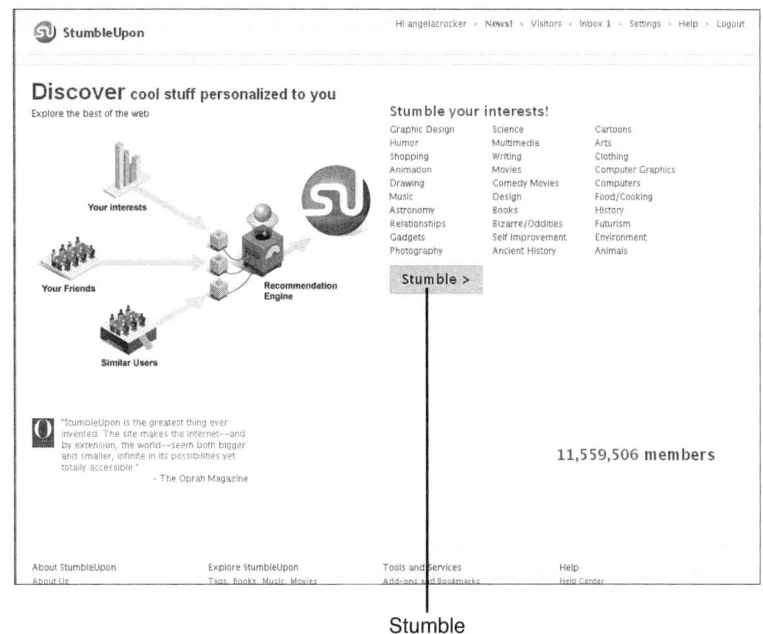

*To explore the content on www.stumbleupon.com, click the **Stumble** button.*

When you click **Stumble** you're taken to a random web page of interest to other StumbleUpon users. Alternatively, you could pick a category from the StumbleUpon home page and be directed to a topical bookmarked site. If you browse categories related to your network, you'll be sure to find content of interest to your members.

When you "Stumble" a site, you will view that site with the StumpleUpon tool bar across the top of your browser window. If you want to share the content you see, use the sharing links. If you don't like what you see click **Stumble** again to see another option.

If science is a focus of your social network, sharing a link to this biography of Albert Einstein (see Figure 10.6) would be terrific content for your network.

In a sense, this is file sharing, except that the files aren't automatically transferred to your computer. Rather, you browse the content online.

Figure 10.6

Results from StumbleUpon for the topic "science" brings us to a biography of Albert Einstein.

Some bookmarking sites also offer a ranking option to rate the value of the resource. This could be a simple thumbs-up or thumbs-down situation, or a more complex star rating system. You might use this *crowd-sourced* evaluation to determine if the content is worth sharing with your network.

> **DEFINITION**
>
> Web content that is **crowd sourced** might win a popularity contest. Good content that receives enough thumbs-up or five-star ratings will increase in popularity as more and more web surfers see the content based on the good opinions of others.

There are many other bookmarking tools to choose from, and you've likely heard of one or more of the following services:

- Alltop (alltop.com)
- Delicious (www.delicious.com)
- Digg (www.digg.com)
- Reddit (www.reddit.com)

Each service offers slightly different features and functions, but all are great resources for content to share.

> **FLICKERS OF INSIGHT**
>
> With so many sources of things to share on your network, you may want to make note of some items and use them later. A notebook on your desk is fine. If you're more digital, try Evernote (www.evernote.com) as a way to gather text, photos, and voice recording with tags for easy reference.

Sharing Photos

The saying "a picture is worth a thousand words" is absolutely true for social networks. Photographs, drawings, and charts all improve a networks ability to engage readers.

Share photographs from company events or social gatherings. Upload images of relevant products and services that will inform members. When appropriate, share humorous or thought-provoking images to spark dialogue. Invite members to share photos of them using your product at home or away.

Digital Camera

Odds are someone in your organization already has a digital camera. If not, please spend the money and invest in one—you'll be glad you did.

There are many different types of digital cameras. The three most popular are:

- A pocket, or point-and-shoot, camera from a company such as Nikon, Canon, or Samsung.
- A digital SLR (single-lens reflex). My favorite is the Nikon D90.
- A smartphone camera built into an iPhone, DROID, or BlackBerry.

Each type of camera has its advantages and drawbacks in terms of cost, speed, and ready availability. The point-and-shoot camera is the least expensive choice, with many models available around the $100 mark, whereas a SLR camera will cost $1,000 or more. The pocket camera and smartphone camera can take only one picture every few seconds, whereas the SLR can capture many images in rapid succession. And then there's the matter of having the camera handy when you need it. Often a phone camera or pocket camera are more likely to be in your purse or briefcase rather than the bulkier SLR equipment. There's also the issue of picture quality, with the phone camera offering today's equivalent of a digital Polaroid versus the higher resolution possible with a pocket camera or SLR.

The point is this: the camera your team or your community members have available will determine the resolution and framing of the pictures that appear on your network—regardless of the content of those images.

Visit an electronics store or your local camera store to get some professional advice on the camera best suited to your needs and budget. Whatever type of camera you have, it will make it easy to capture a candid moment or a more formal portrait to share with your social network.

Taking Pictures

Don't be afraid to take lots of pictures. Digital photography frees us of the old film mentality of "make every image count." You can always delete an image, so go ahead and try new things, make mistakes, or simply take lots of shots to make sure you get a keeper.

In broad terms, there are two kinds of photographs—candids and posed shots. Candids often capture the feel of an event or activity best, while posed shots have a more formal look. Either way, it's tough to get the perfect shot without any eyes closed.

Please remember that any photographs posted by staff members or official network moderators must represent your company's brand or community organization's goals well. It's okay if participants post amateur shots, but official photography from administrators should suit the desired image. This may mean hiring a professional photographer to capture key events and activities throughout the year.

Some people perceive professional photographers as an unnecessary expense, and this is simply not so. Think of photography as another investment in your marketing tool chest. To find a great photographer in your area, do some research. Don't be shy!

Not every budget lends itself to hiring a photographer, though. If you decide to take on the task yourself, then please keep in mind these tips from Wendy D., a highly respected professional photographer in Vancouver:

- Shoot in the highest resolution possible.
- You can always crop a photo later, if needed.

- Check the background behind your subjects. Does anyone have a plant growing out of his or her head?
- Have people turn at a three-quarters angle to the camera lens for a more flattering profile.
- Look for the light and have it shine on your subjects' faces, but don't make them squint.
- Avoid lighting that creates big shadows around people's eyes.
- Plain backgrounds work best and are less distracting in the photo.

Position your camera so it is at eye level or a little above. Shooting from below is not flattering.

Photo-Editing Software

Photo-editing software enables you to alter your pictures. The software ranges from the top-of-the-line Adobe Photoshop to the affordable Corel PaintShopPro X. There are also free programs available, such as IrfanView, that do basic photo-editing tasks.

> **CLOUD SURFING**
>
> You may already have photo-editing software on your computer. However, if you are looking to add some your choices range from the high-end Adobe Photoshop (www.adobe.com/photoshop) to the mid-range Corel PaintShopPro (www.corel.com/paintshoppro) to the freeware IrfanView(www.irfanview.ca).

Some of the things you may want to do to edit your pictures include:

- Cropping images.
- Rotating images.
- Fixing red eye.
- Lightening or darkening a background.
- Adding text or other enhancements.

The benefit of a professional graphic designer is desirable to help manipulate the photos to best advantage. However, if you're on a tight budget, you can make the most of the photos by using basic software tools to make needed changes.

Photo-Sharing Accounts

Photos can be used in many ways throughout a social network. You may have event photo albums and a who's who directory, plus other photos to illustrate discussion topics. Some photos will only be used once, while others will be used frequently both within the social network and on social media outposts.

Whether you plan to use a photo once or many times, I suggest putting the photos onto a file-sharing service such as Flickr (www.flickr.com), SmugMug (www.smugmug.com), or Picasa (www.picasa.com) rather than uploading them from your computer each time they are needed. In doing so, you create an archive of photos for possible future use. Furthermore, your community members can share their pictures through these tools for all to enjoy, as well. Each offers tagging, filing, editing, and sharing tools that make life easier, as well.

Tagging is a particularly useful function, as it allows you to add labels to a photo. As you may recall from Chapter 4, you can tag people, places, or objects in the image, and you can tag the image itself with details on where it was taken, the date it was taken, and who gets credit as photographer. By tagging members of your community, they get validation that you know who they are and appreciate their role in your community.

Ready access to the images will also be useful as you extend your community through social media outposts like Facebook and Twitter. We'll talk more about enhancing your social network with social media in Chapter 13.

My preference is to use Flickr—one of the most accessible and flexible accounts available. It has a free account available to anyone with a limited number of photo uploads each month and a limited overall capacity. One of the drawbacks of the free account is that members can access only a low-resolution version of their images, even if they upload a high-resolution copy. For some members the low-resolution versions are sufficient, while others need higher-quality pictures. Flickr offers a terrific premium membership with unlimited uploads and access to high-res versions for just $24.95 a year. It also stores high-resolution versions of your images even if you let your account lapse back to the free membership level. Upgrade to the premium level again and your high-res access is restored.

Sharing Videos

Videos add variety to the presentation of content within a social network. We all communicate best if we have access to information in multiple ways. Adding video is a great way to make your network an even better communicator.

Video Camera

As with still-image cameras, there are many types of video cameras. In fact, the digital camera or smartphone you already have may also take videos.

If you want video clips of higher quality, invest in a quality video camera. Units like the Flip and the Kodak Zi8 are hugely popular, as they come with a built-in USB port which can be connected to a computer for instant uploads. Videos shot on film can also be uploaded to a computer, although it takes longer to upload and digitize the file.

Taking Videos

Videos can be shot in many different formats, from Quicktime and .avi to .mpeg and .mov. The specific type is usually determined by your camera, and most types can be converted to other formats as needed. The conversion is sometimes necessary because your members will have different software on their computers and may not be able to read all formats.

As with photography, there are many things to consider when capturing video footage. Here are just a few questions to ask yourself:

- What are you filming and when?
- Is the location an indoor or outdoor venue?
- Do you need a weather contingency plan?
- How is the lighting? Is it too bright or too dark?
- How will the footage be used?
- Do you need written permission to use the images of the people in the video? Visit bit.ly/AVRelease for release examples from Florida Atlantic University.
- Who's responsible for the editing and upload?
- What's the timeline to get the video online?

With so many elements to consider, once again it's advisable to find a professional videographer to shoot the video for you. The videographer will work with you to make the video everything you want and need it to be.

If you must do the filming yourself or something unexpected happens and you grab a video camera to capture the spontaneous moment, then keep these tips in mind:

- As best you can, set the scene so that it reflects the story you want to capture.
- Check on the lighting situation. Are people's faces illuminated but not washed out?
- How's the background noise? Is it being picked up on the microphone?
- Are there distractions for the people in the video? Things like trucks going by or crying children will hinder your efforts.
- Are you trying to capture a talking-head interview style, or do you want to widen your frame to show some of the location?

> **FLICKERS OF INSIGHT**
>
> Sometimes you don't need video, if the visuals don't add anything vital to the discussion. Consider using an audio track to share a speech, lesson, or conversation.

Audio-Video Editing Software

Once you have some video clips, you must decide what to do with them. If your network is a casual environment, you may just upload the raw clip without making any changes or edits. Other times you'll want to enhance, edit, or otherwise change your video using a video editing software package. Here are some audio-video editing software options:

- Windows Movie Maker (included with Windows)
- iMovie (for those using Macs)
- Corel VideoStudio Pro
- Cyberlink PowerDirector
- Adobe Premiere Elements
- Final Cut (for serious video-editing needs)

These software packages enable you to do many things, including the following:

- Add titles before or after your footage
- Edit clips from different movies into one bigger movie
- Add still photos or other graphics
- Add music or a voiceover
- Adjust sound levels
- Make videos accessible to users of different types of computers by exporting different video formats
- Upload to your social network and other social sites

> **FLICKERS OF INSIGHT**
>
> There's no one-video-format-fits-all because several different companies developed video technology at the same time. For example, Microsoft developed Audio Video Interleave (.avi) and Windows Media Format (.wmv), while Apple created QuickTime (.mov), and there are others as well. The challenge comes when trying to get certain movie types to play on computers. You can get .avi movies to play on Windows machines, but not always on non-Windows computers. Similarly, QuickTime movies cannot be played on Windows machines without an extra (free) component installed. Many users struggle to add components to their computer and thus can't watch .mov files. The most popular format is .mpeg (moving pictures expert group), as it works across platforms and is supported by the popular browsers.

Video-Sharing Account

Similar to the photo-sharing accounts we discussed earlier in the chapter, there are several tools available for video sharing. YouTube (www.youtube.com) and Vimeo (www.vimeo.com) are both good options, although many favor YouTube as it currently has more influence on search engine rankings. Vimeo has an aesthetically pleasing interface, so it's really a matter of personal preference. For many, search rankings are more important than appearance because they increase the visibility of your network when potential members put relevant keywords into a search engine. You want your network to rank high for greater visibility.

Once content is uploaded to a video site, it can be shared with a simple link or by using embedded code to include the video in a website like your network.

> **AVOID THE FAIL**
>
> Make certain you have the okay of parents or guardians before photographing or videotaping any children involved in your event. Some caregivers have strong objections for a variety of reasons. If in doubt, don't use a photograph or video that includes a minor child.

The Least You Need to Know

- Find relevant news to share from reports and opinions.
- Spark dialogue with thoughtful, open-ended questions.
- Set up Google Alerts and use social bookmarking tools to find interesting, relevant links.
- Share photos and videos with your community.

Okay, Now What?

Part 4

Your network is set up—congratulations! This is the part to read when you want to figure out what to do with your shiny new toy. Start by uploading some preliminary content and cultivating relationships with people who join your community. Don't be shy—read on for some tips to make this painless.

You'll also learn about ways to make money with your network and how to measure your success. Some successes will put money in your pockets while others will be measured in terms of reach and influence. Once you've finished counting, we'll take a detour to cover a few thorny issues that can help or hinder a network. You'll be empowered to avoid common pitfalls involved with issues such as anonymity and authenticity.

Finally, we'll wrap things up with an overview of ways to enhance your network with social media and some recommendations on how to check up on your network. All of your hard work will foster a vibrant community.

Cultivating Relationships

Chapter 11

In This Chapter

- Identifying the types of people you want to engage
- Determining where to find your target audience
- Explaining the benefits of membership
- How to engage a variety of communication styles
- Identifying common objections and appropriate responses

Define the People You Want to Reach

Okay, you've got a network set up and you've figured out what sorts of content you're going to share. That's great. However, you need people to join or you're just talking to yourself. That just won't do.

Now's the time to go back to all the thinking you did in Chapter 2 about connections and objectives. What types of connections have you decided to make? Are you reaching out to businesses, consumers, your peers, or a specific community? What are your objectives? Do you want to focus on education or fundraising, or something else?

Also think about the people you want to reach in terms of demographics and geography. Would you prefer to recruit people from a particular city or region? Are you reaching out to men or women? Parents or retirees? People with means or people with needs?

Determine How to Reach Them

Once you've taken a refresher on your connections and objectives, and have some broad sense of who and what they are, the hunt begins. Finding people to participate in your network is not always easy, but there are things you can do to get started.

Begin with your existing digital connections. Send an invitation by e-mail. Announce the network in your newsletter. Blog about it, and invite others to join in the comment section of other blogs (only where appropriate, please!).

I encourage you to try a combination public relations campaign. Harness both social media and traditional media outlets. If you can afford one, hire a publicist to help get your spokesperson on the radio and TV in your key geographic areas. If money's tight, interact with media types both offline and online and pitch your story. Be sure to take advantage of any free listings or other coverage available in your local papers. Announce your network through Twitter and Facebook. Leverage all media to spread the news far and wide.

> **AVOID THE FAIL**
>
> Publicity is one of those areas where I encourage you to hire an expert. Although you can build relationships with media outlets in your geographic area, it's a time-consuming process to develop a level of relationship where you can pitch a story. Publicists are paid in part for their diverse connections but also for their relationships with the media. The media trust good publicists to act as a filter and bring them only appropriate stories for consideration.
>
> To find a good publicist ask around your community for recommendations. You can also consult your local chapter of the American Marketing Association or a similar professional organization.

Consider building an outreach program to public health units, veterans associations, church groups, or parenting groups—whatever types of groups include your target audience. Offer up complimentary programming, such as a guest speaker, or distribute a how-to pamphlet or other informative brochure, and include an invitation to join the network.

> **AVOID THE FAIL**
>
> Make sure that the spokesperson for your social network is a good public speaker. Ideally, this person will be familiar with your network, well spoken, personable, and comfortable in front of an audience. Think of him as an ambassador for your community.

There's also the personal touch. Get out in the real world and talk to people. Send emissaries to the places your audience gathers, whether that's conferences or community events. Hand out business cards with the network details on them. Maybe even consider a publicity stunt or goofy giveaway to draw attention to your efforts, if that's appropriate to your network.

> **FLICKERS OF INSIGHT**
>
> Publicity stunts are only good if they are memorable in a positive way. At the 2010 Northern Voice conference, two memorable stunts were done. The first happened during the opening session when a delegate sat in the audience dressed in a chicken costume wearing a T-shirt with an Office Max logo on it. At the same event, Travel Masters, a travel agency, distributed branded snack bags with ginger cookies inside and suggestions on how to serve those cookies. Both stunts were noticed by conference attendees and received mentions online.

Once you've engaged the first group, the activity on the network will encourage others to participate. We're a society that likes to join in what others are doing—your first few members will encourage further participants.

As you focus on your recruiting, take a moment to celebrate every hard-won member of your community. It takes time to build these relationships. Don't rush your efforts and expect instant satisfaction. A network is a strategy for the long haul—don't expect overnight results. Enjoy the results as they come along.

Make It Easy to Participate

People are extremely busy. To make it supereasy to join your network, have an obvious "sign up here" button on your welcome page. Don't forget a friendly, easy-to-spot login area for your existing members.

I encourage you to include other sorts of social networks on the welcome page for your site as well. Include a Twitter feed or recent updates from your Facebook page. (We'll talk more about these social media tools in Chapter 13.) Although you want them to sign up for your network, it may be more convenient for them to add you to their Twitter or Facebook accounts. Many users see these streams as a "try before you buy," even if the network is free. Make it easy for them to engage in whatever way works for them.

Figure 11.1

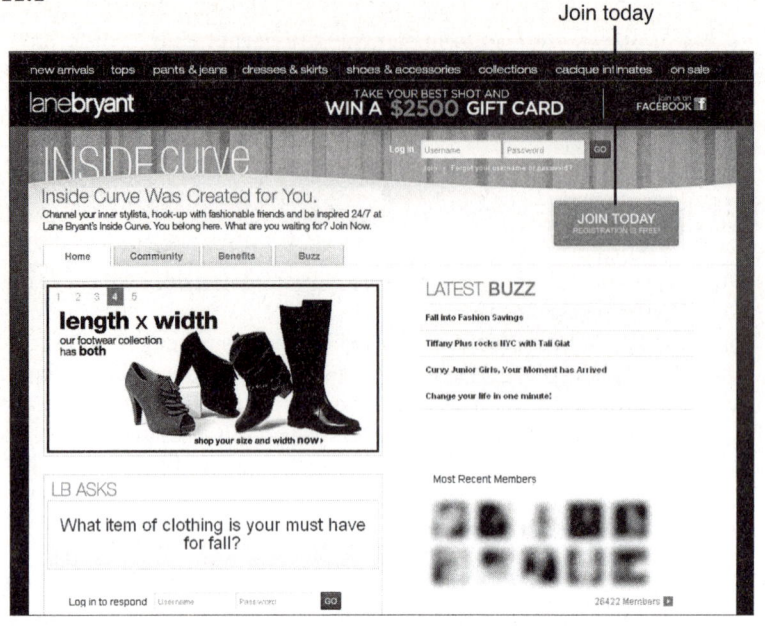

Fashion retailer Lane Bryant makes it easy for customers to join the Inside Curve community, built by KickApps, at insidecurve.lanebryant.com.

Figure 11.2

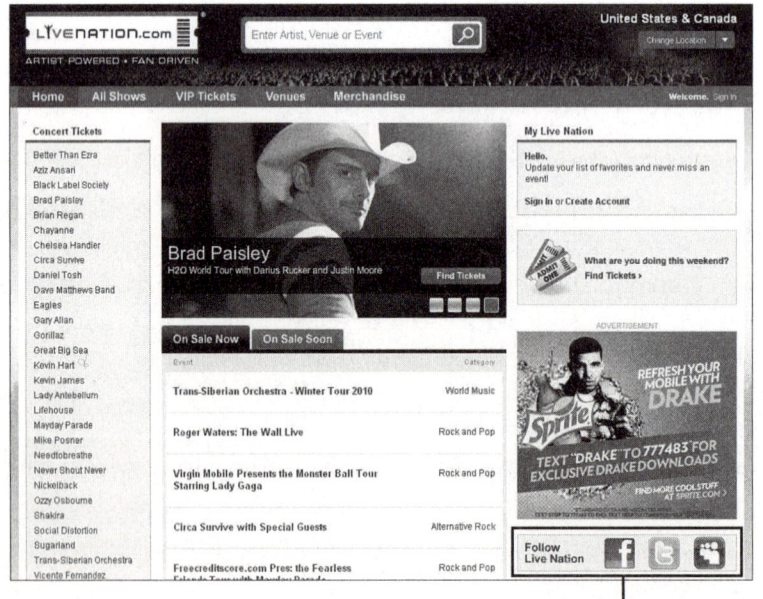

LiveNation.com, built by KickApps, invites members to connect on Facebook, Twitter, and MySpace.

Once a user is logged in, make it obvious how and where members can get involved. Do you have discussion boards or a list of blog posts to comment on? Are there photo albums to browse or a new how-to video to watch? Whatever your features, make them readily accessible.

Articulate the Benefits of Membership

What are you offering? You want people to join your network to help you meet your objectives, but what's in it for them? Your benefits might include the following:

- Rich resources, such as a recipe index
- Free industry reports
- Market research tools
- Newsletter
- A place for dialogue
- Photo gallery
- Event-planning tools
- Complimentary advice
- Stress relief

Think of the win-win. Your win is the opportunity to get acquainted with and engage the member and all that means for your business or organization. What's the win for your member?

This is your opportunity to pitch membership in your community. Talk to them in real life or engage with them by e-mail. As you ask them to consider your community, focus on the needs you will fulfill for the member not the features you offer. This is the time to be a salesperson. Speak or write persuasively and politely pursue potential members.

Consider Communication Styles

Are you familiar with Meyers-Briggs, DISC, or Insights? These are tools commonly used in the workplace to categorize personality types and communication styles. Some employers use them as team-building exercises, while others use them as professional development and self-discovery tools. All of these indices are based on the work of Carl Jung, founder of the Jungian school of psychology.

Your social network will include people with a wide variety of communication styles. As you seek new members, be sure to present your messages in a variety of ways to communicate clearly with all communication styles. This is also useful to keep in mind on an ongoing basis as you share content with your community. Some members will want quick hits of information while other members desire in-depth analysis.

Let me introduce you to four common communication styles. You'll find most people fall into at least one of these categories.

Direct Communicator

The direct communicator knows what he thinks and what he wants. This person doesn't hesitate to communicate quickly, decisively, and efficiently, and expects the same from others.

Quickly provide brief, factual information to communicate well with this group. Make your messages short and to the point, and be prepared to promptly reply to any follow-up questions with equal brevity.

Spirited Contributor

The spirited contributor is a social person who likes to discuss and consider any information. She is looking for dialogue and friendly debate.

Provide information in a conversational style and be prepared to engage in an extended dialogue with this type of communicator. Be ready to respond rationally to any objections that may arise.

Peaceful Collaborator

The peaceful collaborator goes with the flow. He is the one most likely to follow the majority of opinion passively and without debate. He avoids both confrontation and overthinking.

This type of communicator needs to discuss a wide variety of issues, not just the issue at hand. Offer facts about your network but also offer other information based on your mutual interests and the news of the day.

Systematic Methodist

The systematic methodist considers all the facts and organizes the information before considering a decision. She tends to be thoughtful and reflective. It may take some time to reach a decision, but once she does she is steadfast in her point of view.

This group needs time to digest all the facts. Present the information in a way that they can refer to and reflect upon it privately. Responses may seem slow, but once made this type of communicator is extremely loyal to their well-thought-out opinion.

> **CLOUD SURFING**
>
> For a quick snapshot of your own communication style, visit www.personalitytest.net/types to take a Jungian style assessment from the Personality Test Center.

Everyone is some blend of all types. Each of us has one or two categories that are our stronger preferences, and perhaps another category that is challenging to engage. The goal is to understand people's preferences and step out of our own tendencies when necessary to communicate well.

> **FLICKERS OF INSIGHT**
>
> Be sure to consider the communication styles and priorities of various generations interacting with your network. For example, baby boomers (born 1943–1960) have different life priorities than Millenials (born 1982–2002).

As a network manager, it is important to understand that your community will be made up of all communication styles. Ensure that you are offering communication suited to each style.

Overcoming Reluctance

Of course, some people will have an objection to overcome before joining a network. It's just like any sales call where you have to address every concern before you make the sale. It helps to be prepared with knowledge of common objections and how to address them before you get out there and "sell" your community.

Determine Common Objections

If your network is related to an established business, community group, or cause, then you've likely already got a laundry list of objections you've faced in the past. If your network is something new, then you can make some best guesses about what the objections might be and you'll learn more as you go along.

An objection is any reason a person perceives as a reason not to do something. They might articulate this to you if you are conversing in person or through e-mail. However, they may simply be evaluating your community by looking at your website. As this is the more common scenario, try to include content on your welcome page, or on links from that page, that puts any fears to rest. For example, privacy is a common concern. Simply having a link to your privacy policy on the web page and clearly articulated privacy rules can remove this objection for visitors to your site.

Here are some common objections for social networks:

- I'm already using Facebook and Twitter; I don't want to add more social networks to my life.
- I'm too busy and don't have the time to participate.
- I'm having technical difficulty and find the network too cumbersome to use.
- I'm concerned about my privacy.
- I don't see value in it. What's in it for me?
- This is just a sales tool. I don't want to be sold to.
- I'm reluctant to participate, so why join?

By understanding the objections you can develop answers to help people remove these obstacles one by one.

Develop Responses

Once you know what the common objections are, you can develop replies that help people overcome their concerns. You can write these responses in appropriate places on your network. I would also suggest rehearsing these responses before you end up in a dialogue with someone. Here are some examples:

- Our community also has a presence on Facebook and Twitter. Perhaps you'd like to join our page or follow our tweet feed?
- We'd value your membership even if you can only drop by occasionally. There's no requirement to participate.
- Let me have someone from our technical team contact you. I'm sure they can assist and get you started. We also offer a quick video tour that you can take at your convenience.

- We respect your privacy and won't sell or trade your name or personal information. Here's a copy of our privacy policy.

- We offer rich content to our members. What information would be helpful to you?

- Our network is about community, not sales. There's no obligation to buy anything by being a member of our community.

- Your membership alone helps us demonstrate support in the community.

In truth, if someone has objections that you can't overcome, it may mean they are not the right fit for your network. If they're checking you out online you won't know the specific details of why they didn't join, although you will know how many visitors you had and for how long in your Feedburner data. (Read ahead to Chapter 15 for more on that.) Thank them sincerely for their interest and wish them well. No hard feelings.

Warmly Welcome Members

Acting as a gracious host is one of the best parts of being a network manager. When people join your network, welcome them to the community with open arms. Embrace their contribution and enjoy their company.

If your community is on a small scale, you can do this individually with personalized messages and introductions. If your community is larger, with numerous new members joining each day, find other ways to welcome them. Perhaps you could offer a free download as a thank-you for signing up, or send a message after their first week to ask how it's going. Yes, this will have to be a mass e-mail type message, but mail merge technology can allow you to personalize the messages you send.

FLICKERS OF INSIGHT

Free downloads are a common strategy for thanking new members. The download might be a free eBook or webinar related to the subject of your community. It could also be a relevant worksheet, video tutorial, or audio podcast for members to use and enjoy at their leisure.

Most of the social network services allow administrators to message members. This can be done manually or can be automated. You can also use these tools to automatically send pre-scripted follow-up responses at appropriate intervals. Although this is impersonal, members of large communities understand that administrators are doing their utmost to make people feel welcome.

> **AVOID THE FAIL**
>
> In general, I am not a huge fan of using autoreply features as they are so impersonal. However, there are times when high volume or hectic activity makes it sensible to use autoreply. Just remember to use it judiciously.

The Least You Need to Know

- Identify the types of members you want to invite to your social network.
- Figure out a communication plan to find members.
- Explain why membership is valuable and make it easy to participate.
- Understand the variety of communication styles and adapt to suit all needs.
- Be a gracious host.

Foster a Vibrant Community

Chapter 12

In This Chapter

- Ways to start a conversation and keep it going
- How to tap diverse sources to share information with your community
- Conversing with your members by responding to feedback
- Inviting new members and interacting with existing ones
- Some thoughts on autoreply
- Planning a real-world gathering of your community

With lots of great content and a flourishing roster of members, you are well on your way to creating a vibrant community within your social network. However, you cannot rest on your laurels. Instead, you must have a plan to keep members interested, engaged, and participating in your network. There are lots of ways this can be done.

Facilitate Dialogue

Is there someone in your family who keeps conversation flowing at family functions? You know, that person who can ask a leading question or make introductions to get people talking, and then keep that conversation flowing for the entire evening? Social networks require that same sort of social butterfly to keep people talking.

Start by becoming an active listener. Active listeners look for points of interest, things to clarify, and moments of enlightenment. Active listening can both facilitate dialogue and help administrators understand the needs of the community. Through active listening, you can find fodder for the other strategies in this section.

Ask Questions

One of my favorite things to do is to ask nosy questions. These aren't intended to be rude by seeking too much personal information. Rather, ask deeper questions to draw people out in conversation. Don't assume you understand how people perceive the world. Ask them. Look for the deeper layers of their personality and their worldview. What defines them and how does that relate to the focus of your network?

For example, a grief support network might ask the following questions:

- How do you honor your loved one's memory?
- What are the most important elements of a memorial service?
- Share a funny memory about your loved one.
- Where do you like to be on the anniversary of your loss?
- How do you cope when sadness grips you?

You can ask questions through many different features of your network—forums, groups, blog, or chat are all great places to reach out and talk with members. You can also send a message either addressed to each member individually or through a bulk message to all members. By asking probing questions you learn more about members, build and strengthen relationships, and also create some great discussions.

A variation on this strategy is to pose provocative questions. Address the elephant in the room. What's the one thing that everybody has an opinion on but nobody wants to be the first to speak up about? For example:

- An environmental activists network might ask, "What are you going to do to protest the planned incinerator?"
- A traditional family values network might debate, "Do our teens need chaperones?"
- A visual artists network might pose the question, "Exposed breasts—art or pornography?"

Spark the conversation by asking that uncomfortable question, but make sure it's appropriate to your network. A debate on abortion is not appropriate on a knitting network. You're not trying to alienate your membership; rather, you are drawing out a meaningful dialogue that will likely draw lots of participation. A great way to figure out those questions is to play devil's advocate. Consider the prevailing opinion on a topic within your community, and then ask about its exact opposite. You'll be surprised how thoughtful, and sometimes heated, the conversation can become.

> **FLICKERS OF INSIGHT**
>
> Network administrators must carefully consider whether to block or ignore negative comments about the community or individuals. On the one hand, negativity can be misleading or hurtful, but on the other hand allowing a wide range of opinions to appear on the network makes it appear a more balanced and interesting place.

Cite Statistics

There's nothing like a statistic to get people talking. Even though most people understand the number juggling that can create a statistic to support just about anything, there's something magical about numbers. We're impressed by them, or curious about them. Go ahead and quote a relevant statistic now again. Your membership will likely step up with thoughts, opinions, and more great dialogue.

News of the Day

Take a few moments each day to review what's happening in the news. Is there an election imminent or a celebrity scandal in the headlines? Offer up news of interest to your community, and serve the dual purpose of sparking conversation and also informing your members with rich content. News of the day can be referenced with a link, a photo, or a video clip to share some tidbit of news related to real estate, politics, art, current events, or whatever other topics are important to your network.

Don't hesitate to invite new people to join the discussion. Draw them in to dialogue with something like, "Hey, Mary, you know lots about gardening; can you share your advice on Jane's slug problem?" Even if you're inviting someone who's not an expert on the topic, anyone could have an opinion and a point of view to add to a rich dialogue. Make them feel welcome.

Be sure to keep the conversation moving along. It's a lot easier to continue a conversation than it is to start one from scratch. Ask supplemental questions and offer news updates. The goal is to make people feel part of a community rich in dialogue. Dialogue is a two-way conversation and should be filled with multiple replies from one or more people in conversation. That back and forth process keeps the conversation moving along.

Finally, know when it's time to wrap things up. All conversations come to a natural conclusion, and trying to force ongoing dialogue along one subject can start to feel forced and phony. Sometimes conversations just wither on their own. Other times the dialogue has a formal wrap-up filled with thanks. Whenever the conversation ends, go back to the beginning and start a new dialogue.

Share Information

Acting as host to a social network is the perfect time to become the sharer of all knowledge. Don't be stingy with what you know. Offer up information and keep your members in the loop. Help them know what's going on and why it's exciting (or maybe worrying). By sharing information freely you enhance your network's reputation as a central hub for the community.

Community-Specific Information

Talk about the community itself. You could start by celebrating enhanced member features and put the spotlight on new blogs, events, or photo threads. You might also want to highlight and welcome new members. As administrator, you will have access to the member roster and can see who's arrived. Don't put the spotlight on someone who would prefer to remain a wallflower, though. Ask their permission to be introduced to the community before you do it.

For networks with smaller memberships, introductions can be as simple as a message sent to all members. This is impractical for larger networks, as the volume of introductions would be overwhelming both for the administrator and the members. Another strategy is to add a featured new member section on the welcome page for your network. You might also invite the new member to join a group of interest and then make a point of welcoming and introducing them to the group. Depending on how often new members join your network, you can set the pace of introductions be that daily, weekly, or monthly.

> **FLICKERS OF INSIGHT**
>
> You've probably seen community introductions done to great effect at churches, mosques, or synagogues, where new postulants are welcomed to the spiritual family with acknowledgements during the service, a welcome tea, and maybe a new members section in the circular. Embrace this spirit of community and welcome within your social network.

Now, if your community is built around the use of a product or service, you have the power to share information about new product releases, pending retirements, and other company news.

Figure 12.1

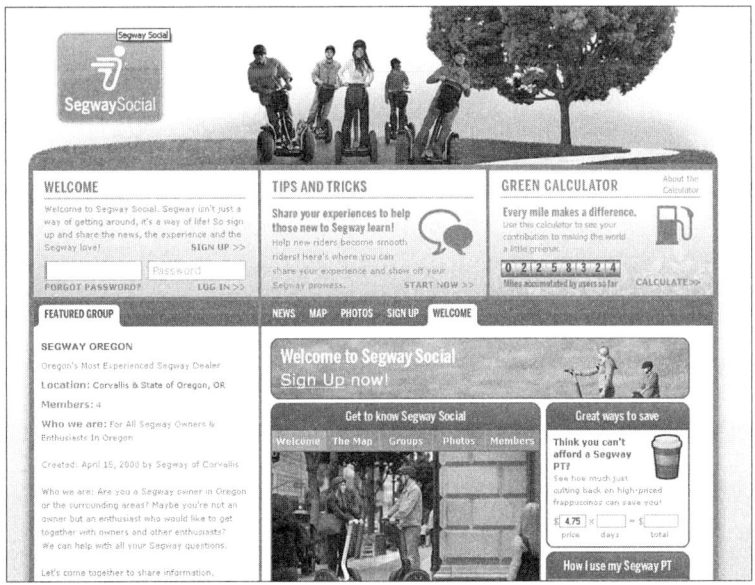

Owners of the Segway people movers are a natural fit for product-focused information sharing through their online community at social.segway.com.

Let's imagine your product is china and your community members are active collectors of your beautiful dishes. You'll have lots of news to share with members on a regular basis. Perhaps you announce the upcoming release of new china patterns twice a year. That's news. And then you might release news about a new artist whose work is featured on your china. More news. And almost every china pattern is eventually retired to make way for new product. This gives you the opportunity to announce the retired patterns and to provide details on where remaining inventory is available. Still more news! This fictional company has a lot of information to share with its community. What product-related details can you share with your community?

> **AVOID THE FAIL**
>
> Don't make the information you are sharing all about products and services. Your members did not sign up for a 24/7 infomercial. Find a balance between company news and community news that satisfies your membership. In general, and every situation is different, you'll want to spend no more than 20 percent of your time talking specifically about products and services for sale.

Upcoming events are a tremendous source of information to share with your community. Think of the sharing in terms of the life cycle of the event itself. You can start by notifying members that an event is in the works. Following that, you can announce the dates, location, and when tickets will go on sale. Next, you can share news about how quickly tickets are selling. There's also news along the way about featured speakers or activities that will be part of the event. You might also have travel partners with hotel and airfare deals to share with members, not to mention special offers from event sponsors. Then there's the event itself, with lots of news generated during the formal sessions and informal social events. After the event, there's news to share of major decisions, memorable moments, and the photos and videos taken of real-world participants. While events are a lot of work, they can be a tremendous source of news for online communities.

Sharing information about breaking news (both general interest and news specific to your community) can be a service to your community. What do you know about your organization that would be important news to your community? Make sure your social network community is among the first to hear the news directly from your organization. As for broader-scope breaking news, I can't predict for you what breaking news will hold the interest of your community. You'll decide what's appropriate to share when we are next affected by events similar to Princess Diana's death, the events of September 11, 2001, or the 2010 Haiti earthquake.

An important type of information sharing is to let members know about pending changes to the network service or function. By sharing news of change ahead of time, members will feel better prepared to cope with the change. Springing significant change on your community without warning is a guaranteed way to get them riled up and irritated with you. For example, if your network has been storing high-resolution, large photo files for members and then decides to change the policy to store only low-resolution, smaller photo files, you'll want to inform members well in advance so they can archive the high-resolution images elsewhere. If you fail to inform them in advance and the only high-resolution copy is stored on the network, members will become angry and upset. By announcing the change well in advance, you can prevent some of this ire.

> **AVOID THE FAIL**
>
> It can be tricky to know how often to send repeat information to members of your network. Some members will expect a message only once and be annoyed to receive the same information again. Other members might ignore the first message and assume you'll tell them again if it's really important. You'll have to get to know your community and figure out which style of communication works for most.

Subject Matter Experts

On a totally different tack is the idea of retaining subject matter experts (SMEs) to share information with your community. Is there someone doing research relevant to your network or an experienced physician with an appropriate specialty? SMEs don't have to be professionals in the traditional academic sense, although you may seek information from a doctor, lawyer, teacher, or police officer, for example. Open your scope to allow for other kinds of experts—a mom to four kids, a traditional healer, or a wise woman can all provide rich and interesting information depending on your community.

While many SMEs will share their knowledge out of the kindness of their hearts, it is only reasonable to retain them as contributors if you expect ongoing contributions to your community. By paying for content you both honor the contributions of the expert and guarantee ongoing quality information for members.

The cost to retain a SME varies widely, and it's difficult for me to tell you what to budget here. There are many writers keen to be published and willing to work for a modest fee—let's say $100 per article. However, other writers are aware of the value of their expertise and might charge significantly more, perhaps $1,000 per article. The fee might vary depending on the size of your network, the length of the articles required, and the frequency with which you expect them. You may also consider putting SMEs on a monthly retainer of anywhere from $250 to $5,000 or more as compensation for all the content they provide in a month—articles, photographs, facilitating chats, answering questions, and responding to comments. The fees you offer should be in keeping with the quality of content your members expect and the going rates in your industry.

Respond to Feedback

Earlier we talked about facilitating dialogue, and much of that advice holds true for responding to feedback as well. Listen actively, ask questions, and provide appropriate facts and statistics. Your members want to be heard and you should listen to their feedback.

Positive feedback comments are a bit like candy for network administrators. That pat on the back indicates members' interest in the content that's being shared and, to some extent, validates all the effort of creating and maintaining the community. Don't just bask in the glory; be sure to respond to positive comments so the members know that you heard their point of view.

Negative feedback also requires a response, but often it's harder to reply to. As with anything negative, it's tough not to take things personally. Try to remember that the network is not you. Many of us struggle with this, so before you respond, get over your personal reaction and reply in the voice of the network. Perhaps the negative comment resulted from a misunderstanding or technical glitch. Address the issue professionally, promptly, and politely.

A majority of feedback is benign, as in it is neither positive nor negative—it's just a comment. It's still good practice to respond to those comments even if it's just a simple thank you. The power of a thank you cannot be underestimated. It illustrates in two simple words the courtesy and respect that members can expect from the administrators.

Finally, be sure to review feedback and look for member questions. Are they seeking further information? Are they lost? Has something changed to confuse them? By answering questions, you can enrich their experience within the network and the opinion they will share outside the network.

Invite New Members

There's nothing like new members to foster a sense of community. New members bring new opinions, experiences, and energy to the network. This can have a recharging effect on existing members who are keen for new information and connections. We talked about cultivating relationships in Chapter 11 and I encourage you to review that chapter again if you're on a membership drive. Here are some ways to go about getting new members.

Your current members are truly your best advertising. If you have engaged and satisfied the needs of your members, they will share their good experiences with family, friends, and colleagues. On occasion, ask current members to invite new members to join. You can do this informally or you could create an incentive to motivate them further. Be careful with incentives, though, because you want to encourage new membership without having people sign up just so their friend can get the swag you're offering.

Let's clarify that an invitation is simply the question, "Would you like to join our network?" It doesn't have to be a fancy card like a wedding invitation or even a postcard with a casual invitation. Use what you are already creating both in print and online and add the words of invitation to your copy.

If you're a business or community group, ask your customers and clients to join your network. You may have asked them before and they declined, but there's no harm in inviting them again once in a while. You never know when they're going to decide to make that digital leap in your relationship. Also remember that if your business is thriving, you are probably gaining new customers regularly. Those are ideal candidates for invitations. Make them feel special. Thank them for their business and extend a personal invitation. Be sure to explain what the community has to offer that might be of interest. Done correctly, this will be perceived as great customer service even if they decide not to join.

Perhaps your organization hosts events from time to time. If so, make it easy for participants and audience members to join your network. Have your social network information available on-site. If appropriate, have a computer available where they can sign up on the spot. At the very least, have a printed takeaway that includes information about the network. Invite them to join. Again, you want to make them feel like part of your community.

You can also look for new members amongst those who are subscribed to your newsletter or engaged through your social media outposts. (We'll talk more about enhancing with social media in Chapter 13.) People who are engaging with you through other sources are a natural fit to receive invitations to join your network.

Finally, you have the option to seek out new members through traditional and online advertising. Perhaps Google ads or Facebook ads make sense to reach your target market. Or, if you are a geography-bound community, consider advertising in your local media. Remember that your online efforts, including your network, are aligned with your real-world efforts.

Interact One on One

Depending on the size of your community, it may be possible to interact with members one on one. Even if your community is very large, you can still reach out to some members (maybe just *superusers*?) now and again.

> **DEFINITION**
>
> All networks have technically minded members who learn and use all the features of the network. These members are often called **superusers.** Their familiarity with the features is often on par with network administrators.

Private messages are just that—private. Think of messages as a simple internal e-mail system that allows administrators and members to communicate privately with one another even if one of them is currently offline. Usually organized with a simple inbox and sent items file structure, members can review their messages at their leisure and keep an archive of old messages for future reference.

Often these messages can be sent to groups. Usually the user must have a friend connection or common group membership with each recipient before the messages are delivered. This prevents spam-type messages in members' inboxes.

As we discussed in Chapter 11, I suggest you, as administrator, start with a welcome message when someone joins your community. If your community is relatively small, you could manually generate the message. For larger communities or membership that expects an instant response, set this up as an autoreply. Thank them for joining and ask if they have any questions. Maybe share a bit about yourself or the organization that would be new information for them. You could include a small digital gift, such as a code for a free workshop or game token. Think of this message as the Welcome Wagon for your community.

It's also worth taking the time to check in with members at regular intervals. Maybe you pop them a message after their first week or month as a member. Certainly an anniversary message is appropriate. Some check-in messages ask for feedback while others are simply a hello and thanks so that members don't feel the onus of replying. We'll talk about the importance of checking in in Chapter 17.

On occasion, send a personalized private message to selected members. You might join them in celebrating their marriage, the purchase of a new home, or completion of a college diploma. You might also send wedding anniversary or birthday greetings. If your relationship is more business focused, then send congratulations on new premises, a redesigned logo, or a years-in-business milestone. Some messages may be less positive if there is need to send a get-well note or condolences on the loss of a loved one. The details of these life experiences come from communication on the network in members' activity feeds, forum posts, or chat discussions. Show your community that you are listening and know who they are and that you care.

Moderate Comments

Another very valuable investment of time is to moderate comments on your social network. This could be blog post comments, notes in *microblog* threads, comments on events, photos, or other content. Wherever you build interactivity, you need to monitor and moderate that activity.

> **DEFINITION**
>
> **Microblog** refers to text-based communication tools such as Twitter or Foursquare, where the text communication is limited to 140 characters.

Moderating comments isn't just a matter of reading what's been said and sharing it with colleagues over lunch. There are four key functions:

- Delete spam
- Remove slanderous comments
- Respond to criticism
- Give thanks for praise

First of all, delete any spam that gets through your spam filters. Unless it's relevant to your subject, you don't need offers of sexual enhancements, requests for international financing, or pharmaceutical sales offers clogging up the legitimate content on your network.

Next, you want to be vigilant about removing any *slanderous* comments that appear. Refer back to Chapter 7 to refresh your memory on the participation guidelines in your code of conduct to decide what needs to be removed. A comedian training network focused on buffoonery will be much more tolerant of personal attacks said in jest than a parenting group, for example.

> **DEFINITION**
>
> A comment is **slander** or libel if it demeans, berates, or otherwise harms the reputation of a person or brand. If the comment is made orally, it is considered slander while written attacks are libel.

I sincerely hope criticism will appear rarely in your network, but if it does, be sure to respond to it. Don't delete it; rather, add a constructive response, such as:

- Thank you for your feedback.
- We are aware of that problem and are working to fix it.
- A free upgrade/fix/patch is available here *<link>*.

Most often, you will receive praise for not only your products but for the engaging, informative community you have created online. At every opportunity, give thanks for this praise. Please don't use a generic statement for every expression of appreciation. Be specific—acknowledge people by name, express your pride in the product mentioned, and ask how you can help further. This sort of personalized response will engage your participants even more.

> **FLICKERS OF INSIGHT**
>
> Take a moment to celebrate any comments published on your social network. Some statistics suggest only 1 percent of those reading any website will leave a comment, so you could multiply each comment by 100 to get a sense of your reach.

Systemwide Messages

Your community may need daily systemwide messages that reach all members. Perhaps you share a daily reflection or offer an activity of the day that enhances your members' community experience. Systemwide messages can, of course, be sent less frequently. Some communities anticipate systemwide communication from the adminstrators only when there is a major event announcement or the occasional down period for network maintenance.

Whatever the frequency, systemwide messages should be short and clearly communicated with members. Brevity and clarity are key so that members actually read your missive rather than ignoring what you've got to say.

Get Together in Person

Sometimes fostering a vibrant community means throwing a party. Well, okay, it doesn't have to be a party, but it's fun to bring people together in the real world.

Get-togethers are such a great idea that there are social networks, such as Meetup, devoted to bringing people together. Your network may use a tool like Meetup or perhaps you've got an event planning feature built into your social network. (Pop back to Chapter 4 if you need a refresher on the events feature.) Either way, it's a good idea to bring people together in real time.

So what kind of get-together should your social network host? There are lots of options with many variables. You can spend a little or a lot. You can have a few people or thousands. You can create a free event or charge admission. Whatever you decide, always make sure it's the right kind of event for your community. Let's talk about some specific ideas.

A gathering could be as simple as descending on a local coffee shop or bar. Whether your group wants a coffee clatch or a beer night, there's nothing too formal about this event. Pick a time and location and let your people know. If your group is going to be more than 10 people, it's a good idea to call the venue manager and give them the heads-up that you are sending business their way. They can then staff appropriately to serve your group.

Other options include ticketed events like a luncheon with a special guest speaker or a cocktail party with ice breaker activities. It's common for the costs of these events to be shared with attendees who pay a modest fee to cover the room costs, speaker fee, and a plated lunch or some appetizers.

Figure 12.2

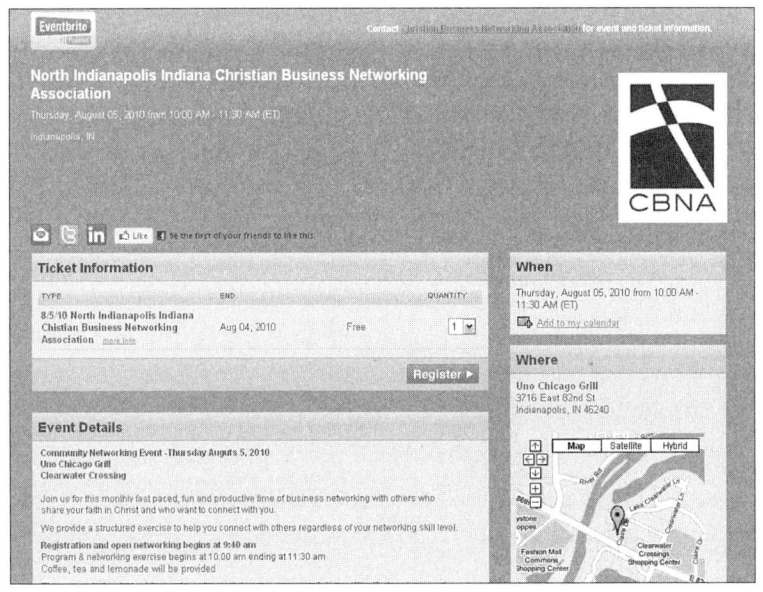

For a nominal fee, anyone can use the event planning and ticket sales tools at www.eventbrite.com.

Perhaps your organization has access to some of those subject matter experts we talked about earlier. Why not offer a seminar and give your network members a chance to learn more directly from the expert?

On a bigger scale, you could organize an entire conference, or maybe just add on an event for your community when many members plan to attend the same conference. Either way, it's an opportunity to see and be seen in the real world.

If your network is specific to a single city, then planning events is easy—you simply host them in your hometown. However, many networks have membership spread across many cities. If that's you, consider replicating a particular type of event in multiple cities over the course of the year. Your members will love that you took the time to come to them.

Patience

Remember that patience is a virtue. Even highly visible, well-known brands take time to build an online community. If you are building your brand profile at the same time you're building your network, bear in mind that you will need to be doubly patient.

The size of success will vary from one business to another. Some businesses will be delighted with 100 participants, others will wait to pop the champagne cork until they have thousands. Whatever your threshold, it will take time to add each relationship to the network. Please don't abandon early adopters because there's only a few of them. Stick with it and over time you will foster a vibrant community.

The Least You Need to Know

- Act as both host and moderator in conversations.
- Engage members personally.
- Be strategic and purposeful in your use of autoreply.
- Consider organizing a real-world meeting of network members.
- Be patient, as it takes time to build a community.

Enhance with Social Media

Chapter **13**

In This Chapter

- Deciding what social media tools work for you
- Popular social media sites and ways to use them
- Establishing your daily routine to manage social media

No matter what features and content become part of your social network, you have established a home base for your community's online presence. While your community may grow and flourish in its own location on the Internet, I encourage you to establish some social media outposts to engage potential members in other places on the web.

Your participation in sites such as Facebook, Twitter, and LinkedIn creates an easy point of entry for new members. These outposts are also useful for engaging those on the periphery of your community who may not be interested enough to join the community but still have some level of interest. There are added benefits such as brand awareness and strategic alliances that can also be a boon to your core network.

In order to be effective in your use of social media outposts, you must map out your activities with purpose. We'll talk in general terms about the functionality of each site, but each of these deserves an entire how-to book so I encourage you to seek additional resources (including those listed in Appendix B) to help you figure out how they function.

Make a Social Media Plan

As we talked about in Chapter 1, the terms "social media" and "social networks" are often used interchangeably. For our discussions, we defined social networks as community and social media as content. Of course, this gets muddled because communities form within social content sites. Occasionally you'll even see all-content communities called "social media networks." As we move through this chapter think of social media as any site other than your own network that includes content of interest to your community, even if that content is unrelated to your topic.

To give your network the maximum possible reach, seek out your target audience by engaging in general interest social media sites like Facebook, Twitter, and LinkedIn—and, perhaps, some niche social media tools as well. For example, consider Corkd.com if your community is for wine lovers or Blip.fm if your focus is music. In truth, you are networking in the most traditional "get-acquainted-how-can-we-help-one-another" sense. In doing so, you raise your profile, make your information more accessible, offer to help others, and make it easy for potential members of your network to get acquainted with what you do.

> **CLOUD SURFING**
>
> If you're looking for niche communities, explore Knowem.com. This user name checking service is a useful place to explore the variety of social media sites available in various niches including design, entertainment, health, photography, and other categories.

If this prospect overwhelms you, remember that all forms of networking have many dimensions—from conferences to coffee dates. To have the largest networking circle possible, you must engage in a variety of activities. To be most effective, do the same online—join the group conversations and find one-on-one conversations of interest. Introduce yourself and participate where it's appropriate.

"Appropriate" is a key word here. You want to genuinely insert yourself into the conversation. Be curious and interested and offer help. Don't barge into a conversation and say "join my network" to get what you want. The backlash from that sort of poor behavior would undo all the good work you'd put into creating your network.

To get the best impact, carefully select a few social media tools that suit your needs. Are you a "professional service"–type business? Then you likely want to be on LinkedIn and Twitter. Are you a "personality"-based business? Then Facebook and Twitter might be the right combination. Or perhaps you're a "bricks-and-mortar" business, in which case Facebook and Foursquare might be your top choices.

Once you've selected a handful of the most appropriate social media outposts make a plan to put them in action. Your first step should be to sign up for the selected services. Secure your accounts for them all at the same time, if you can. This will then ensure that you have your preferred name consistently across different sites. However, please don't start using them all at once. For most people, adding one new social media tool every three weeks works well. Give yourself time to get familiar with the tool and adjust the settings to maximize the value you're deriving from this extra effort. If you fully master the tool in less than three weeks by all means start on the next one. Also, give yourself permission to take longer if you need more time.

Next, prioritize the social media sites into the sequence you plan to use them. Will you add Facebook or Flickr first, or is YouTube your top priority? Or maybe your core focus is LinkedIn supported by Twitter?

As you activate each site in your plan, spend some time optimizing your accounts with a biography, photo or logo, and other information. (Chapter 8 offers lots of tips about profiles.) Next, spend some time exploring the tool. Figure out how to navigate and what different links do. Multitask this exploring time by listening and observing what others do with the site. Try to get a vibe for the tone and energy level of participants.

Finally, decide what kinds of content to share on each site and try for a balance of original content and referenced content. As for the content, that should follow the 80:20 rule—80 percent about others and 20 percent about your social network. (Remember our discussion about content in Chapter 9? You can use that advice outside your network, as well.) Your plan should also outline how often you'll participate in each site. We'll talk more about something I call the Daily Routine at the end of this chapter to determine the frequency.

Options to Consider

There are literally hundreds of social media tools that could become part of your social media plan. Some are household names familiar even to those without a computer, while others are newer or simply less well known. In fact, in the time lag between writing this book and your first opportunity to buy it, there will be tools that pop out of obscurity and into the limelight. Your task is to pick a few that make sense for your network and ultimately your organization.

Remember that this is something you are simply trying out. Give it your best shot and embrace those tools that work for your social network. If something isn't working, ask yourself, why? If the interface is frustrating you, then you'll likely want to seek out some training to make it easier for you. However, if the functionality isn't giving you the kinds of results you want, then it may be time to reconsider your social media mix.

> **FLICKERS OF INSIGHT**
>
> There are two trains of thought about promoting your social media outposts on your social network site. On the one hand, if people have already found your community and your goal is to engage them there you don't want to distract them with links to your outposts. At the same time, there are those visitors who aren't ready to sign up but have some interest. By highlighting your social media outposts you make it easy for them to date you before accepting your marriage proposal.

Facebook

Facebook (www.facebook.com) is the largest social media network, with more than 500 million active users. As we mentioned earlier in the book, Facebook users spend an average of 55 minutes per day on the service. That's a lot of sharing and connecting all in one place. This truly is the party to attend.

Celebrities, causes, and consumer brands engage a lot of customers through Facebook, and your social network can do the same.

> **FLICKERS OF INSIGHT**
>
> A new type of social media network called Diaspora (joindiaspora.com), an open-sourced social community, is being developed at this time. The creation of Diaspora is, in part, a reaction to Facebook's centralized model where Facebook, the company, controls the community. Diaspora is planned to be a decentralized, user-controlled community with transparent operations. Users will be able to see clearly where their data is going and how it is being used. An early version of the open source code for Diaspora was released to developers in September 2010 and the community is expected to launch in early 2011.

Facebook users will be familiar with the different types of accounts that appear within this community—profiles, groups, and pages. You'll want to choose the type that works best to support your network.

Profiles are for individuals. According to Facebook's terms of service, each individual is allowed one account, so users must marry their personal and professional selves into a single profile. Status updates posted to a profile appear in the news feed of that person's friends. Profiles are permitted a maximum of 5,000 friend connections.

Figure 13.1

Sean Cranbury's profile page on Facebook.

Groups are used to gather people with like interests including study groups, community organizations, and event planners. This category was Facebook's first service that connected people without requiring them to be friends. Groups can be made public or private—giving the option for a secluded space to interact within this huge community. The number of members of a group is unlimited; however, it is helpful to bear in mind that the group's administrator can send a message only to the first 5,000 members. Also, status updates posted to a group appear in the news feed of members only occasionally, which puts the onus on members to check the group wall for information.

Figure 13.2

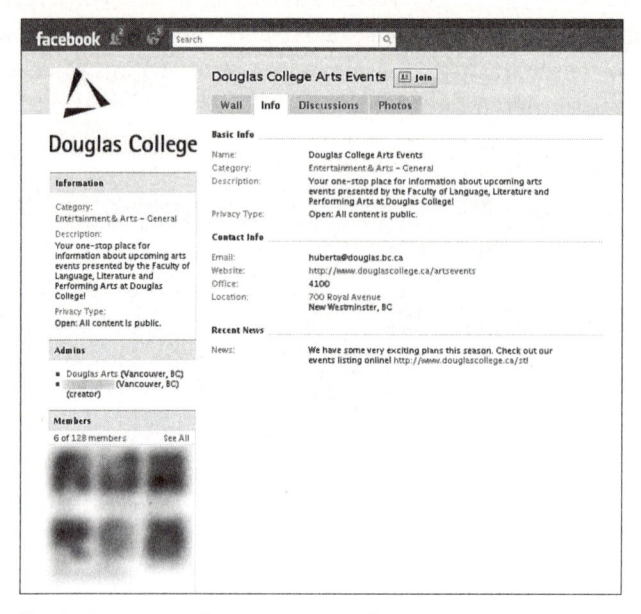

This Facebook group gathers supporters of arts events at Douglas College.

Facebook offers two kinds of pages—business pages and community pages. Business pages are for personalities and brands, while community pages are for causes and interests. Given the number of fan pages (the old Facebook lingo for pages) set up before the community page option was offered, this distinction is pretty blurry. The essential difference is in the set-up process. If you select a community page, you're not asked to categorize yourself into a particular business or celebrity category.

> **FLICKERS OF INSIGHT**
>
> Make it easy for people interested in your network to find you on Facebook. Go to www.facebook.com/username to set your custom Facebook web address. Twenty-five people must 'Like' your page before you can do this.

Pages have many desirable features, including an unlimited number of fans, the ability to add multiple administrators, and the opportunity to gather valuable data, called Insights, about users.

In general, I recommend businesses and organizations set up a business page to take full advantage of the limitless fans, multiple administrators, and the Insights data.

Include content from your blog, but also make a point to post items unique to the page. And be sure to engage in dialogue with anyone who comments on your status updates.

Figure 13.3

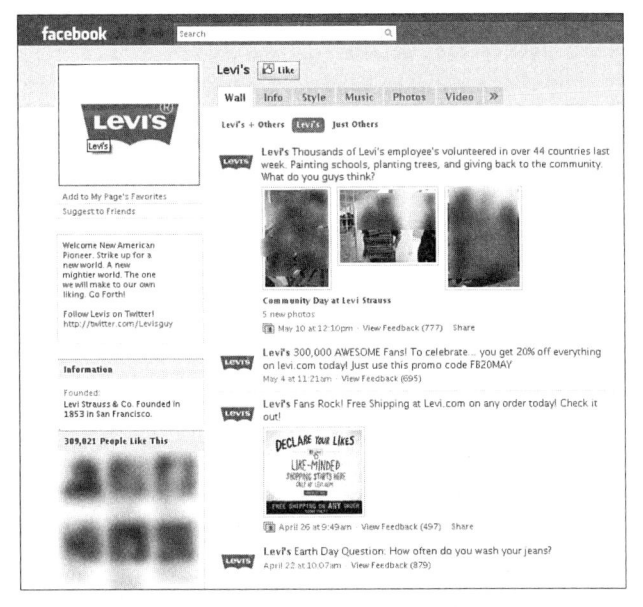

Fans of Levi jeans gather to share their enthusiasm for this iconic denim brand.

Twitter

If your social network is interested in engaging with professionals, consumer brands, academics, and parents then consider Twitter as a social media outpost. Some of the most successful accounts on Twitter are tied to big brands. Check out Whole Foods Market's efforts (www.twitter.com/wholefoods) and Domino's Pizza Chicago (www.twitter.com/Ramon_deLeon) for some great examples of brands connecting with customers on Twitter.

Twitter is a microblogging tool that allows users to share 140-character messages called "tweets." These short messages can contain all sorts of information, from brief status updates, some with photos, to conversation-starting comments with links to blog posts for more detail.

Once dismissed as a tool just for those with time to waste sharing details of their breakfast and bowel movements, Twitter is now considered a powerful tool for networking, research, and opinions.

> **FLICKERS OF INSIGHT**
>
> While many brands successfully participate on Twitter, those with the greatest success tend to be accounts for individuals. It has to do with the relationship building and conversational potential of tweeting. Success isn't about the number of followers or the number of tweets, it's about the quality of communication and the depth of relationships built. For a variety of examples of interesting Twitter users, visit www.twitter.com/CleverAccounts.

Within Twitter, all users sign up for the same sort of account. The connection between users is a one-way relationship. Each user decides who they want to follow. If they follow someone, then that person's tweets will appear in their news feed. In Twitter lingo, accounts you follow are those you are "following" and accounts that follow you are your "followers." Are you with me?

Figure 13.4

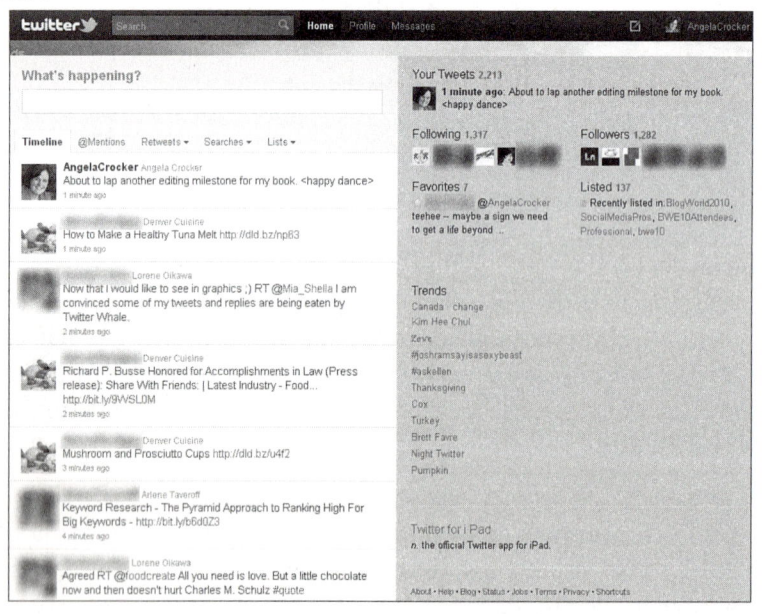

A typical Twitter home page.

Twitter messages can be used in several ways but all are limited to 140 characters. When a user tweets a status update other users can forward, or "retweet," that message. Both tweets and retweets can include mention of specific Twitter users using the @ symbol. For example, to mention me in a tweet you would include "@AngelaCrocker" in the message. (Go ahead and try it—I'd love to hear from you!) All of these messages are public and visible to anyone reading the news feed. Users can also send private messages, called direct messages or DMs, within Twitter by substituting the letter D for the @ symbol. Unfortunately, direct messages have become a haven for spammy autoreplies and genuine messages can get lost in the junk.

To help users organize the way they see information on Twitter, Twitter lists were developed to enable users to categorize people into groupings that make sense for them. These lists can be public, or locked for private viewing only. The public lists can be viewed by others who then have the option to follow lists of interest.

Figure 13.5

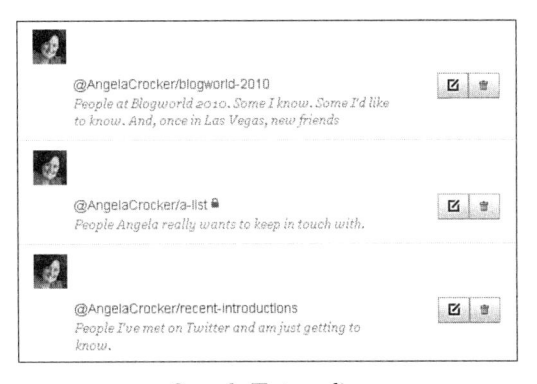

@AngelaCrocker/blogworld-2010
People at Blogworld 2010. Some I know. Some I'd like to know. And, once in Las Vegas, new friends

@AngelaCrocker/a-list
People Angela really wants to keep in touch with.

@AngelaCrocker/recent-introductions
People I've met on Twitter and am just getting to know.

Sample Twitter lists.

There's lots to know about Twitter so let me share a few more useful tips. When considering how you will use Twitter, please reflect on the quality versus quantity issue outlined in Chapter 16. Also, take advantage of search.twitter.com to look up keywords related to your topic and to find people of interest. Finally, make good use of *hashtags* to participate in discussions—this will help people find you.

> **DEFINITION**
>
> Within Twitter, conversations threads are noted using a **hashtag.** The hashtag is simply the "#" symbol followed by a short string of characters. You'll see conferences often announce an official hashtag such as the #BWE10 used for the 2010 Blogworld New Media Expo. Hashtags are also used to mark topical conversations such as "#parenting," "#mustread," or "#politics."

Foursquare

Foursquare is a location-based microblogging tool that allows users to "check in" at a particular location. Driven by the GPS service built into many smartphones, users decide when to announce their presence at a given location.

Figure 13.6

Sample check-ins on Foursquare from the iPhone app.

From a relationship-building point of view, users can use Foursquare to connect in the real world. Say you were a store owner and you were connected via Foursquare to your best customers. If these customers check in while at your store, you then know they are in the building and can give them the special treatment they deserve. Foursquare users see special offers when they check in at a given location; if they want to take advantage of the discount, bonus product, or other perk they identify themselves to the clerk. Even if there's no offer available at that location there's still the fun of earning points and badges from Foursquare.

> **FLICKERS OF INSIGHT**
>
> Gowalla is another location-based microblogging tool to keep an eye on. Similar to Foursquare, it offers the fun of trip-building functionality.

Foursquare doles out fun rewards for participants. The person who checks in most frequently at any given location is declared mayor, while all users can earn badges based on their check-in activities. Badge milestones include everything from your first check-in, which unlocks the "newbie" badge, to your first check-in at sea to unlock the "on a boat" badge.

When they go to check in users see a list of nearby locations based on their position relative to the GPS. If their place is not currently listed, they have the option to add that place and check in anywhere.

Foursquare is also interesting because participants can "shout" messages to one another, with either broadcast updates similar to tweets on Twitter or more specific messages like finding someone at a crowded carnival.

LinkedIn

LinkedIn is considered the professionals' social media site. With its simple text interface filled with rich information, many use this tool in lieu of a deskbound address book. This contact list stays with you no matter where your career takes you, as these are your relationships.

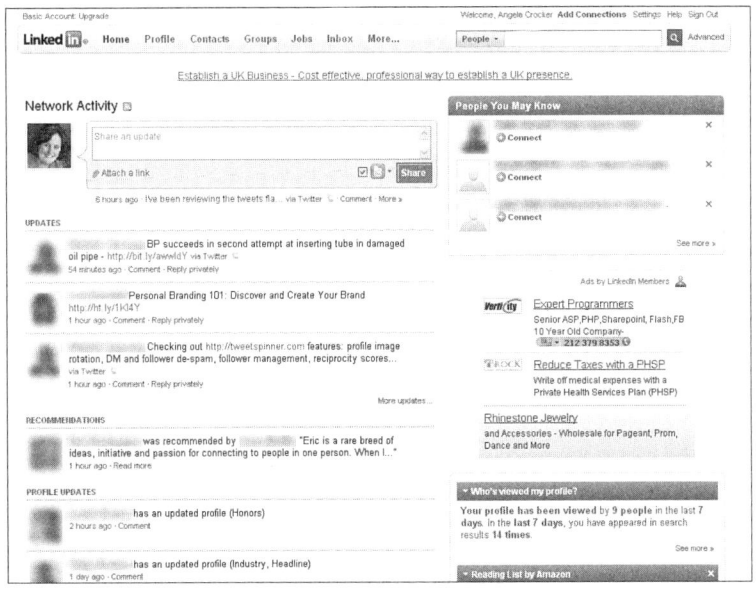

Figure 13.7

Your LinkedIn home page provides a wealth of information about what's happening with your connections.

LinkedIn includes the opportunity to make connections with people you know, and also get second- or even third-hand introductions to people you don't know. You can categorize your relationships to sort out colleagues from friends and classmates.

LinkedIn also has a wealth of special-interest groups, with rich dialogues occurring on discussion boards every day. There's also a chance to connect with people by posting compliments, called "recommendations," on their profiles.

Special-Interest Communities

Along with thousands of others, your social network is a special-interest social media community. Although you are trying to build your own network, it may be worthwhile for you to join one or more of these communities.

From CafeMom.com for parents to Blip.fm for music lovers, carefully selecting one or more special-interest communities to participate in will keep your network's brand top of mind.

Finally, don't rely solely on the brief introductions and quick tips provided in this chapter. There's lots to know about every social media network. There are great books and websites listed in Appendix B to direct you toward resources with more detailed how-to information.

Create a Daily Routine

Making the decision to participate in social media to enhance your social network requires discipline. Signing up is not enough—you must join the conversation. To do so, you need a presence management plan, something I call the daily routine.

Everyone's daily routine is something unique to their particular accounts and objectives. Many people think of these as additions to their existing routine. Here's an example:

- Check voicemail
- Check for deliveries
- Check e-mail
- Draft blog post
- Update Facebook status
- Check for comments on previous Facebook status

- Schedule tweets for the day
- Review one hashtag for relevant tweets
- Respond to direct messages on all platforms

To that list you might also add some weekly tasks to enhance your efforts:

- Check Facebook Insights
- Review followers on Twitter and follow back, as appropriate
- Make one sincere recommendation on LinkedIn
- Thank people who have been helpful throughout the week

Although I am certain you will post nothing but the most interesting information on your network and your social media sites, most people will not engage with you that closely. As such, you can connect some of your tools together to share that content elsewhere. For example, use Networked Blogs software to have blog posts feed into your Facebook status. Consider having Foursquare check-ins appear as tweets on Twitter, and so on.

The Least You Need to Know

- Social media will enhance your social networking efforts.
- Of the many social media tools available, popular choices include Facebook, Twitter, LinkedIn, and Foursquare.
- Participate in special-interest communities that are in keeping with your social network objectives.

Chapter 14

Making Money

In This Chapter

- An overview of ways to make money with your network
- Understand why sales are important—even when you're not selling goods or services
- The pros and cons of selling advertising on your site
- How to utilize e-commerce on your network
- Managing your advertising program
- Using sponsorships to garner cash and in-kind support for your network

Using a social network for business or community purposes is all about sales and marketing. You have the opportunity to host a 24/7 virtual party to honor those interested in your product or service. That's a truly amazing privilege. If you do it right, users are going to trust in your network to keep them informed, entertained, and supplied.

Many networks are created by businesses with hopes of generating revenue, either directly or indirectly. Although selling might not be the primary objective of your social network, it can be used to generate sales. You might sell products or services directly online, or indirectly at an offline location that benefits from the promotional efforts that are an inherent part of your network.

In many ways, social networks are the ultimate *handselling* opportunity, even if you are selling high volumes. Each relationship is valued on its own merit. Personal selling, even if several customers have the same needs, is a terrific form of customer service. If you've ever purchased a book in a retail store, odds are the bookseller helped you find a book to meet your needs.

> **DEFINITION**
>
> **Handselling** happens when a sales clerk, in the real world or online, walks you through the features and benefits of a product suited to the needs you have expressed.

A well-planned social network will result in natural promotion and product placement. Please don't become a smarmy huckster, though! Instead, take the time to build a real community based on trust and valid information—if you do, your network will become the go-to source for those who are interested in your topic. Sales and marketing just happen along the way.

But I'm Not Selling Anything

Some readers might now be protesting that they have nothing to sell to members of their social network. I beg to differ. Even if you're not selling products or services in exchange for cash, you may be selling ideas and opinions in exchange for moral support or volunteer hours.

Figure 14.1

The PeoplePodcastProject (www.seattle.peoplepodcastproject.com) in Seattle is selling people on the idea of sharing and listening to podcast stories. No money changes hands.

What Can I Sell?

Social networks can be used to sell all sorts of products and services. What you offer for sale depends on the nature of your community and what products you have available that suit your members needs and interests.

Here are some examples of products commonly sold through social networks:

- Sports equipment
- Event tickets
- Books on related topics
- Nutritional supplements
- Crafts and craft supplies

Services can also be sold through your network. Here are some ideas:

- Webinar training courses
- Weight-loss programs
- Coaching or counseling sessions
- Fashion advice
- Music lessons

Please don't limit yourself to these examples; your sales potential is as adventurous as your entrepreneurial spirit. Your sales can occur either through direct sales on the network or through indirect sales that happen outside the network. The indirect sales can happen both through online retailers and offline in stores.

E-Commerce

The process of selling goods and services online is called e-commerce, an abbreviation of the longer "electronic commerce." This is also sometimes referred to as e-business. Network administrators who want to monetize a social network have to decide how e-commerce will be part of their overall community.

Most often, networks sell goods and services that enhance a member's experience of the community. For example, a weight-loss community might offer scales, vitamins, food, training DVDs, or other goods for sale that support the efforts of members.

This assumes that the network has developed products or sourced them for sale to members. Similarly, a community facility such as a recreation center might make things convenient for network members by providing an online registration and payment system for dance classes, art programs, and sports leagues.

Figure 14.2

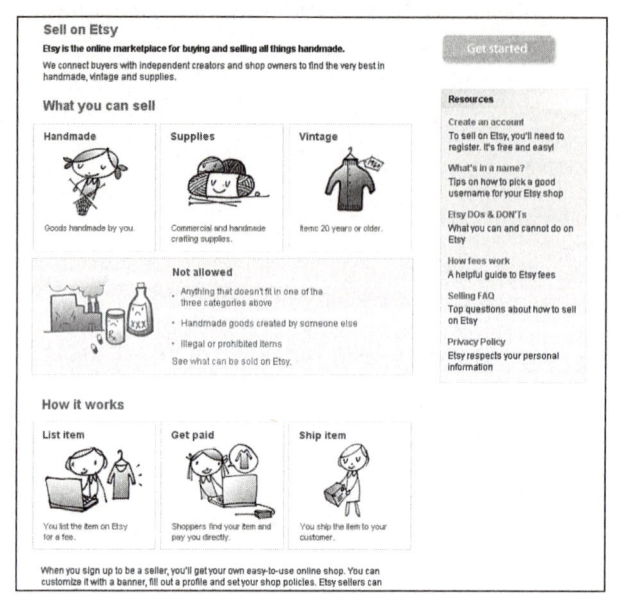

Handcrafted items can be bought and sold through Etsy's e-commerce system at www.etsy.com.

If your network needs a means to sell products or services, plan on some added expenses, as the free network services do not include a shopping cart feature. There are tools available to add the shopping cart functionality necessary for e-commerce to your network. For example, a SocialGO network has access to a member billing feature as part of the $150 per month all-inclusive Concierge-level fee. The same feature can also be added to the $25 per month Premium level for an additional monthly cost of $20, resulting in a total cost of $45 per month. Similarly, BuddyPress networks can add shopping functionality with the Shopp (note the two *p*'s) plug-in (shopplugin.net) for a one-time $55 fee. There are additional costs if your network would like to integrate banking or shipping services.

As the old adage goes, it costs money to make money, but these fees won't break the bank. Of course, the custom sites built with services like KickApps and ONEsite can also have e-commerce functionality. The key is to decide if you need to build these services into your network, and then to explore the options currently available for your network service.

Of course, e-commerce can happen using external tools available for websites that don't include a social network. You might use PayPal (www.paypal.com) or e-mail money transfers to your existing bank account to accept payments for member purchases. Services like Eventbrite (www.eventbrite.com) can be used to sell events. You could even handle the sales transaction over the phone, although the time required can overwhelm a network administrator if a product or service proves popular, and there are trust and security issues around sending unsecured credit card details.

> **CLOUD SURFING**
>
> 1ShoppingCart is a popular e-commerce tool. Visit www.1shoppingcart.com to learn more about e-commerce.

E-commerce is a complex mix of banking protocols, credit card processing, security certificates, shipping rates, automatic responses, and customer service. If you decide to include sales through your social network, then plan carefully and be sure to test your system thoroughly for any difficulties before making sales available to your members. Even if you decide to focus on indirect sales through online retailers or offline in stores, make sure your products or services are available and ready for sale.

Advertising Opportunities

First, you have to determine if you have control over advertising that appears on your network. The free network services on Wall.fm and SocialGO include advertising for the services' brands, and network administrators do not have control over paid advertising that appears on their network nor do they benefit from the advertising revenue. (This is a classic nothing in life is truly free moment.) Paid packages on Wall.fm and SocialGO give network administrators the opportunity to remove network service branding and to gain control of ads. Similarly, all levels of Ning networks have this type of control, as do the custom network services on KickApps and ONEsite.

If you are using a free network platform like Wall.fm, SocialGO, or KickApps, your community is likely seeing mentions of the social network service throughout your site. That's the trade-off to support the existence of your community. Generally speaking, the logo and text mentions are obvious but unobtrusive.

Figure 14.3

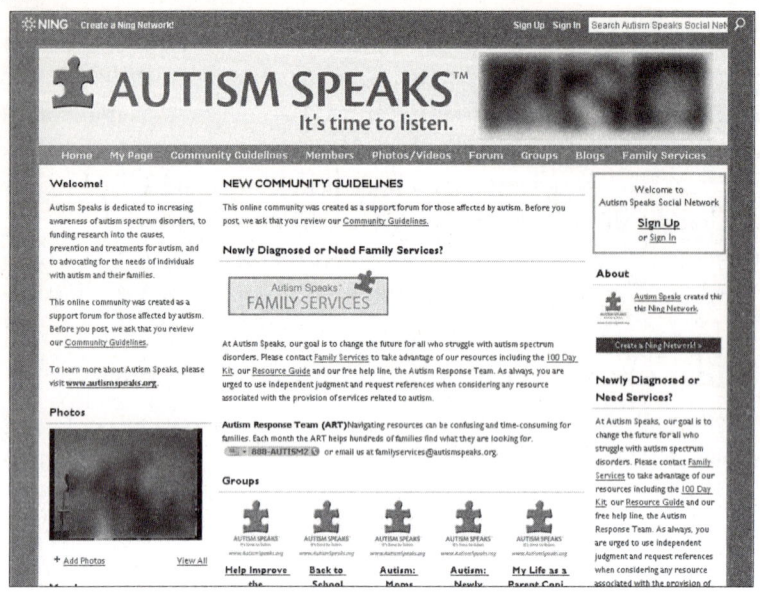

On this Autism Speaks network page (autismspeaksnetwork.ning.com), Ning's logo appears in the top-left corner along with an offer to create a Ning network.

If you have control of advertising on your network, you have an assortment of advertising options available to you. Do you want to have ads, or ban them? Do you want to lease space on your network for others to sell ads, or would you prefer to take on the sales process yourself? Let's consider the options.

While some networks successfully generate revenue from Google ads, the amount is often modest. Many networks suffer a backlash from their users who find the ads to be distracting clutter on the network page. There is also concern that you do not control the ad content, so the ads can be on any topic—including offering your competitors' goods or services to your hard-won customers!

You could just leave the network as a showcase for your product or service without any paid advertising. In a sense, the entire network is advertisement for your brand. Make the decision consciously and understand that you may be leaving revenue on the table. Many networks do not include advertising, and that's okay.

Figure 14.4

BabyVibe, a community for expectant moms at www.babyvibe.ca, only includes advertising content that reflects its own products—in this case, a baby fair and their DoggyVibe service.

Ads can take many forms. Some ads change each time the page is reloaded, allowing for multiple advertisers to use the same space. Two of the most common are text ads and image ads. Text ads are made of type only and always include a link back to the advertiser. They resemble classified ads in newspapers. Image ads resemble the display ads you've seen in magazines and newspapers that include text, graphics, and, sometimes, photography. Text ads are the most common, but you'll still spot display ads on the web regularly.

AVOID THE FAIL

Members of your network are most likely savvy web surfers who have been trained to spot an advertisement from a million miles away. Web surfers typically ignore ads that they recognize as ads because they don't want to be sold to. That being said, you can be creative with the placement of advertising on your network so that it flows more naturally in the graphic interface and doesn't scream *"I'm an ad!"* quite so loudly.

Figure 14.5

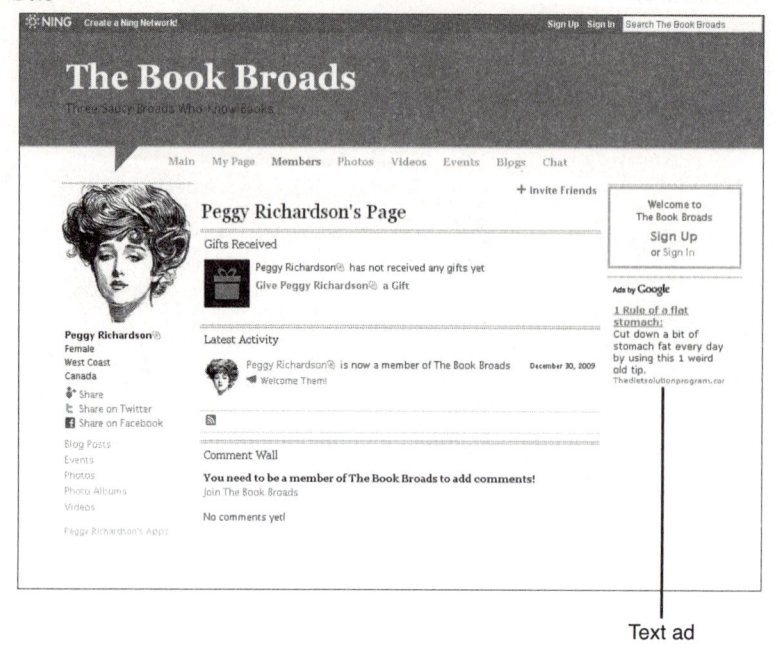

Notice the "1 Rule of a flat stomach" Google ad in the far right column, an example of a text-only ad.

Figure 14.6

In this example, The Columbus Dispatch (www.dispatch.com) has sold display advertising in the far-right column.

If you are interested in including text ads or display ads on your network, you now have to decide how to manage your advertising sales. Do you want to sell the ad space yourself and manage relationships with advertisers? Or would you rather sign up for a service that takes care of that for you?

Google AdSense

Those websites looking for an advertising service often turn to Google. Google's advertising system has two sides:

- Google AdSense: For those with advertising space to sell
- Google AdWords: For advertisers with ads to place

As a network administrator, you'll want to sign up with Google AdSense to earn some cash.

> **FLICKERS OF INSIGHT**
>
> When you sign up for a Google AdSense account, you'll be asked whether this is an individual account or a business account. Answer that question according to how you want to be paid. Should payments be made out to you personally or to your organization? Decide wisely now to avoid banking hassles later.

In brief, here's how Google AdSense works. You begin by signing up for an account at www.google.com/adsense. Once your request for an account has been approved, you then place a bit of HTML code provided by Google on your website. This code informs Google's ad engine where to find your site and place ads. At any time, you can log in to your Google AdSense account and edit the size and type of ads that appear on your network. There are horizontal and vertical options, as well as decisions to make about text ads and display ads. You can also control things like the color of ads and the way the type is displayed.

The intricacies of maximizing the money you make with Google ads are many and varied. This chapter introduces you to the basics, but I would recommend reading up on Google AdSense before you begin.

Google AdWords

The flipside of Google AdSense is Google AdWords (www.google.com/adwords). This is the place where advertisers place their ads. Each advertiser decides on the keywords they are looking for to promote their products. For example, a cloth diaper service might look for the keywords "newborn," "baby," and "mothers" so that their ads are placed on websites where expectant and new parents are likely to visit. Websites that include these keywords in their content (i.e., their blog posts, photo captions, etc.) become potential advertising space for advertisers seeking those keywords.

Of course, no ad appears on every website that includes the desired keywords. Instead, the advertiser provides a budget to indicate how much he or she wants to spend. To keep the math simple, let's assume our cloth diaper service has $1,000 to spend on Google ads. The advertiser also sets the amount he or she is willing to pay per click (PPC). So if our cloth diaper company is willing to spend $1 per click then it knows it will get 1,000 leads, most of which will be from web browsers who are prequalified leads. I say "most of which" because sometimes people click on links by accident or they end up not being interested in the product or service being sold.

The money-making part comes when advertisers have placed their ads through Google AdWords, and Google AdSense has placed the ads on relevant websites. Each time a visitor clicks on the ad, the site host, or in our case the network host, earns some money. The exact amount varies because it depends on how much the advertiser was willing to pay for the click and also depends on Google's formula for paying a percentage of that amount. Estimates suggest that percentage is about 75 percent, but even that's just an educated guess. So in our example, each click on the cloth diaper ad might earn 75¢. That's $750 in your pocket! Part of the success of Google's advertising tools is that the exact placement and payment process is a well-kept secret, so that those smarmy hucksters we talked about at the beginning of this chapter can't manipulate the system.

> **FLICKERS OF INSIGHT**
>
> If an advertiser sees they are getting consistently strong leads from a particular site, they may change from a pay-per-click method to a pay-per-impressions method. This means their ad will always appear on that site and the site owner gets paid a set amount for every thousand views or impressions.

Network administrators have no way of knowing how much money the space allocated for ads will generate. Google insists that they optimize the potential revenue for each Google AdSense subscriber, but you'll have to take this on faith. The amount of money you will make depends on the number of site visitors you have and the number of clicks or impressions your network provides. The price advertisers are willing to pay for those clicks or impressions can vary from 5¢ to $25 or more. Some sites make coffee money, while others make hundreds or even hundreds of thousands of dollars.

The other thing to consider is that networks providing space for Google ads have limited control over what kinds of ads will be placed. Adjusting the settings for ads that might appear requires considerable skill and familiarity with the AdSense system. Even those with a strong understanding have ads appear on their websites that surprise them. For many networks, this won't be a problem, but what if you are a weight-loss community and your competitors' ads appear on your network because the keywords "exercise," "diet," and "fitness" appear repeatedly on your site? As network owner, you'll need to consider the potential impact of ads that are not in keeping with your business objectives.

Sell Your Own Ads

Those who want more control or believe they can earn more money on their own can forgo AdSense in favor of a self-administered advertising program. Of course, increased content control and financial gain also means increased pain. If your organization is going to start selling ads, then you've just added a whole new layer of customer service to your business. Ask yourself the following:

- Who's going to decide what ad space is for sale?
- Do you plan to offer text-only ads or image ads?
- What is the impact—positive or negative—on your members?
- Who sets your prices and creates a *rate card?*

> **DEFINITION**
>
> A **rate card** is the menu advertisers review when buying ad space. It outlines the size of the ad space, the rates, frequent purchase discounts, and the technical details on how and when to deliver the ad.

- Who's going to seek out prospects and pursue them as advertisers?
- Who's going to take care of the technical aspects of posting the ads?
- Who's going to collect the payments from advertisers?
- Who deals with complaints when the network has some down time, or a user says something negative about the advertiser?
- Is all this hassle something you're willing to take on?

If you think your network team has the skills to accomplish all these tasks and sell your own ad space, then go for it. If not, then figure out how you are going to accomplish these tasks well. If you can't do them well, then I'd suggest not doing them at all.

Figure 14.7

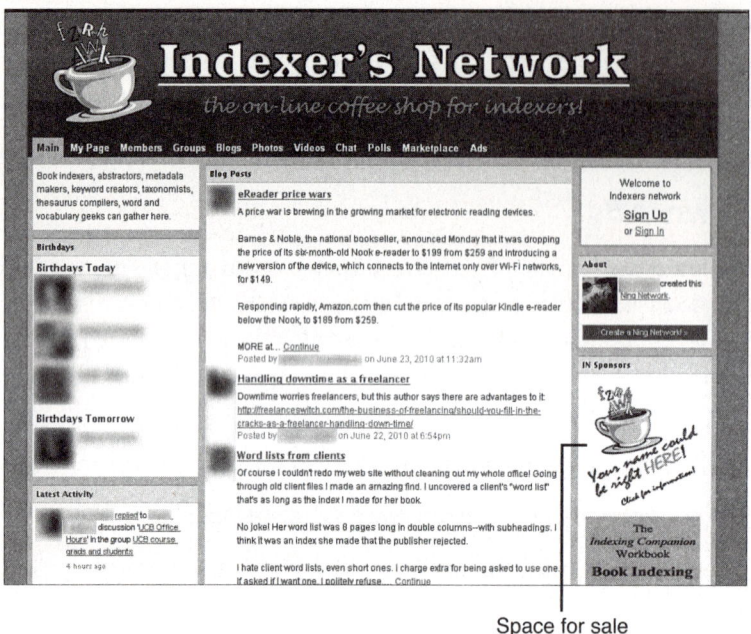

The Indexer's Network, a Ning network at www.indexing.ning.com, offers space directly to advertisers in the right column.

Let's talk a little bit about what to charge. You need some rates for your rate card, right? Pricing is influenced by the size of the ad, the frequency with which it appears, the uniqueness of the niche market you are offering, and how many people you reach. Determining the exact amount to charge will be a matter of trial and error. Often sites establish a rate card and then discount it for the first few months to secure their first few advertisers. Advertisers will also want to know the size of the audience you deliver. In terms of a network, this is the number of members you have subscribed and, possibly, the number of prospective members who visit your site. You can also share figures for the number of hits you get on your network, the frequency of those visits, the number of unique visitors, and the duration of any visits to help illustrate the value of the audience you are providing. As with all things on the web, it's hard to illustrate as there isn't always a direct relationship between ad and consumer action.

Finding advertisers is just another form of sales. You have advertising space that will provide other organizations visibility to your audience. It helps if you can articulate the demographics of your members. Are they men or women? Older or younger? Married, widowed, or single? What's their salary range? Where do they live? Statistics like this can be generated by looking at aggregate data from your members profiles. You can also define your members based on their interest in your network's topic. As with all sales, you've got to network and seek out prospects. Attend networking breakfasts or participate in social media to meet people. Do research and identify companies that are complementary to your network. Are you a community for foodies? Then they need kitchen equipment and table linens. Find suppliers who advertise these goods. This requires time and energy to find the prospective advertisers.

Affiliate Marketing

Your network may also generate revenue from affiliate sales. If your community has interests in products or services beyond the ones your company or organization already provides, you may be able to increase your revenue with referral fees from other companies seeking your target market.

Affiliate marketers will pay either a commission or a fee per lead for those names that you provide to them. For example, if you talk about books on your network, you might want to have an affiliate link with an online bookseller like Amazon or Barnes & Noble. When members of your community click that link to make a purchase, the retailer gives you a commission based on the size of the member's purchase. Alternatively, you might have members who seek legal advice or medical information on a particular topic. Pharmaceutical companies, law firms, and many other businesses will pay a flat fee for each qualified lead provided to them. The fees range from a few dollars to hundreds of dollars per name.

Affiliate marketers are looking for e-mail, search, or SMS leads. If you generate appropriate leads and fit an affiliate campaign into the culture of your community, this can be a lucrative stream of income. To find a partner affiliate marketer, network online at places such as www.affiliatesummit.ning.com and offline by attending trade shows like Affiliate Summit and AdTech.

FLICKERS OF INSIGHT

There are strict rules regarding e-mail marketing, including the United States CAN-Spam Act. Essentially, these laws require marketers to honor users requests to opt out of a marketing list. Read more from the Federal Trade Commission at www.ftc.gov/spam.

Figure 14.8

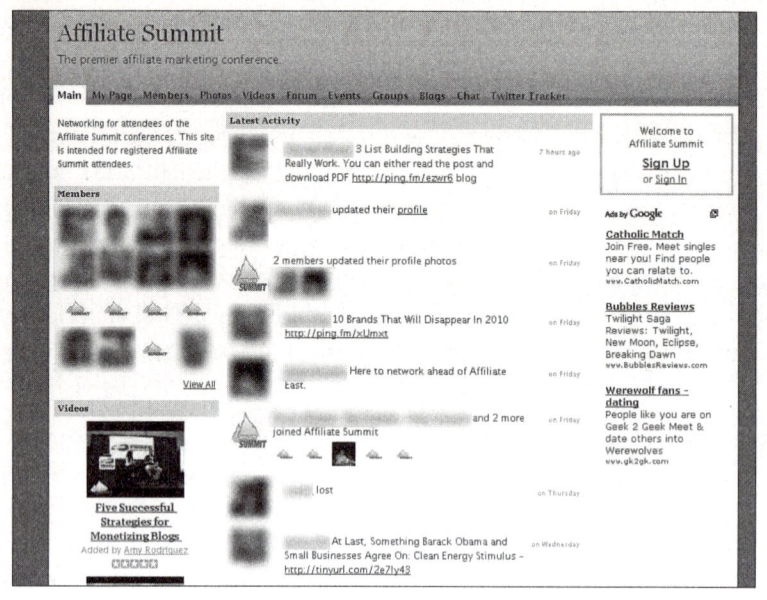

Those engaged in affiliate marketing gather at the Affiliate Summit each year. They also connect through a social network at www.affiliatesummit.ning.com.

Sponsorship

Another potential source of revenue is sponsorship or other types of paid promotions. This differs from advertising in that the advertiser's brand, goods, or services are incorporated into the content of the network rather than being advertised next to the content. Sponsorship can be as simple as a statement such as "This community is sponsored by Kellogg's" or a more complex relationship that includes product placement.

> **AVOID THE FAIL**
>
> Understand the importance of disclosure if pursuing sponsorship support. This is especially true in the United States, where legislation now requires bloggers to specifically state when they are talking about something they've received as a promotional sample or complimentary review copy.

Selling sponsorships involves cultivating relationships with companies that are interested in your community's demographics. The difference is advertisers buy space based on demographics and reputation, while the most effective sponsorships grow from mutual understanding and shared needs.

Sponsorship can take the form of cash or in-kind products and services to support your network. In exchange for their contribution, the sponsor will expect you to deliver all the promises made in the sponsorship agreement. This might include logo placement, product placement, an opportunity to message or survey all members, a sampling program, or any one of dozens of other possibilities.

> **FLICKERS OF INSIGHT**
>
> Sponsorship can happen on a small scale with requests for financial support from members. Ning offers a donation button for this purpose.

Selling sponsorships is not easy or quick. Often it takes a year or more to cultivate the relationship to the point where network representatives can ask the company to give. Even then there's no guarantee that they will make a contribution, nor a promise they will renew after the first year. There are many things to consider with sponsorship and it's advisable to bring in fund-development professionals to help with selling sponsorships.

Consider Your Competition

While it's always good to be a leader in any sales or marketing initiative, in this new era of social networking it's also a good idea to look at what your competitors are doing every once in a while. Ask yourself:

- Are they doing something you should be?
- Is there the potential for a strategic alliance?
- Are they creating classic "don't" examples to use in training your staff?

Whatever you glean, time spent observing the activity of your competitors is well worth the effort. As in many aspects of business, competitive intelligence is key.

Understanding the Relationship

As host of a network, you are in a trusted position. Your members are your most valuable asset; you want to ensure that they find value within your network and that they do not feel taken advantage of. Your management of this unique relationship will make your network a success or a failure.

If you decide to make revenue from your network, I encourage you to make careful choices that respect your members and their experience within the community. If you need to raise funds to pay for the existence of the network, let them know. If they see value in the community, they'll support efforts to keep it going. If your network is business oriented and might include the sale of goods or services, make it clear that your community is driven by a business. Again, members will accept this if they see value in the community.

Here's an example of what *not* to do: a network is created as a community for writers and bills itself as a helpful place for writers to find the resources and support they need to publish a book. Once signed up for the community, the user then discovers that the network host is actually an author services company that will gladly provide the promised resources and support, but for a fee. The host preys on the publishing dreams of the writer, and emptying her bank account and filling her basement with poorly edited, badly designed, unsellable books. This social network host did not respect and uphold a trusting relationship with its members.

Thankfully, there are also lots of good guys out there. I want you to be one of them. Deliver what you promise, and then some. Go above and beyond members' expectations. Forge relationships built on honesty and trust. And figure out how to increase your revenue along the way.

The Least You Need to Know

- You can make money with your social network.
- You are selling something, whether it's goods, services, or an idea.
- By upgrading to a paid network service, you can control advertising that appears on your network.
- Advertising revenue opportunities are available to you either through Google AdSense or a self-directed advertising program.
- Affiliate marketing is another source of potential revenue.
- Your competition might be doing the same thing or something different. Pay attention.
- Never abuse your trusting relationship with network members with too much emphasis on sales to benefit your organization.

Measures of Success

Chapter 15

In This Chapter

- Evaluating the success of your network in terms of reach, influence, and action
- Advice and suggestions for deciding what to measure
- Methods for gathering data
- Ways to assess the data gathered, including monetary and nonmonetary success
- Making a plan to continue improving your network

For some, simply creating a complete network will be a huge success. Please take the time to celebrate that momentous accomplishment. Shortly after the party, please be sure to define other ways to articulate your community's success from month to month and over the years. In this chapter, we will look at some ways to measure both monetary and nonmonetary success.

Success Metrics

Measuring social networks is an inexact science. While a highly respected part of a marketing campaign, the marketing business has yet to come to an agreement on how to best measure the value of a social network. In part, this is because there are so many variables to consider. Another contributing factor is that much of the value and purpose of a network is about the community and relationships. This means there aren't always direct correlations to sales or other actions.

In this digital era, we are blessed with an abundance of empirical information. We can track clicks and comments and other interactions along with rising (or falling) membership rates and the all important volume of sales. All that bean counting is terrific, but what are we really counting and what do the numbers tell us about our community?

I suggest that we can evaluate a successful network by considering three things:

- Reach
- Influence
- Action

Your *reach* is the size of your community. How many people do you reach? You're looking at the number of first-hand connections between you and the members of your community and, don't forget, the members of your social media outposts who are on the outskirts of your community. Remember that every member of your community made a conscious decision to become a member. That has tremendous value.

Reach can be simply a head count, or you can further define your reach by demographics or geography or some other defining factor that makes sense for your community. You might define your count by generations—how many do you reach from Generation X or the baby boomers? Or you might define your reach by how many are in a particular city, state, or country depending on your market. Pick logical, purposeful subcategories when defining your reach, but don't forget the overall head count as well.

> **DEFINITION**
>
> **Reach** is the size of your community, or rather the number of members who have joined your network plus those you reach through social media outposts.

Next, consider your *influence*, the extended reach possible through the connections of your community members' friends, fans, and followers. You may interact with only one person, but the influence that person has over his or her connections can be of tremendous value to your community. Recall the old Faberge Shampoo commercial where the model with glowing hair tells two friends, and they tell two friends, and so on.

> **DEFINITION**
>
> **Influence** is the number of people whose opinions will be swayed by those that you reach.

What sort of support do you receive from your community? Are they talking about you outside the social network? Most likely they are because their experience in the network is part of their overall life experience to share.

Consider the impact of their influence. Do they reach thousands of people who don't really listen to them and thus have limited influence, or is it the opposite? Or do they reach a modest size group of peers with tremendous influence? What is the pass-along effect of their connections—the told-two-friends-and-so-on phenomenon? Do you seek influence within the community or outside the community, or both?

Firsthand opinions and reviews are among the things most likely to sway someone to join your community. The exponential potential of influence is a very valuable asset for your social network.

> **FLICKERS OF INSIGHT**
>
> You may see or hear reference to the expression "social graph," a diagram or drawing that illustrates the interconnections between the people, groups, companies, and organizations within a social network. It shows how each piece interrelates to the others. In some circles, the term "social graph" has come to be a synonym for "social network."

The third consideration is *action*. Has your communication within the community included calls to action? Have you asked your members to do something? This process is sometimes called engagement. You can tabulate the number of actions and use this information in assessing your success.

> **DEFINITION**
>
> **Action** is any click, comment, or content where members of your network do something—in other words, they take action.

How do you define engagement or calls to action within your community? It's up to you. For instance, have you asked people to join your community, comment on content, download some content, participate in an event, or make a purchase? Don't limit yourself to thinking of responses in terms of cash sales. What else is measurable? Remember that social networks are about building relationships and community. Sales are important and often come from social networks, but they are not the primary purpose.

What to Measure

Before you can gather the data to assess your success, you've got to figure out what to measure. But to know what to measure, you need some sense of how you're going to measure success.

I suggest you begin by brainstorming some preliminary questions to define success. As you start to define what questions you want to ask, it becomes easier to decide what things to measure.

Perhaps you want to know how the size of your membership is changing. Growth can be an indicator that you are reaching new levels of success. Perhaps your community is shrinking. Is it a good thing because there are fewer smokers to join your quit smoking community? Or is it a bad thing because your community is not engaging members and retaining them? Or maybe your group remains the same size. Whatever the change, the size of membership is important to all social networks as this is a baseline measurement for your reach.

Another question you might want answered is about prevailing opinions. Are you receiving glowing reviews or negative missives? Opinions can be positive, negative, neutral, or mixed. As the old publicity adage goes, all coverage is good coverage because it is exposure. However, for social networks built on community, more opinions on the positive side means your community is serving its membership well.

These are just two common examples of questions that might be crucial in the assessment of the success of your community. As we turn our attention to a list of things you might measure, consider how these items can be used to assess your success.

What are you going to count? In Chapter 4, we talked about the different features available to your users. Here, we'll list questions you might ask related to most of those features. Please don't plan on counting answers to every one of these questions. You'll have too much data to be meaningful and I want you to remember to focus your attention on your community and its members, not on endless statistical analysis.

> **AVOID THE FAIL**
>
> As with any sort of number crunching, keep in mind statistical significance. While the numbers represent facts, they don't always represent meaningful information.

Think of the following questions as a shopping list from which to choose those questions that best measure the performance of your network. Choose just the ones that make sense in your case.

As we've discussed, your membership is the core of your community. So consider asking:

- How many members do you have in total?
- How many people have been invited to join?
- How many new members have joined?
- How many members have left the community?
- How many members are participating?
- How many inactive accounts are there?
- How many members have updated their profile?

Communications are the most basic of actions within any social network. So ask yourself:

- How many members are contributing content?
- Are there active contributors who share more content?
- What types of content are being added?

Subsets of your overall community gather in groups to discuss topics of mutual interest. How is your community using the groups feature?

- How many groups are there in total?
- How many new groups have been created?
- How many groups have been closed?
- How many active or dormant groups are there?
- Are some groups only active seasonally?
- How many discussions per month in the forums?

Comments and messages are simple ways members can take action within your community. Ask yourself:

- How many comments are posted each day, week, or month?
- What percentage of members are leaving comments?
- What is the volume of private message traffic?

Rich content sharing may also be an indicator of your network's success. Calculate:

- How many photos are being shared?
- How many songs, photos, and videos are available?
- How many members have uploaded songs, photos, or videos?
- How many times has each song, photo, or video been downloaded?
- How many ratings were added?

Notes, blogs, and microblogs are also rich content within your community. Consider:

- How many new notes, blogs, or microblogs have been shared?
- How many have been read?
- How many have been shared outside the community on Facebook or Twitter?
- How many comments have been left in response?

Do you offer calendar or event features? Is so, then measure:

- How many events are planned?
- How many activities are noted on the calendar?
- How many users utilized the event or calendar features?
- How frequently do members interact with the calendar? (Daily? Weekly? Monthly?)
- How many page views? By how many users?
- How many people attended events? (Virtual events or real-world events?)

Other possibilities for your list of measures include:

- How many notifications have been sent?
- How many tags have been entered?
- How many have responded to tags?
- How many have taken each poll?
- How many badge downloads have there been?

On the administrative side, there are more things to measure. This might include:

- The number of requests for help.
- How many minutes or hours of downtime.
- The sort of feedback you have received.
- Any reports of spam or abuse.

Outreach beyond the community is key to its success. Outreach through social media tools is the crux of Chapter 13. Consider sharing through social media tools both in terms of efforts by the community and by administrators. Audit things such as the following:

- List your social media outposts.
- How many fans on Facebook?
- How many status updates were posted?
- How many followers on Twitter?
- How many tweets sent?
- How many tagged replies appeared on Twitter or Facebook?
- How many times were your messages forwarded on Twitter?
- How many connections on LinkedIn?
- How many guest blog posts did network administrators post on other sites?
- How many comments on those guest blogs?

As you start to define what questions you want to ask, it becomes easier to decide what things to count. These measurements should become part of a regular assessment routine. We'll talk about how to do that assessment later in this chapter, but first we need to talk about how to measure your social network.

> **FLICKERS OF INSIGHT**
>
> When you first set up your network, take baseline measurements. You must have a starting point to compare with.

How to Measure

The tools to measure social networks are still evolving. Your social network platform may have some metrics built in to your administrator access, particularly if you are using a custom label service. At the moment, some counting must be done manually, though, which is both time consuming and potentially inaccurate. To manually count, you'll have to sit down at your computer and count what you see. Manual counts make it difficult to discount duplicates and get a real sense of your true numbers. However, best-guess numbers are better than no numbers at all.

Consider how often to gather your numbers—the tallies, figures, and facts that answer the questions you've selected to assess your network. For most networks, a monthly review will be sufficient. This is frequent enough to see trends over time and also infrequent enough not to be too onerous a task. On occasion, ramping up to weekly reporting or backing off to quarterly reports will work. Do what's best for your network.

> **AVOID THE FAIL**
>
> Please remember that monitoring your network communications and social media channels is a daily task. Only measurements for assessment should be done monthly.

Data Gathering

I suggest you start with a basic web analytics package to provide you with all sorts of data about unique visitors, inbound links, and the amount of time people spend in your community. You may already be familiar with tools like Google Analytics. You can sign up for a free account at www.google.com/analytics. Google makes it easy to use the system and there are lots of help files to teach you how to set up, read, and interpret the analytics if you need some help.

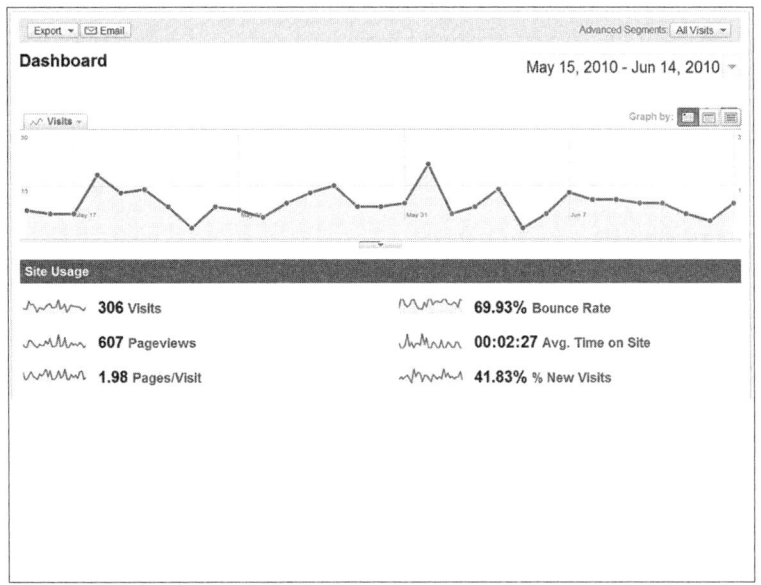

Figure 15.1

This Google Analytics dashboard provides an overview of visits, page views, and other information for a one-month period.

Analytics are a helpful way to gather numbers and show you how they change over time. I suggest recording the numbers at selected moments and graphing the results over time. Beyond analytics, you can do manual tallies. Of course, sitting at your computer counting every blog post, comment, and community member is only practical if your community is small. When the volume gets too large to count in a timely way, you'll need to move on to an automated method. Google Analytics can be helpful, and there are paid services measuring influence and engagement.

Both Radian6 (www.radian6.com) and Vocus (www.vocus.com) offer sophisticated tracking, measurement, and analysis tools that can be used to monitor social networks. Paying for a service can save you time as you'll only have to read and assess the reports provided. The service takes care of gathering the numbers and presents them to you with lots of customizable detail for review. These services are also useful because they can be configured so that network administrators can have access to the data simultaneously. Of course, keep in mind the cost of such a service. Radian6's fees start at $500 per month for 10,000 results and go up from there.

Figure 15.2

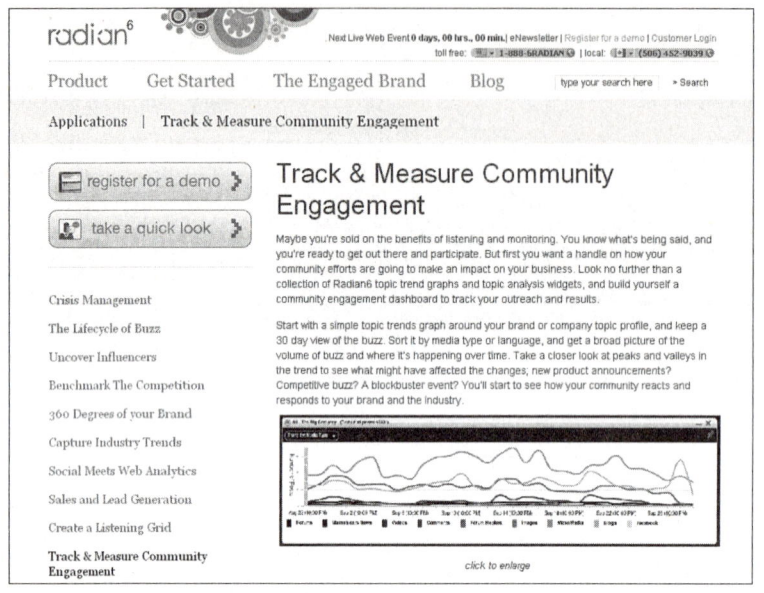

Visit www.radian6.com for a quick video introduction and to sign up for a free demo.

> **CLOUD SURFING**
>
> The measurement services discussed in this chapter are by no means an exhaustive list. You have many other options—including www.attensity360.com, www.trackur.com, and www.postrank.com, among others—that offer similar tracking, engagement, and interaction tools and assessments. Seek out the provider that suits your needs and your budget.

One area where you will most likely do a manual tally concerns your time spent on administration. The degree of success of your network is, in part, related to how much effort is required to generate that success. While self-reporting can be inaccurate, it is important to evaluate time spent on the community and supporting social media outposts. Remember our discussion about the cost of time in Chapter 5. Count the hours spent on administrative functions, creating and uploading content, and also the time spent interacting with your community. Most networks will have more than one team member so make sure you count everybody's hours. An informal time sheet is all that's needed. You can compare your other results in relation to the amount of time spent. Is your time well spent? Or are you wasting time?

Assessment

Figuring out what to measure and how to measure it is a big task, at least the first time that you do it. Now comes the all-important assessment phase when you figure out what all the data means. Now's the time to think like an accountant. Audit what you are doing by looking at the numbers.

Until someone develops an all-encompassing tool to do this, I suggest you create your own dashboard of information in a simple spreadsheet. From the dashboard, look for key figures and trends that indicate the health of your network. Look for numbers that have increased, decreased, or remained the same. Have you grown, remained static, or shrunk?

Figure 15.3

	January	February	March	April	May	June
Membership						
Total Members start	350	380	416	437	432	462
New Members	34	38	22	4	33	38
Lost Members	4	2	1	9	3	0
Net gain/loss	30	36	21	-5	30	38
Total Members finish	380	416	437	432	462	500
Content	January	February	March	April	May	June
Status Updates	30	60	90	60	60	75
Blog posts	4	7	11	8	4	6
Photos	15	18	22	17	16	23
Videos	4	5	6	7	4	6
Sales	January	February	March	April	May	June
Books	3	3	6	5	6	7
Book $	$ 30	$ 30	$ 60	$ 50	$ 60	$ 70
Tickets	0	0	123	150	75	0
Tickets $	$ -	$ -	$ 12,300	$ 15,000	$ 7,500	$ -

A simple dashboard for a fictional network.

While it's fine and dandy to subscribe to some services that count and analyze your social network's metrics, in the end someone in your organization needs to review and consider the numbers and what they really mean.

Try to find a story or narrative in the figures. Are your numbers increasing or decreasing? Is that change statistically significant for the size of your community? Here are some examples of the kinds of information you might see in your numbers.

- Are members interacting with blog posts but not videos?
- What features are used most often?
- Is there a pattern to when members of your community are online? What's their prime time?
- Does an increase in blog post frequency correlate to an increase in sales?

The facts will give you insights into your community and how it is changing.

> **FLICKERS OF INSIGHT**
>
> Be realistic about your expectation for success with your network. Your community is not going to be a viral entity embraced by millions in the first week. More likely, you'll plod along over time with (hopefully) a steady influx of new members.

Monetary Success

Many networks are associated with businesses and organizations that are trying to earn some money. If revenue is among your goals, then you need to assess what activity related to your network has resulted in sales or donations.

Some sales will be direct sales, where a member clicks on a link in your community and makes an online purchase right then through your e-commerce system. As owner of the domain, you can track how many people visit the relevant page, and also capture details on where the purchaser came from within your shopping cart system. Some direct sales will be for downloadable products, while others will be for products that need to be shipped by mail or courier. Either way, you'll have summary data on the number of units sold and be able to track where those buyers came from in your analytics data for the network traffic and from your shopping cart software.

Your network may also benefit from offline sales. By this, I mean the sales that are made in a retail location or at an event as a result of activity within the network. For example, a network for triathletes might start a discussion about must-have items for athletes preparing to compete. Someone might mention how useful Body Glide is to prevent chafing under a wetsuit, a product that is available from the network's store. This discussion may prompt a corresponding increase in Body Glide sales.

> **FLICKERS OF INSIGHT**
>
> It can be really difficult to measure online activity if it's something driven by offline interests. For example, a child's interest in ballet may prompt a mother to join a dance community even if she doesn't share the same interest. If the child needs ballet shoes, the parent will interact with the community to get advice solely for the benefit of the child.

If you have decided to include advertising in your community, then tabulate how much revenue you've earned. Revenue from Google AdSense is easily calculated by adding up any payments you've received. If you elected to sell your own advertising, you'll want to look at your net advertising income—that is to say, the amount of advertising sold less the costs of staff time and other expenses related to making the advertising sale.

There are also payments to add up related to your affiliate sales. If you've only joined one affiliate program, then the math is simply the total payment received. If you participate in more than one affiliate program, add them all up. When participating in multiple programs, it may be easiest to tally your affiliate revenue on a particular day each week or month, as every pay schedule is different.

Finally, there's your sponsorship revenue. Calculate how much sponsorship money your network brought in. You can also count the value of any in-kind contributions. In some cases, free products and services that are needed for your network are as good as cash because you would have spent the money anyway.

Each of the subtotals above adds to your overall influx of cash. Add them up for a grand total of your monetary success.

Nonmonetary Success

The success of social networks is not always about money. There are many other factors that indicate success, and the results can often be quantified.

Size of Community

Celebrate each and every member of your community. Size matters, but don't get caught up comparing your community to others. Not every network is going to be the next Facebook with 500 million users. Think about the scale of your efforts. Have you created a network for parents at your child's school? Then your maximum size of community is the 200 families at the school, but you know that not everyone will be interested in participating online. So in this case, success is tied to a small number of potential members. Is your community wider reaching? Then evaluate success based on your percentage of the market.

> **FLICKERS OF INSIGHT**
>
> Social networks and social media are about building relationships over time. Don't dismiss or abandon your network after just a few weeks. Note the numbers as facts and celebrate or lament changes in those numbers with action, as needed.

Calculate and track growth rates rather than straight numbers. A community with 10 members that attracts 10 new members suddenly has a 20-member group with 100 percent growth. Those same 10 members would be statistically insignificant within a community of 10,000.

Also evaluate your net gain or loss. If you lost 345 members and gained 355 members, your net gain is 10 members. Reverse the numbers and you have a net loss. This change in membership is called churn.

> **AVOID THE FAIL**
>
> Don't assume the people that leave your network have departed with negative opinion, bad feeling, or for some other nefarious reason. Instead, they may have checked out what you have to offer and decided it's not for them. That's okay, as you want to engage people who are genuinely interested in your topic.

Look for patterns in your numbers. What moves network members from strangers to evangelists? Can you see a trigger that inspires them to take action? What's the funnel that moves them up the levels of engagement?

Consider a community for new parents hosted by a public health unit. In response to a retailer's objection to a woman breastfeeding in public, the network administrator posts a blog about the benefits of breastfeeding and advocating for a community that supports mothers in doing so. This public declaration may rally parents and others who are part of the group to talk favorably about the network and to join further conversations with like-minded parents.

Quality of Interactions

The quality of interactions can be an indicator of success. The sheer volume of interaction can be evaluated based on positive, negative, neutral, or mixed opinions. You can also consider how deeply committed the user had to be to undertake an interaction. Does adding a rating have the same value as writing a comment? If there are back-and-forth dialogues between members, that can be a healthy indication of interaction, too. You decide what's a quality interaction for your community.

> **FLICKERS OF INSIGHT**
>
> There is some debate about whether a community should have a passive approach to engaging members in action as opposed to an aggressive approach. You'll have to decide what's best for your community.

What to Do Now

So now you know where you've been according to the numbers. The time has come to take the data and related assessment and decide what to do next.

A little goal setting is a good way to start. I suggest you set time-bound goals for your community. You many even want to set a realistic goal and a stretch goal. The stretch goal may motivate you to exceed your expectations and increase the popularity and activity of your network faster than planned. Goals might include targets for the amount of content shared or the time spent in dialogue with members.

If your assessment reveals things you're not happy about, then take action. If change is needed to extend your reach, explore new membership, or create more revenue, then decide what needs to be done. Even if you're not sure what action will get you the results you want, make a plan. Test some possibilities and reevaluate after you have some results to gauge your success.

You'll also want to schedule further reviews. As I mentioned earlier, monthly reviews are common or you may need to adjust for daily, weekly, or quarterly reviews. Remember not to put all of your attention on gathering data and assessment. The bulk of your time should be spent maintaining the community itself.

However you define success for your community, look at the numbers as painting a picture of the success of your network. Then go out there and create the community that matches the image in your mind's eye.

The Least You Need to Know

- You can evaluate your network by considering reach, influence, and action.
- You need to know what you're going to measure.
- You must select key questions and gather relevant data to assess the success of your community.
- Monetary success might include direct sales, affiliate sales, and offline sales.
- Nonmonetary success can include the size of your community and quality of interactions.
- Assess the data you gather and make a plan to improve your network.
- Don't spend all your time gathering information; put most of your energy into engaging your network.

Develop Network Savvy

Chapter 16

In This Chapter

- Understanding why users want to be anonymous and when it is acceptable
- Tips for ensuring the security of your network
- The importance of a privacy policy
- Fostering a community where people can be their true selves
- The issue of quantity versus quality

You've established a vibrant, useful social network for your business or organization. As you continue to work with your community, there are a few issues that we should talk about to ensure your ongoing success. The issues are all potential pitfalls, and if you take the time to read up you'll avoid many of these common "fails."

Anonymity and Obscurity

The usual goal of a social network is to connect with real people in an online context. However, in some situations participants may hide behind a pseudonym or make themselves anonymous.

Many legitimate reasons for anonymity are acceptable. Perhaps the participant is part of a custody battle, or closely related to a public figure. He or she might suffer from an illness such as depression or HIV, which sometimes still have unfortunate and inaccurate stigmas attached to them. Maybe the user is on an injury claim and may risk the claim if he or she even talks passionately online about particular recreational activities. Many reasons are understandable if honorably motivated.

> **FLICKERS OF INSIGHT**
>
> While personal details of anonymous users are invisible to the lay person, there are clever technical people who can usually track down a person's approximate location, based on their IP address. Armed with their user name and a map it is often possible to determine their identity. Fortunately most users don't perform this unethical action but it underlines the need for security and the importance of making your members aware of the possibility if your network is vulnerable.

The problem with obscuring one's identity is that there are, sadly, many malicious users who hide behind false names to participate in a community. They do this to mine information, to stalk individuals, or for other nasty purposes. The existence of this sort of anonymous user then creates a sense of distrust amongst legitimate users of the social network.

> **AVOID THE FAIL**
>
> If anonymity is appropriate to your social network, set up a way for participants to indicate that they are using an assumed identity. Consider an example such as, "participating as Peggy Plumley" or "guest starring as Graceful Ella."

In truth, anonymity undermines the whole point of social media—creating meaningful connections amongst like-minded individuals. With this in mind, the host of any social network has to establish ground rules that are appropriate to the community for anonymous participants.

There are certain networks on which hiding your true self and taking on an assumed identity is expected online. These social networks are set up with the assumption that participants will interact under assumed names, appearances, and other traits. For example, social networks devoted to LARPing (live action role play) use alter egos to create fictional real-world experiences. They might LARP based in a vampire culture or the reenactment of a Roman battle. Participants in Second Life, a virtual reality world populated by millions of alter egos, is also a place where anonymity is accepted.

> **CLOUD SURFING**
>
> Second Life is a highly detailed online community. Users create avatars to represent themselves as they participate and interact in the community. Second Life (www.secondlife.com) can be used for all sorts of experiences like shopping, work meetings, cultural experiences, and much more. New users receive an orientation on Welcome Island where they learn how to walk, talk, and even fly.

Figure 16.1

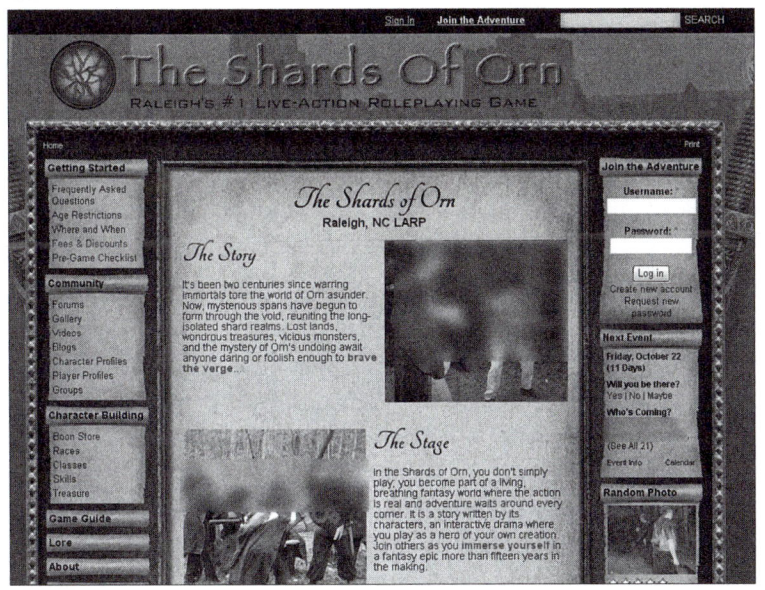

This social network is for The Shards of Orn (www.ornlarp.com), a LARPing group, in Raleigh.

Safety and Security

Chapter 8 offered specific advice about creating strong passwords, but there's more to safety and security than just that.

In the rush of enthusiasm to play in the network you've created, some may share information that compromises their security. Encourage participants to avoid announcing things that could compromise them in the real world, such as the following:

- "Leaving for three weeks in Europe."
- "Attending niece's Sweet 16 at the Hard Rock Cafe."
- "Taking my son to Town Center Park for some one-on-one time."

All of these examples give away too much information that opens participants up to unwanted experiences such as robbery, a party crasher, or child abduction. Instead, users should share their news in more general or past-tense terms:

- "Just back from three fabulous weeks in Europe."
- "Sending my niece special Sweet 16 wishes."
- "Time to take the little man for some swing time."

Location is one of the latest darlings of social media, and we've got to agree it's fun to know where friends are through services like Foursquare and Gowalla. As explained in Chapter 13, mobile phones use GPS (global positioning satellites) to allow you to "check in" at any location and announce your presence. It is anticipated that social network services will add location features. This will be particularly useful to communities that are based in a specific place or those that are tracking marketing activities in different locations.

> **CLOUD SURFING**
>
> To experiment with location-based check-in communities download the mobile applications available from Gowalla (www.gowalla.com) or Foursquare (www.foursquare.com).

As a network host, you are entrusted with an amazing amount of personal data on your members. It is your responsibility to have the technology in place to protect your members. Sadly, there are talented hackers who will access any vulnerable system. They'll try to mess with your settings or distribute your members' data or other nefarious activities. Protect yourself!

If your social network service is hosting your community, you already have considerable protection for your community. If you have your community hosted elsewhere, please consult the services of an IT professional who specializes in your particular server system. You'll want to talk to them about some core issues such as firewalls, backup systems, redundancy, and other technical things. If you don't have expertise in this area, please don't try to DIY.

Privacy and Terms of Use

A privacy policy for your network is highly recommended. Your staff members must honor every word of it. This is a legally binding understanding between you and your participants. Trust and confidence are key to the success of your network. To create a policy start by reviewing examples made available by Social Media Governance at socialmediagovernance.com/policies.php. As this is related to legal statutes on privacy, it is recommended that you consult a lawyer to ensure your privacy policy is most effective.

> **FLICKERS OF INSIGHT**
>
> If you create your community on a service like Ning or Wall.fm, I suggest informing your members that members of your social network can only see what's happening in your community. What other communities they belong to and how they participate in those social networks remains private.

Many networks are created without any formal consideration of privacy issues, which could get them into trouble. For example, what if a member abused the information he or she had access to in order to create an e-mail list to spam other members? Without a privacy policy, the network administrators have no recourse.

I'm sure you've visited a website or signed up for an e-newsletter with a privacy policy. Do you read them all word for word? Most users simply click on "Agree to the terms" and just want to get on with participating in your network.

Every network will have a policy unique to its particular community. Your policy might include things like:

- Type of information collected and for what purpose.
- How people's personal data is stored and for how long.
- Who has access to personal data and why.
- Assurances that data will not be sold to a third party.
- Who to contact if the member has any privacy concerns.

Authenticity

In an ideal world, opinions and actions are authentic. That is to say, individuals participate with their true beliefs, and we're not talking about religion. Rather, the information shared online should be a person's true point of view on a given topic—whether the choir is changing its rehearsal time, the local rotary club is shifting its philanthropic focus, or the government is considering a new tax.

> **AVOID THE FAIL**
>
> In social networking, transparency means being up front about who is controlling, or at least orchestrating, the content that appears online. Is it the group's founders? Is it elected participating members? Is it a free-for-all managed by the group as a whole? Or is it some outside influence, such as a sponsor? Details on who's behind the scenes can be shared on the home page or on the "about this network" page. You might also include a line about this in your welcome letter to new members. Transparency like this will enhance the authenticity of your community.

Network administrators can only vouch for the authenticity of the content they share on the network. Users' authenticity can't be verified. However, the administrators' good example can help create a culture within the network where authenticity is understood to be the expected behavior.

You might wonder why this is so important. The reality is that social media is driven by genuine interaction. If someone acquiesces to others, too often they may stop participating in the social network. If people make up false opinions, the conversation is wasted. If voices aren't heard from all points of view, then the dialogue is unbalanced. All instances of inauthentic participation may result in decreased participation as members get frustrated with the garbage content. Of course, some networks lend themselves to unbalanced discussions because the members share a common political, religious, or other specific point of view. The key is that all people who are part of the community should be encouraged to present themselves as they truly are.

Quality vs. Quantity

Another factor to consider is the quality versus quantity argument. In social networks, this point arises in two different contexts—participants and interactions.

When we talk about quality, we're talking about the value—the social net worth—of each participant or interaction. Conversely, quantity is the sheer numbers game of counting how many members you've got.

There are a great many theories about the ideal number of people to have participating in your community. One argument suggests that the human brain can maintain only about 150 relationships. Another theory is just the opposite—I call it "Go Big or Go Home"—where the goal is to have tens of thousands, if not hundreds of thousands, of followers. If you're on Twitter, I'd be willing to bet that you've had a so-called Twitter guru offer to sell you thousands of followers if you send them just $79.95.

For me, the ideal number is somewhere in the middle; the exact answer depends on your business and your social networking objectives. (Pop back to Chapter 2 if you need a refresher on your objectives.) Consider the volume of people you need to make the network work for you by asking yourself a few questions:

- Do you want to have 10,000 quantity followers with only 1 percent of them genuinely interested in what you have to say? Or, is 100 people enough?
- Would you rather have 500 quality followers with 80 percent of them genuinely interested? That means 400 of those 500 relationships engage with your cause, products, or services.
- Are you looking for repeat customers?
- How many customers do you need to make ends meet?
- How many customers do you need to retire early?

Which is better—quality or quantity? It truly depends on your purpose. If you're an electronics store wanting to sell discount televisions to those seeking bargains, then the quantity of followers is probably your preferred scenario, as not everyone will buy a TV every time you have a sale. On the other hand, if you are a writer who publishes a new book every couple of years and gives regular seminars, then the quality followers may be your preference.

> **CLOUD SURFING**
>
> Writer, blogger, and noted thinker Kevin Kelley suggests that the sweet spot is to have 1,000 true fans. (Read bit.ly/1000True.) The idea is that if you have a fan base of 1,000 people who truly love your work or believe in your cause, then they will buy all your products and participate in all your events. Furthermore, these fans will share their enthusiasm for your work with their contacts, creating the ultimate word of mouth promotional effort. According to Kelley, this is the number of fans needed to be successful in whatever you do.

The Least You Need to Know

- If appropriate, create a mechanism to allow people to participate anonymously on your network.
- Provide recommendations and guidelines to keep your members safe online and offline.
- Take responsibility for privacy issues on your network.
- Create a network culture built on authenticity.
- Understand the value of quality and quantity, and determine which strategy is best for your network.

Keeping It Going

Chapter 17

In This Chapter

- Checking in with your membership to provide the network that suits your needs
- Surveying members' opinions
- Making decisions about what functions to add or delete

Here we are near the end of this book, and you may have the feeling your work is done. In reality, the work of hosting a social network is never done. There will always be content to create, comments to moderate, and fires to put out. Let me share some strategies to keep your network moving forward.

Six-Month Check-Up

Dentists recommend a six-month check-up to keep your teeth healthy, and the same holds true for your social network. Once established, it's easiest to just keep plugging along the way you'd originally planned without checking your *heads up display* to see what's really going on.

> **DEFINITION**
>
> A **heads up display** is a transparent computer screen that is available to users without having to change their point of view. This might mean a transparent display monitor, a helmet with visor, or even a pair of sunglasses. The expression has also become a reference to being aware of what's going on around you. Maybe you've shared information with someone recently or given them a heads up?

It's important to review what's happening with your network to make sure you're putting all that effort in for the right results. You want those results to correlate to the objectives you defined back in Chapter 2. Depending on your network, you might do a check-up every six months, annually, or some other interval. Pick the timing that makes sense for your unique community.

While a check-up every six months, works for many communities, you may end up monitoring different things throughout the year. Let's make an example of a fictional network about fly-fishing in the Pacific Northwest with a BuddyPress network.

Daily: Check for feedback and questions and respond. Upload content as planned and add spontaneous content based on the news of the day.

Weekly: Review social media outpost participation. Are you on target? Acknowledge anglers with the "big catch" story of the week.

Monthly: Consider how your resources are being spent. Check in on the financial health of our community. Also look at human resources for the month to come. Is anyone going on vacation?

Quarterly: Review content shared in the previous quarter. Was all desired content posted? Did members interact with the content? Was their reaction positive or negative? Map out an editorial calendar for the next quarter.

Semi-annually: Conduct a member survey. Send out a note of appreciation to members for being part of the community. Review back office statistics about storage, bandwidth, and so on, and plan for changes, as needed.

Annually: Consider the year in review. What were your biggest challenges? Capture the lessons learned. Celebrate your successes and make New Year's–style resolutions for the year ahead.

This list is by no means the entirety of the monitoring you'll do over the course of the year, but note that some parts of your network check-up can happen on a schedule like this.

What Features Are Being Used?

Have a look at the features that are being utilized by members of your network. Are they uploading pictures, posting status messages, and using the event feature? Maybe the discussion boards are blank with no dialogue happening. Try not to get caught up in the why—just quantify what's happening and make note of the tallies for analysis.

You might also look at usage in terms of the time of year. Is there a spike related to a seasonal holiday or a conference-type event? Is there less traffic during the summer months? Looking for patterns will help you time critical community activity during periods of highest participation.

What Do Participants Say?

Empirical data is great, but what do your participants say? Pose the question on a message board or in an e-mail to all members. Ask something like:

- What do you value most about this community?
- How can we support the community to serve you better?
- How'd we do this year?
- What three features do you use most often?
- How can we improve your experience here?

Make it clear that you want to make the community what they want—make it about them, not you.

Figure 17.1

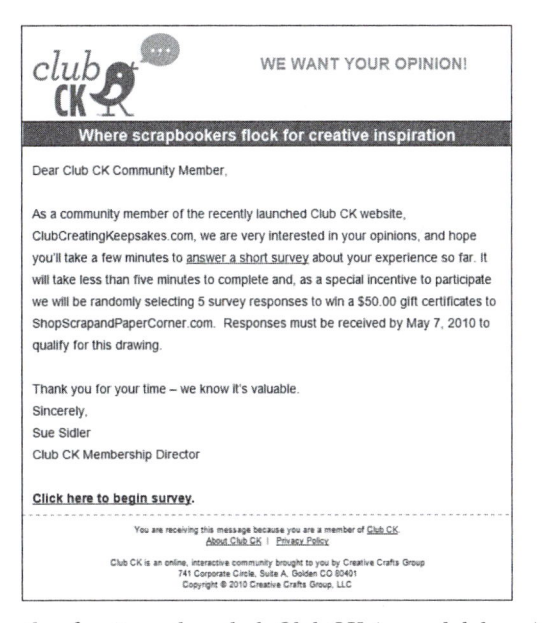

A few months after it was launched, Club CK (www.clubck.com) sent an e-mail asking members to take a short survey.

Creating a survey is easy using tools, and there are many online tools to help you gather your data including:

- SurveyMonkey (surveymonkey.com)
- Polldaddy (polldaddy.com)
- SurveyGizmo (surveygizmo.com)
- Google Docs' forms feature (docs.google.com)

Try to keep your survey short and sweet—you need to respect members' time. If the survey is too long or too complicated, they won't take the time to give you the valuable information you seek.

Figure 17.2

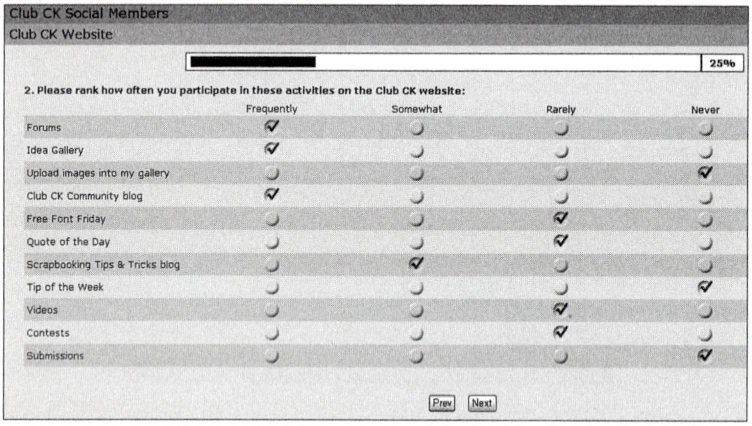

In your survey, ask participants to rate various components of your network and how they use them, as Club CK did in this example.

When crafting your survey, include different styles of questions. Some should require simple yes or no answers, while others can invite people to click all that apply from a series of options. You'll also want to ask some opinion questions where members can give feedback on a scale from most favorite to least favorite. You can also ask open ended–questions, with an opportunity for more specific feedback.

Questions you might ask members of your network include:

- What do you value most about our community?
- Rank the following features from most useful to least useful.
- Tell us any suggestions you have for improvements.

More, Less, or Stay the Same?

Based on the tally of activity and the aggregate responses to your survey, analyze what members like and use and what they don't like or ignore. From there, decide whether to add more features, remove some features, or keep things just as they are.

As much as possible, detach yourself from the results. Try not to read emotion or other implications into the responses. By focusing on the numbers, you'll see a story in the data.

Continually Adapt

Keep up with any new features available from your social network service. Have Ning, Wall.fm, or KickApps added new functionality? You shouldn't add every new thing that comes along but do consider those that would work well in your network.

Also, keep an eye on your competition. What are they doing? Is there some special functionality that a competitor employs that could draw members away from your community? Are there opportunities for joint activities or other strategic alliances?

Use Search

As we talked about in Chapter 10, search can be a useful tool for generating content. It can also be a powerful means of checking up on your network.

Inside Job

Within your own social network, search for keywords and phrases. Are the topics and content you intended being added to the conversation or has the community evolved to discuss other things?

> **CLOUD SURFING**
>
> Peggy Richardson from WizardofeBooks.com, a company focused on words in the digital realm, has a very useful white paper on keywords available for free at www.keywordcheatsheet.com. This brief document offers an introduction to keyword research for beginners and step-by-step instructions to establish keywords for your website, blog, or network. It's a quick and easy read full of terrific information to get you started.

For example, is your social network intended for fans of car racing? If so, you might expect certain key phrases to come up time and again—NASCAR driver, Formula One, engine blocks, wheels, and tires. However, over time, you may find the conversation moving away from your intended purpose. Maybe the content has moved your community to be a fan site for specific teams or drivers?

If there is a change, it's not a bad thing. It's just an organic process of any community in conversation over time. As network owner it's good to be aware of this shift so that you can continue to support and engage members.

Search Engines

Also look outside your network. How are you rating in the search engines like Bing and Google? Consider your Alexa.com rating as a benchmark for the relative influence of your site.

> **CLOUD SURFING**
>
> Alexa.com provides free traffic metrics, search analytics, demographics, and other data for websites. Of particular interest is the Alexa Traffic Rank, which is calculated using a combination of average daily visitors and page views over the previous three months. Sites like Google, Facebook, and YouTube are always in the top ten most popular sites. To increase your Alexa ranking work to have more visitors and more page views.

Once again, Google Alerts (see Chapter 10) can be useful as you check up on your community. Keep an alert set up for the name of your network and any logical variations or misspellings to see what's being said in the wider web.

Often it is a good idea to reply to both positive and negative coverage. This is a great opportunity to invite people to be part of your network.

The Least You Need to Know

- It's a good idea to do a six-month check-up on your network.
- Gather data on who uses what features.
- Poll the membership for opinions and ideas.
- Keep your network current with new functions, when appropriate.

Social Network Service Tutorials

Part 5

The social network services featured in this book are all pretty user friendly. With a little bit of computer know-how and an understanding of how you want your social network to work, you're well on your way to creating a new community. In the next five chapters, we'll walk through set-up instructions to help you create your first community on Ning, Wall.fm, SocialGO, BuddyPress, or KickApps. The step-by-step tutorials will take you from the first welcome screen through the sign up, download, and feature selection processes, as applicable. Think of these tutorials as your orientation guide to getting started with each social network service. Now spread your wings and fly!

Ning Tutorial

Chapter 18

In This Chapter

- How to set up a Ning network at www.ning.com
- An overview of the pricing plans
- Creating an account
- Payment and billing arrangements
- Creating a Ning network

In this tutorial, we'll build a Ning network. To get started, direct your browser to Ning.com and click on the **Get Started Now** button.

Ning offers three levels of service—Mini, Plus, and Pro. A 30-day free trial is available at every level, but you'll still have to select a service level to set up your network. Monthly fees range from $2.95 for Ning Mini to $49.95 for Ning Pro. Ning also offers annual discounts if you prepay for the year—for example, subscribers can secure a Ning Mini for one year for $19.95. The annual savings options won't appear until you get to the payment stage. In our example, we'll select Ning Pro.

Figure 18.1

*Click **Get Started Now** to begin your Ning network.*

Figure 18.2

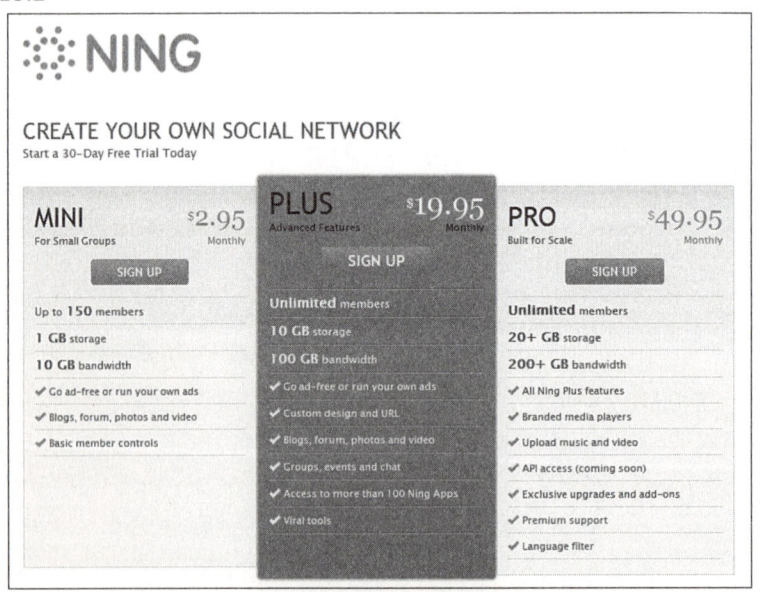

Select a service level for your Ning community.

To create your network you must have a Ning account. If you already have one, simply click **Sign In** on Ning's home page. If you need a Ning account, complete the sign-up form with the following information:

- Full name
- E-mail address
- Password
- Captcha phrase

Once the form is complete, click **Sign Up** to create your account.

Figure 18.3

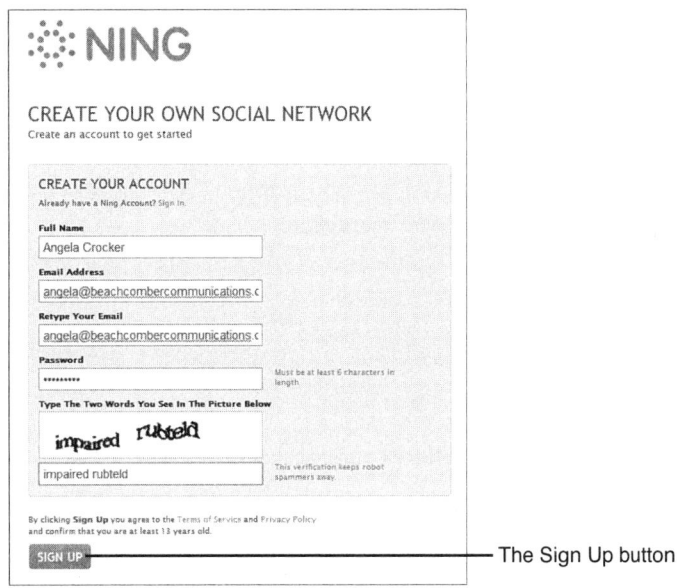

Input your name, e-mail, and password to quickly create an account.

> **FLICKERS OF INSIGHT**
>
> You can use the same Ning account with multiple Ning networks. This account can be used to create more than one network and can also be used to become a member of Ning networks administered by others.

248 Part 5: Social Network Service Tutorials

Next, Ning requires your payment information. Ning offers a 30-day free trial, but they ask users to provide banking information when the network is set up. They claim this reduces interruption to network services and streamlines the process for the network administrator.

You can arrange to pay your monthly or annual fee by PayPal or major credit card. Enter your preferred payment type and click **Enter & Select** to continue.

Figure 18.4

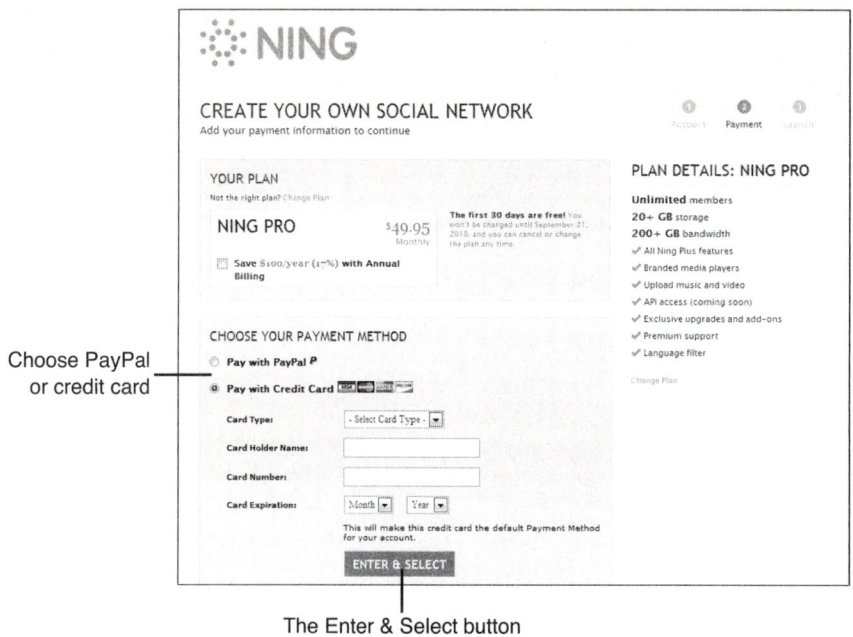

Select your payment type.

Either payment method will walk you through the process of preauthorizing Ning to charge the monthly or annual fee to your credit card or PayPal account. In our example, we elected to pay by PayPal. Click **Agree and Continue** to finish the basic setup of your Ning network.

Figure 18.5

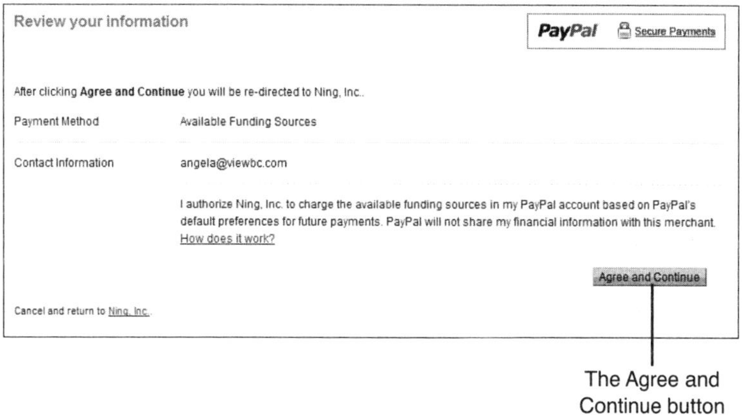

Authorize Ning to draw payments from your available funds.

We're almost done setting up the network. All that's left to do now is answer the seven questions in the "Set Up Your Network" form.

Begin by providing your network name and selecting a network address (*yourname.ning.com*). If your first choice is unavailable, Ning will prompt you to make another selection.

Then identify the country where your network resides. The pop-up menu provides options from Afghanistan to Zimbabwe. If your organization should operate in more than one country, select the country where your head office is located or wherever you do the majority of your work.

Next up is to choose the language for your network. English (U.S.) is the default, but networks can be launched in any number of languages from French, Italian, or Spanish to Romanian, Polish, or Chinese. Simply select your desired language from the drop-down menu.

You must also choose a category for your community. Is your group sports focused, business oriented, or all about entertainment? Select the category that best describes your community from the drop-down menu.

Next decide whether your network is public or private. Do you want your content visible to anyone or do you want to restrict access to members only?

Finally, provide a contact phone number. Ning will use this to contact you if there are any problems with your network or billing issues.

Once the Set Up Your Network form is complete, it's time to click **Launch** and your network is published immediately.

Figure 18.6

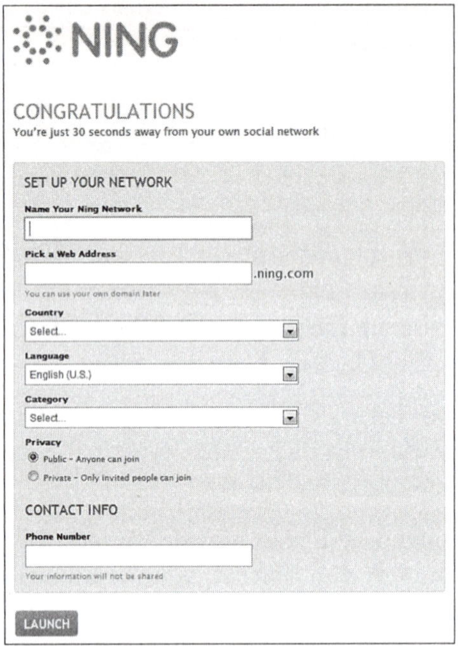

Seven questions to set up your network.

Once you've created your network, Ning redirects you to your administrator's dashboard. From here you can add or update features, make changes to the appearance of your network, and invite members to join. You could spend days exploring all the options.

Figure 18.7

Explore Ning's dashboard.

> **CLOUD SURFING**
>
> www.creators.ning.com is Ning's social network for those building Ning networks. It offers a frequently asked questions section, discussion forums, information about upcoming changes, and so on. You'll also find assistance available at help.ning.com.

You'll also want to visit the network address of your newly created community—yourname.ning.com. There you'll see the default features and appearance included in your Ning network. You'll also see your community the way it will appear to members. If you want to change something, visit your dashboard and make adjustments to suit your needs.

Figure 18.8

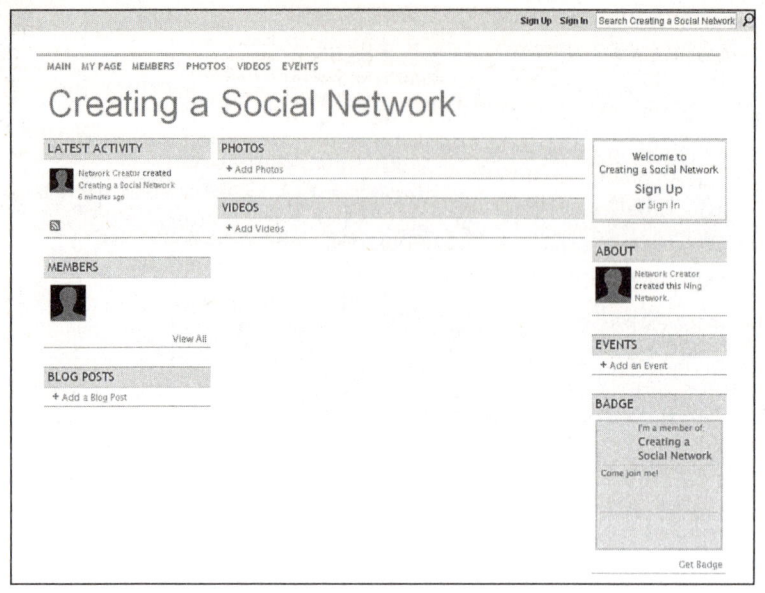

The Creating a Social Network community at angelacrocker.ning.com.

The Least You Need to Know

- You can build a Ning network at www.ning.com.
- You'll need a Ning account in order to set up a network.
- All networks come with a 30-day free trial.
- Ning bills monthly or annually as per the payment arrangements you make at the time of setup.
- Cost savings are available if you pay for a year at a time.
- Networks can be customized in the dashboard.

Chapter 19

Wall.fm Tutorial

In This Chapter

- How to set up a social network on Wall.fm
- Creating your Wall.fm account
- Selecting the appearance of your community
- Moving your community to a custom domain

To begin setting up a Wall.fm network, direct your web browser to Wall.fm. You'll find a welcome screen that looks something like Figure 19.1:

Figure 19.1

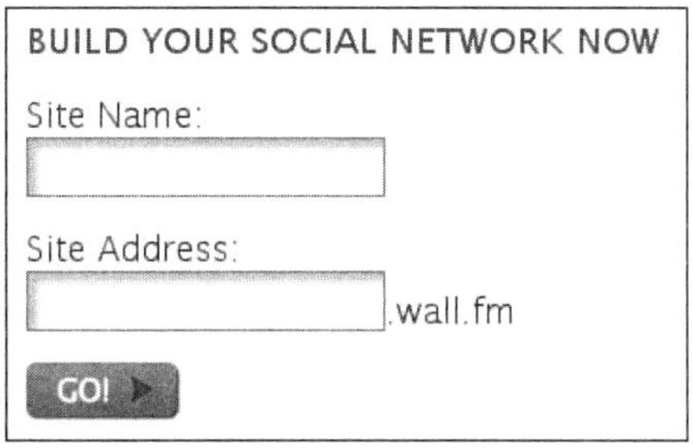

> BUILD YOUR SOCIAL NETWORK NOW
> Site Name:
> [   ]
> Site Address:
> [   ].wall.fm
> GO! ▶

The welcome screen of Wall.fm home page, formerly known as Wackwall, is where you'll begin.

To get started, fill in the "Site Name" and "Site Address" boxes under the headline "Build Your Social Network Now" and click the **GO!** button.

Part 5: Social Network Service Tutorials

Figure 19.2

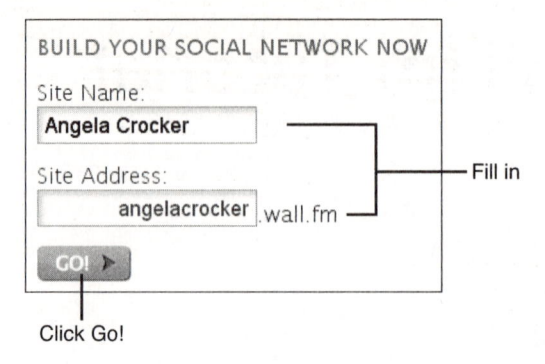

In this example, the network name is Angela Crocker and the network address is angelacrocker.wall.fm.

On the next screen, there is a five-part form for your basic settings. The top two boxes have already been autopopulated for you—network name and address. You'll want to add a tagline and a description of your community in the boxes provided. When that's complete, check the box that indicates you agree to the Wall.fm terms of use. Once you're satisfied with your answers, click the **CREATE** button.

Figure 19.3

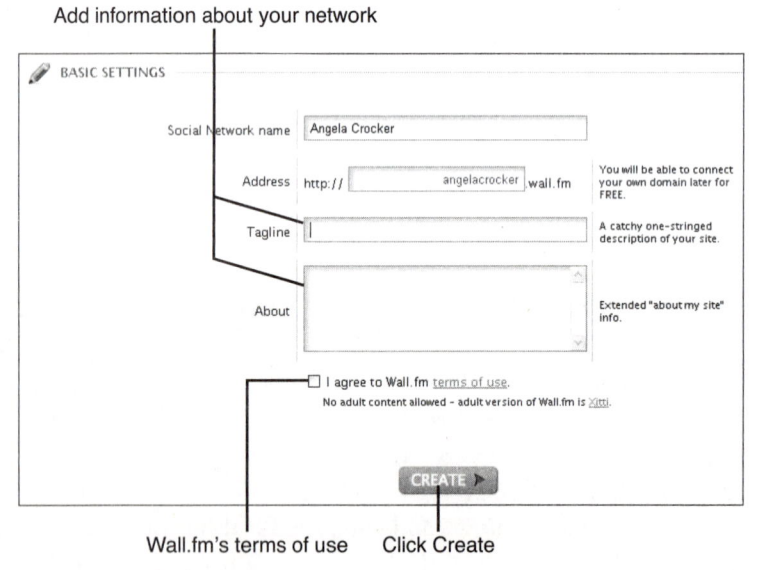

Wall.fm provides the opportunity to include a tagline or catchphrase, and some further details about your network.

Now you get to choose the theme, or the appearance, of your network. When I created this network there were six options available. On the left side of the screen you'll see the available options with names like Basic, Aerial, and Green.

The check mark in the circle indicates which theme you are previewing on the right side of the screen.

Figure 19.4

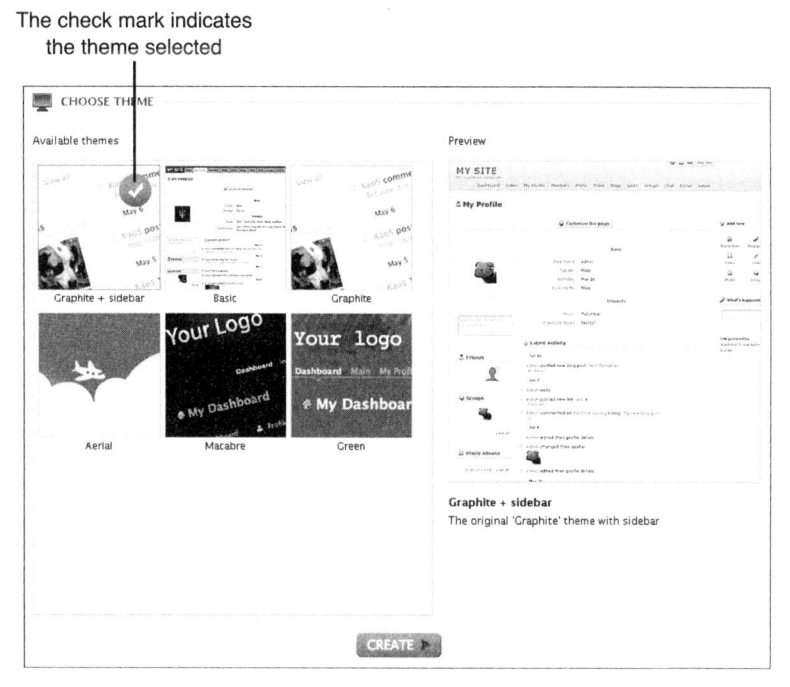

In this example we preview the Graphite + sidebar theme.

Part 5: Social Network Service Tutorials

Click on a different thumbnail to preview a different theme.

Figure 19.5

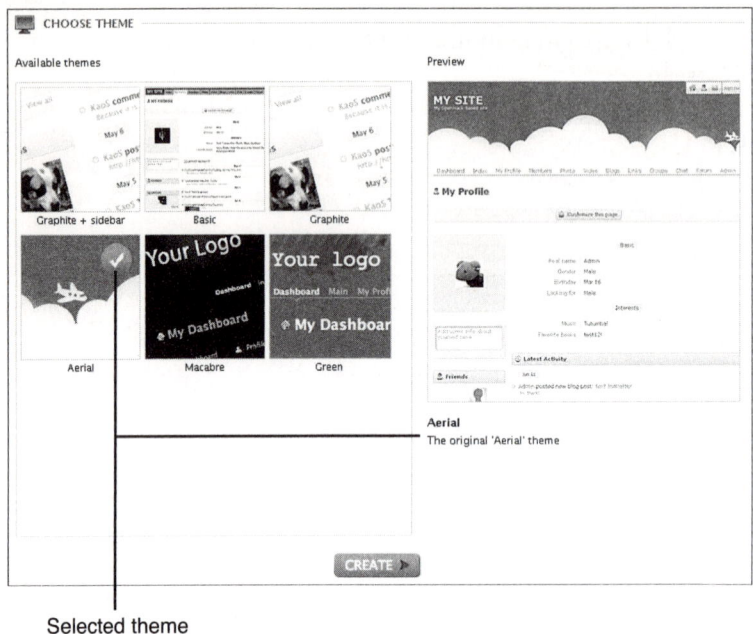

This selection previews the Aerial theme.

Once you've selected the theme you want to use, click the **CREATE** button at the bottom of the page. Even if you're not sure, choose a theme as you can always change it later. This will take you to the last step—sign-up.

If you already have a Wall.fm account, click the **Sign In** button in the top-right corner. If you don't have an account, you can create one by filling in the web form with your e-mail, user name, and password, and clicking on the **SIGN UP** button.

Figure 19.6

Wall.fm offers several ways to sign up for a free account.

If you'd prefer, you have the option to sign in using an existing integrated account on Facebook, Google, Yahoo!, OpenID, Windows Live, or AOL. Click on the icons for these social media services and a pop-up window will give you larger, clickable links to the specific service.

Figure 19.7

You can sign up for Wall.fm using any of these social media accounts.

When you click on any of these familiar logos, you'll be taken to the relevant integrated sign on page and asked to verify that you want to allow Wall.fm access.

Whether you've signed in or signed up, there will be a few seconds pause while Wall.fm creates your account. Once it's been created, you'll be redirected to the user dashboard.

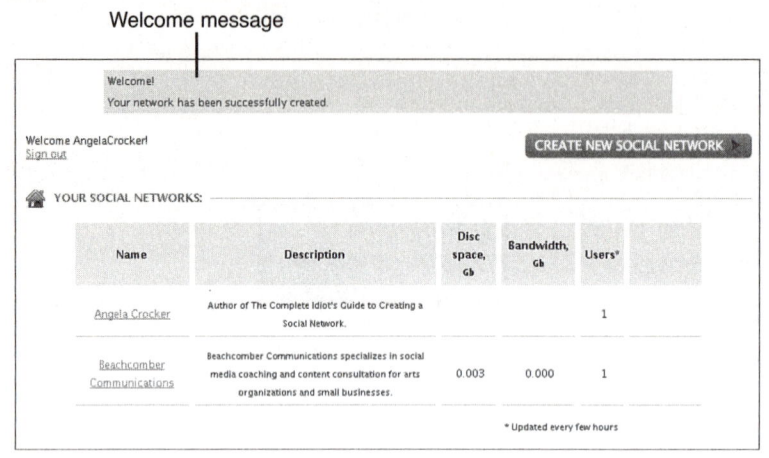

Figure 19.8

[Screenshot showing the Wall.fm user dashboard with a "Welcome message" callout pointing to "Welcome! Your network has been successfully created." The dashboard shows "Welcome AngelaCrocker!", a Sign out link, a CREATE NEW SOCIAL NETWORK button, and a YOUR SOCIAL NETWORKS table with columns Name, Description, Disc space Gb, Bandwidth Gb, Users*. Rows: Angela Crocker — Author of The Complete Idiot's Guide to Creating a Social Network. — — — 1; Beachcomber Communications — Beachcomber Communications specializes in social media coaching and content consultation for arts organizations and small businesses. — 0.003 — 0.000 — 1. Note: * Updated every few hours.]

Wall.fm says "Welcome! Your network has been successfully created."

The user dashboard lists all of the networks associated with your Wall.fm account. If you're new to Wall.fm, there will be only one network on the list—the one you've just created. If you have already built other networks on Wall.fm, they'll also be listed.

> **CLOUD SURFING**
>
> As mentioned in Chapter 6, there is an online help resource available at wall.fm/help.php to assist you as you create your Wall.fm community.

Hover your mouse over the network name and you'll notice the entire row of information, from name to bandwidth to storage space, is highlighted in gray. You now have three choices:

- Click on the network name to visit your community.
- Click on the "o" to edit the network settings.
- Click on the "x" to delete the network.

Figure 19.9

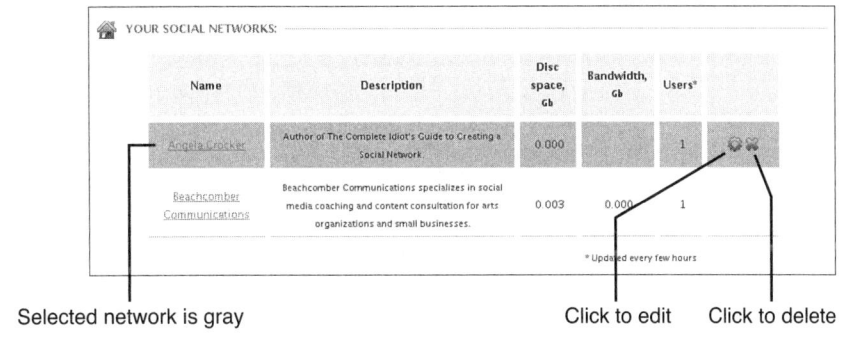

Take your first network administration steps from the dashboard.

If you click on the "x," your network and all of its data will be deleted.

If you click on the circle, you'll be taken to a screen that gives you the option to move your Wall.fm to your domain name for free. You'll want to do this if you'd prefer not to have a network address like angelacrocker.wall.fm. If you arrived at this screen by accident, don't check the "Use my own custom domain" box and click **SAVE** to return to your network without changing its domain name.

If you do want to move your Wall.fm network to a custom domain, be sure to read the link with further information before you do anything. You'll need the DNS information for your website to complete this task. If you don't understand the instructions about registering and changing your DNS, ask your go-to tech for help.

Figure 19.10

You can move your network to a custom domain on this screen.

To move your network to a custom network address, click the box next to "Use my own custom domain."

This opens up a box for you to enter the domain name where your Wall.fm community will be hosted. Once you save this change, your network will be available at the custom location. Remember that custom domains are a paid feature on Wall.fm and you will be asked to pay for this service once your free trial is over.

Figure 19.11

Move your network to a custom domain.

Now let's return to your network either on Wall.fm or your custom domain. You'll see your network name and tagline in the top-left corner of the screen. The colors and design are those of your selected theme.

Figure 19.12

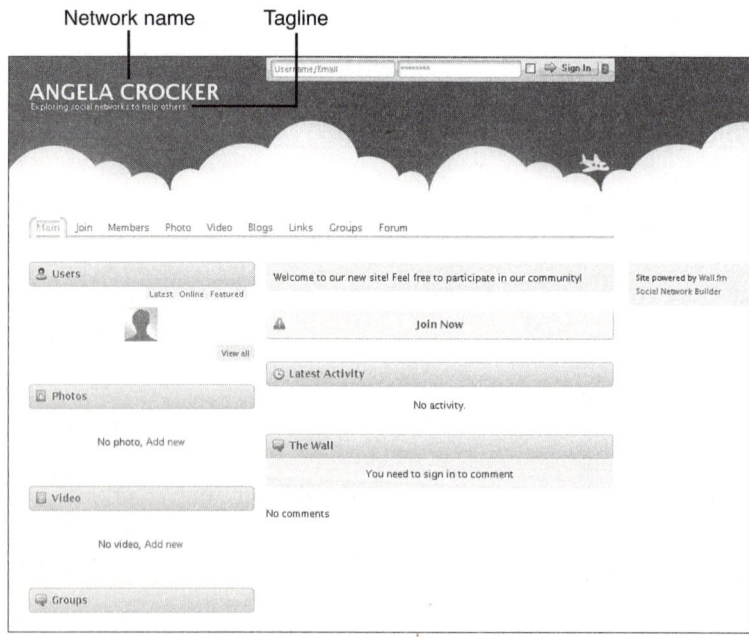

In our example, we return to angelacrocker.wall.fm.com.

You'll notice that several features are preinstalled on your network. With Wall.fm, all features are activated on every network. These include users, photos, videos, and groups in the left column, while latest activity and the wall appear in the center column.

As we dicussed in Chapter 3, I suggest you upload some content to your network to give it a more polished and lively appearance before inviting members. Once you've done that your Wall.fm network is now ready to receive visitors. Start inviting members to join your community and begin to share content for your community.

The Least You Need to Know

- Try Wall.fm's service at Wall.fm.
- Select the appearance of your network by choosing a theme.
- Create an account on Wall.fm or use an existing social media login from Facebook, Yahoo!, Google, or others.
- Host your community with this social network service or move it to your own domain for free.

SocialGO Tutorial

Chapter **20**

In This Chapter

- A step-by-step tutorial on how to set up a social network with the SocialGO service
- Upgrades available for networks to remove SocialGO branding, enable member billing, and access premium features
- Where to find assistance if you run into difficulties

If you'd like to give SocialGO a try, then direct your browser to www.socialgo.com. You'll arrive at their home page, which looks something like Figure 20.1. Click on **Start your free network now** to begin.

Figure 20.1

SocialGO users can build a free social network in minutes.

SocialGO offers three levels of service—Concierge, Premium, and Free. You can do a trial of their Premium version for 30 days or you can set up on their "free forever" version. You can upgrade or downgrade your level of service at any time. That being said, I recommend you try the Premium version for 30 days because networks set up on the Free level cannot upgrade and get a 30-day free trial. The Premium version of SocialGO includes all the available features so it's worth exploring those as well.

The first step directs you to SocialGO's pricing and features grid. Each column clearly explains what's included at each level and the monthly cost. At the bottom of each column is a "Continue" button. We'll click on the **Continue** button in the center column for a 30-day free trial of the Premium service.

Figure 20.2

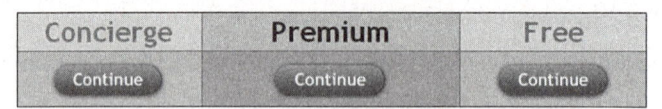

*Select a level and click **Continue**.*

The Premium level is available for $24.99 per month (after the 30-day free trial), and there are three optional add-on expenses:

- $19.99 to remove SocialGO branding
- $19.99 to enable member billing
- $9.99 to add the Go IM Premium service
- $349.99 for setup and design service

We'll add Go IM Premium to our trial network. Click **Continue** to move on to Step 1, where we enter our network details.

Figure 20.3

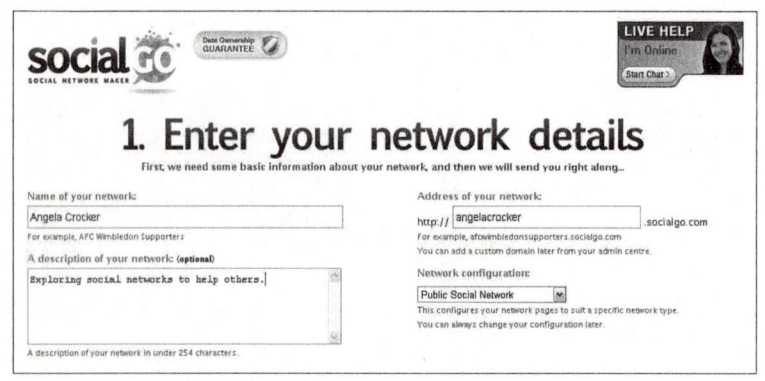

Fill in the blanks to start creating your network.

As you type, the contents of the network name box on the left automatically populate the network address box on the right. If you don't like the address provided you can edit this. In the example in Figure 20.3, the space between the two words in the network name created a hyphen in the network address. I was able to go in and delete the hyphen. Once completed, SocialGO will tell you if your selected network address is available. If not, then you'll have to select a different address.

Once you've filled in the network name, network address, and network description, you must choose the type of network configuration you want:

- Public Social Network
- Private Social Network
- Blog with a Social Network
- Forum with a Social Network
- Website with a Social Network
- Business Intranet
- Education Intranet
- Organization Intranet
- Event website

For this demonstration we'll choose Public Social Network. Your network configuration can always be changed later.

Figure 20.4

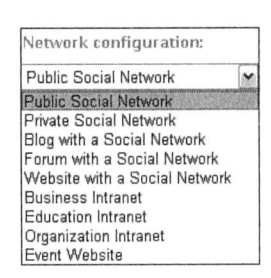

Select a network configuration.

Next up is Step 2—network design. Select one of the premade designs for the look of your network. You can change your selection, customize your choice, or design an original look later.

You'll be able to make further refinements once your community is launched.

Figure 20.5

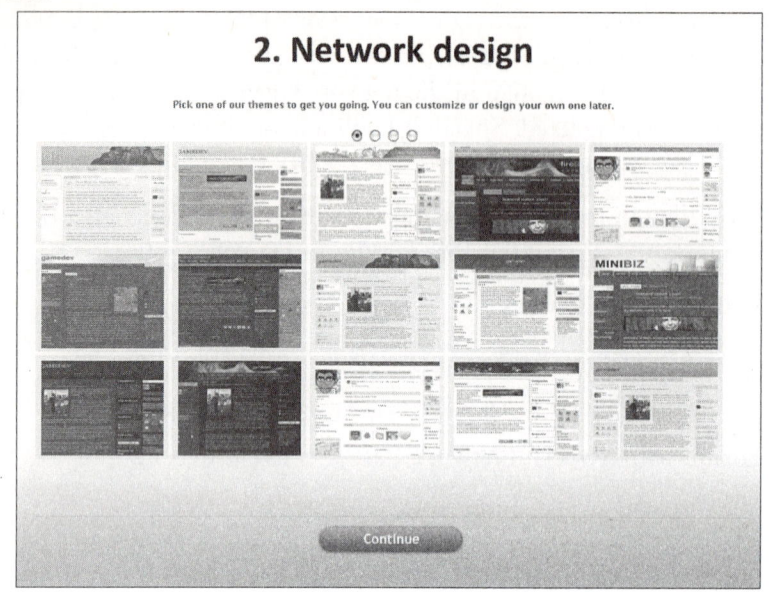

Design options for your SocialGO Network.

Once you've made a selection, click on **Continue** at the bottom of the screen.

This brings us to Step 3, the account details screen. Because this free trial will expire in 30 days, SocialGO asks users to provide billing details and payment information at the time of setup. You will not be charged until your trial period is complete. If you cancel before the trial is over, you will not be charged. Once you've completed the form, click **Continue**.

> **CLOUD SURFING**
>
> If you need any help with SocialGO, visit www.owners.socialgo.com or www.socialgo.com/help for assistance.

After completing your payment, voilà! SocialGO instantly creates your network. Your browser will redirect to your site and you'll receive an e-mail from SocialGO welcoming you as a customer.

When your site launches, SocialGO's introductory video walks you through 10 steps to optimize your network and get started on content before you invite your contacts to join. The video also introduces you to the SocialGO Admin Centre, which is the hub of your administrative access to the community.

Figure 20.6
SocialGO Admin Centre

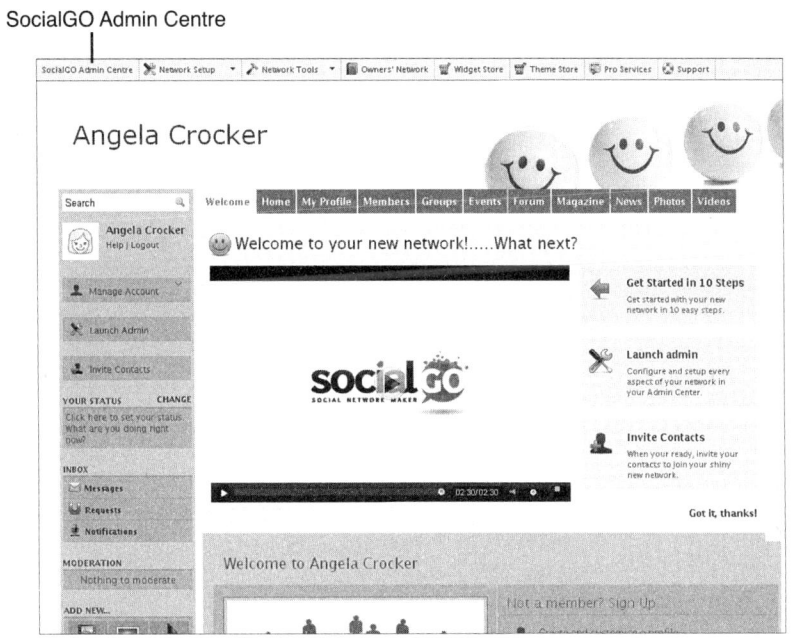

Here is the community created at angelacrocker.socialgo.com.

The SocialGO Admin Centre gives you easy click access to network-related functions, as well as the widget and theme stores. You can also access the SocialGO owners' community through the admin bar or by visiting owners.socialgo.com. I encourage you to experiment with the features and tools that are most useful to your community. Figure out what meets your objectives and suits your needs and work on building your community from that foundation.

The Least You Need to Know

- Try SocialGO's service at www.socialgo.com.
- SocialGO offers a "free forever" service with limited features.
- To test all the features, you should subscribe to a 30-day free trial of SocialGO's Premium service.
- Use the SocialGO Admin Centre to explore customizations and features available to your network.

BuddyPress Tutorial

Chapter 21

In This Chapter

- Understand that BuddyPress is a WordPress plug-in
- Where to get the free BuddyPress software
- How to install BuddyPress
- Selecting a theme to dress your community
- An overview of the dashboard controls
- Introduction to the widgets available

BuddyPress is an open source, social network service that is compatible with WordPress. WordPress is a popular blogging and website design tool used to create 10 million or more websites.

To create a BuddyPress network, you first need a WordPress website. Once WordPress is in place, you can add the BuddyPress plug-in to create your community. In this chapter, we'll walk through how to do just that.

Before you go to the trouble of installing BuddyPress on your domain, you can explore and examine BuddyPress's capabilities at the BuddyPress Test Drive community at testbp.org. This demonstration site uses the default settings to illustrate how BuddyPress operates immediately after it has been installed. It was created to allow prospective users a sneak peak and a chance to explore the technology.

Figure 21.1

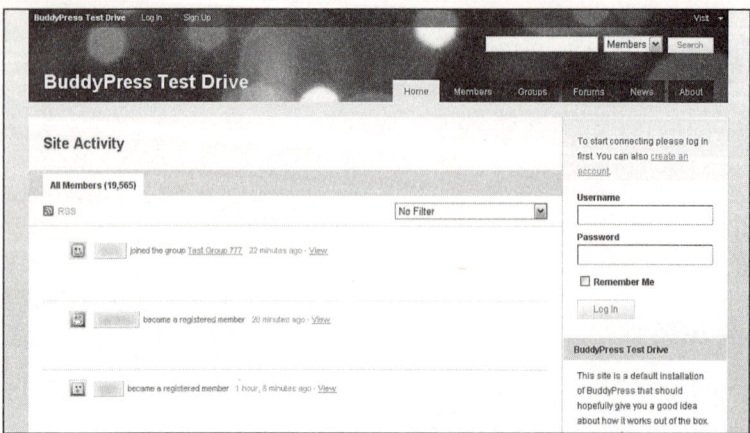

Explore a live demonstration of BuddyPress at testbp.org.

Begin by clicking **create an account** in the top-right corner of the screen. Enter a user name (lowercase letters only), e-mail address, and password, plus your name, a brief biography, and country into the Create an Account form. This generates an autoreply e-mail with a verification link. After verifying your account, you can then log in to the BuddyPress Test Drive Community.

The BuddyPress Test Drive landing page includes a news feed similar to Facebook or Twitter feeds. Members can enter and post a brief status update to share with the test drive community. Most of the messages are brief, inconsequential notes as others try out BuddyPress.

BuddyPress includes navigation tabs across the top of the page to find further information about Members, Groups, Forums, News, and About. As you browse the following images and explore the site itself, imagine your network's name in place of "Test Drive" to visualize how the network might work for you.

The Members tab (see Figure 21.2) leads to the Members Directory, a listing of all members of this community. The members list can be sorted according to Last Active, Newest Registered, and Alphabetical. The directory includes members' avatars and most recent status update post.

Figure 21.2

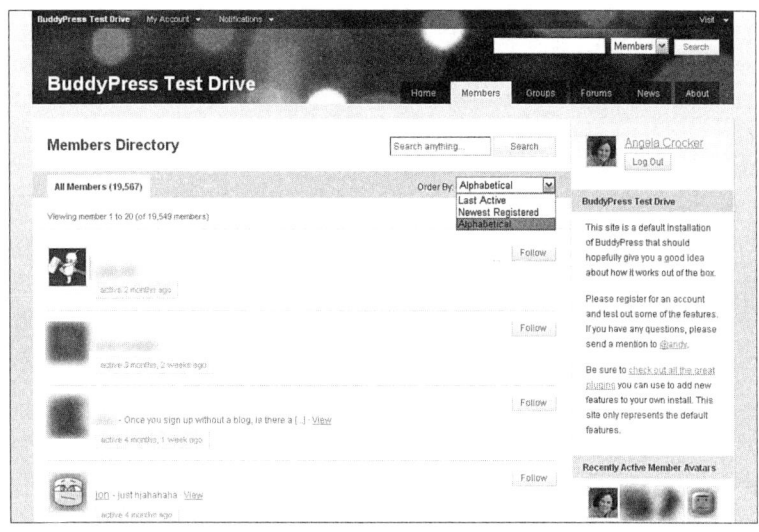

The Members tab in BuddyPress Test Drive.

The Groups tabs (see Figure 21.3) navigates to the Groups Directory. This page also allows users to browse a list of existing groups. The groups can be sorted by Last Active, Most Members, Newly Created, and Alphabetical. New groups can also be created from this page. Go ahead and create a group to see how it works. This group doesn't have to be a real one but it will show how easy it is to set up a group.

Figure 21.3

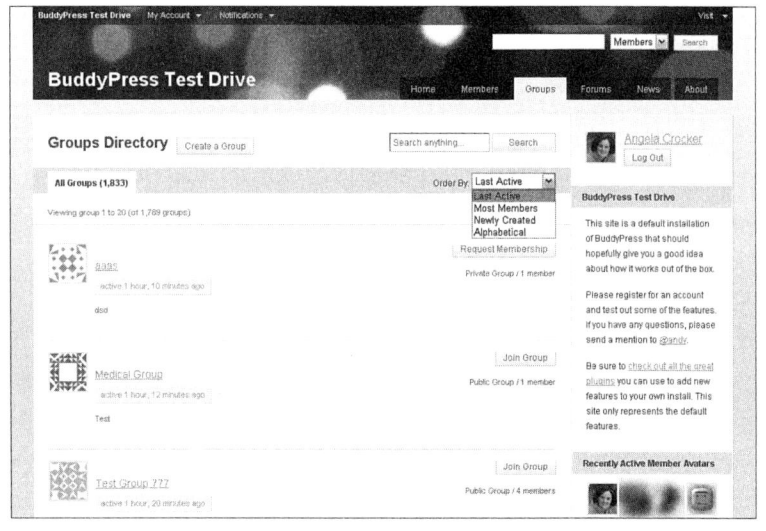

The Groups tab in BuddyPress Test Drive.

272 Part 5: Social Network Service Tutorials

The Forums tab (see Figure 21.4) directs users to a list of all the discussions within the various groups. Once again, the discussions can be sorted according to Last Active, Most Posts, and Unreplied. New topics of conversation can also be started from the Forums area.

Figure 21.4

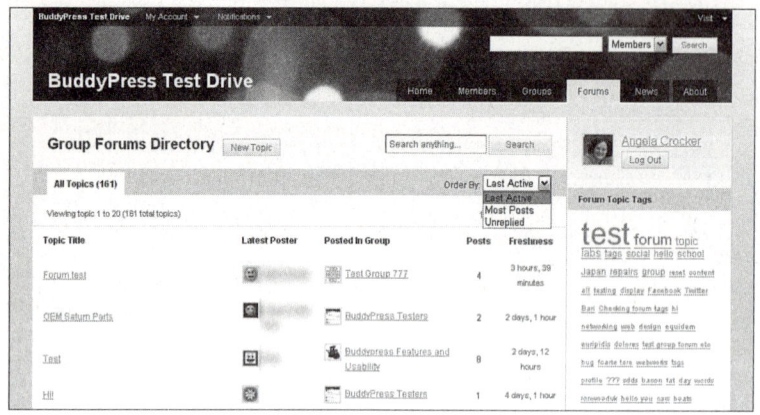

The Forums tab in BuddyPress Test Drive.

The News tab (see Figure 21.5) directs users to a recent blog post pulled from the connected WordPress Blog. Community members can comment on the post within BuddyPress.

Figure 21.5

The News tab in BuddyPress Test Drive.

The final tab, About (see Figure 21.6), is simply information about the BuddyPress community. It's the community's biography, if you will.

Figure 21.6

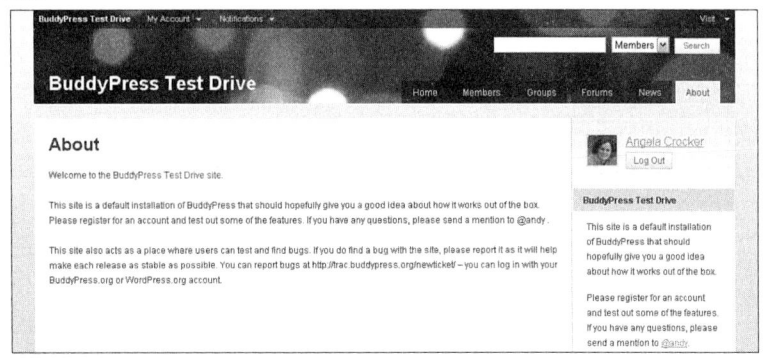

The About tab in BuddyPress Test Drive.

You'll notice in all the previous images that the navigation bar across the top and the right column remained the same for all screens, providing users with a constant frame of reference. This makes for easy navigation and a cohesive appearance.

Beyond the default features illustrated in the BuddyPress Test Drive community, there are 125 (and many more in development) additional BuddyPress plug-ins that can be added to extend the capabilities of any BuddyPress community. Tools like Tweetstream and Facestream allow users to share their BuddyPress experiences on Twitter and Facebook. There are also tools to create secure contact forms, enhance SEO, and generate maps, as well as dozens of other add-ons.

Install BuddyPress

Let's walk through setting up a BuddyPress community and further explore the features of BuddyPress from an administrative point of view.

Of course, you must have access to a WordPress site in order to set up BuddyPress. If your organization already has WordPress, you'll need an admin login and password to access the dashboard. If you need WordPress, visit wordpress.org and click download for information on getting this set up.

To get started with BuddyPress, visit BuddyPress.org/download and follow the instructions to get the BuddyPress installation file. Save it somewhere on your hard drive where you will be able to find it again. Do not unzip the file yet.

Next, log in to your WordPress dashboard, the administration panel. Then follow these steps to get started:

1. Click **Plugins** in the left column.
2. Click **Add New**.
3. Click **Upload**.
4. Click **Choose File**.
5. Select the Buddypress.zip file you saved to your computer earlier.
6. Click **Install Now**.

Figure 21.7

Install a WordPress plug-in here.

Once you click **Install Now**, the BuddyPress file automatically uploads, unpacks, and installs itself into WordPress. This should only take a few minutes.

Figure 21.8

The BuddyPress plug-in automatically installs itself.

Once the installation is complete, the BuddyPress plug-in appears in your list of installed plug-ins. You must click **Activate** to turn it on.

Figure 21.9

List of plug-ins installed.

Once the activation is complete, you'll see a message informing you that "BuddyPress is ready."

Figure 21.10

The BuddyPress plug-in is now activated.

Your next task is to activate a BuddyPress-compatible theme. Recall that themes are the way your community looks, including its colors, layout, and design. BuddyPress includes a default theme that you can use right away. You also have the option to change your WordPress theme to a theme that is BuddyPress compatible. For now, we'll use the included default theme by clicking **Activate** below the image of the BuddyPress default theme.

Figure 21.11

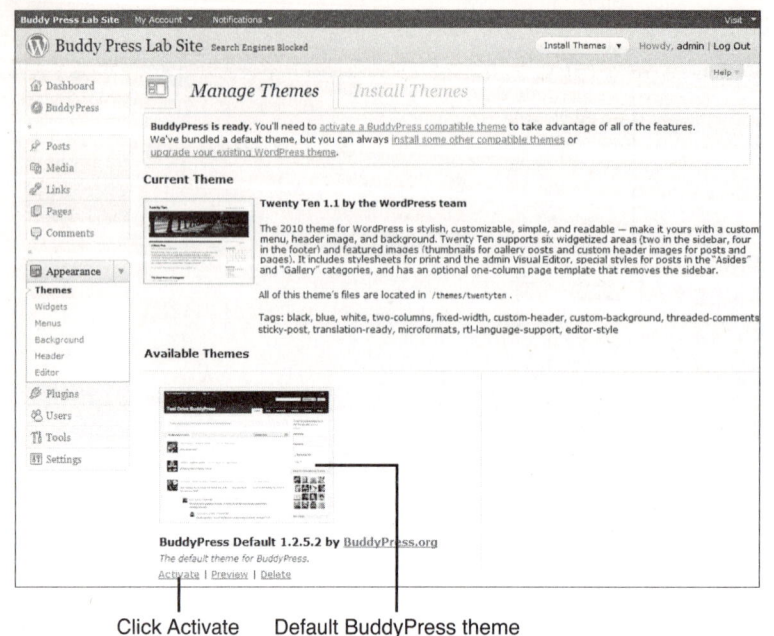

You must activate a BuddyPress compatible theme.

Now let's explore BuddyPress and the many aspects that administrators can control. Look for the word "Dashboard" in the top-left corner of your screen. Below that, select BuddyPress just above a list of four options including:

- General Settings
- Component Setup
- Forums Setup
- Profile Field Setup

Let's start by reviewing the General Settings. Each setting is preset with a default selection. Fill in the blank or click a different button to change the answers for your community. From this page you have control over things like group names, avatars, and the activity stream.

Figure 21.12

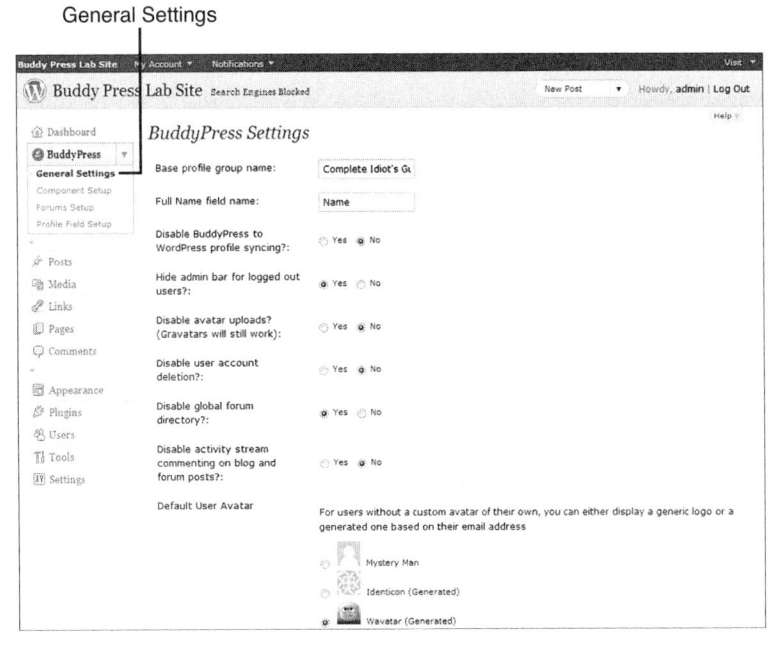

BuddyPress General Settings.

Next click **Component Setup**. BuddyPress uses the term "component" to describe user features. These are the same as the features we've discussed throughout this book. Things such as activity, friends, groups, and private messaging should be familiar by now. Select **Enabled** or **Disabled** for each component to include the features you desire in your community.

Figure 21.13

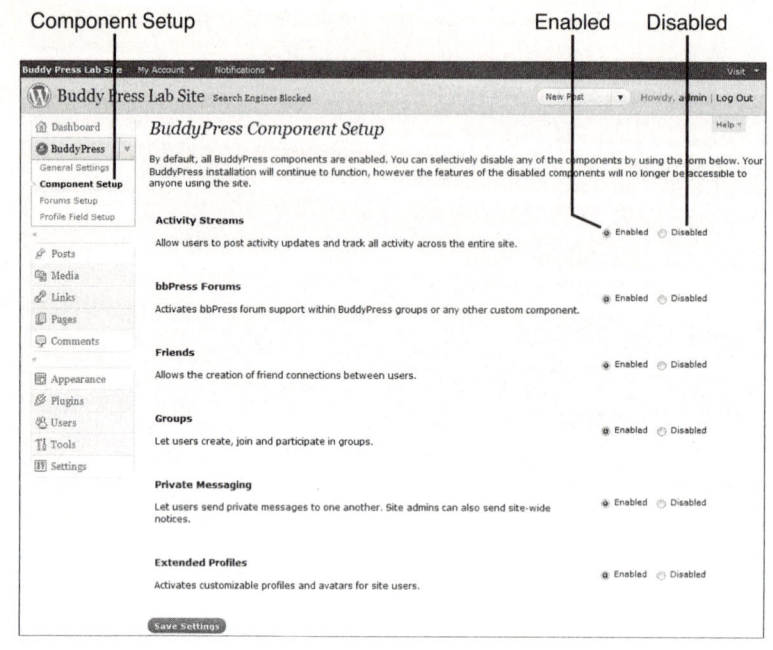

BuddyPress Component Setup enables or disables features.

Once you are satisfied with your component selections, return to the left-hand menu and click **Forums Setup**. Recall that forums are the place where members engage in much of their conversation. BuddyPress gives you the option to create a new forum or use an existing installation. As this is a new community, you'll want to click **Set up a new bbPress installation**.

Figure 21.14

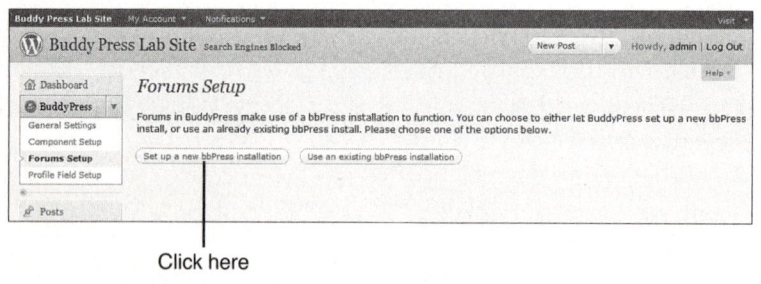

Create a new forum for your BuddyPress community.

Having made the "new" selection, you'll arrive at a page that confirms that you want to make a new forum. If so, click **Complete Installation**.

Figure 21.15

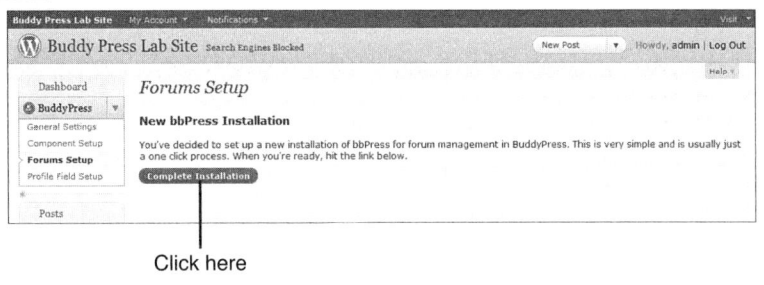

Click here

Confirm you want to create a forum.

After a few moments, your forum will be established and you'll receive confirmation with an "All done!" message.

Figure 21.16

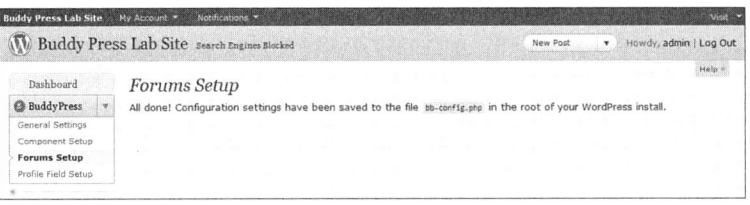

A successful forum setup.

Once again, we can turn our attention to the left-hand navigation list and, this time, focus on Profile Field Setup. This allows BuddyPress community administrators to control what member information is requested as they build user profiles.

BuddyPress profiles have fields of information. Each field is a different fact—name, city, interests, and so on. BuddyPress allows administrators to create Field Groups so that users add information at different times. The first Field Group is always the information that will be requested at sign-up. As we discussed in Chapter 8, you'll want to keep this as simple as possible. Further questions can be put in a different Field Group for users to fill in at a later time, if they so choose.

Figure 21.17

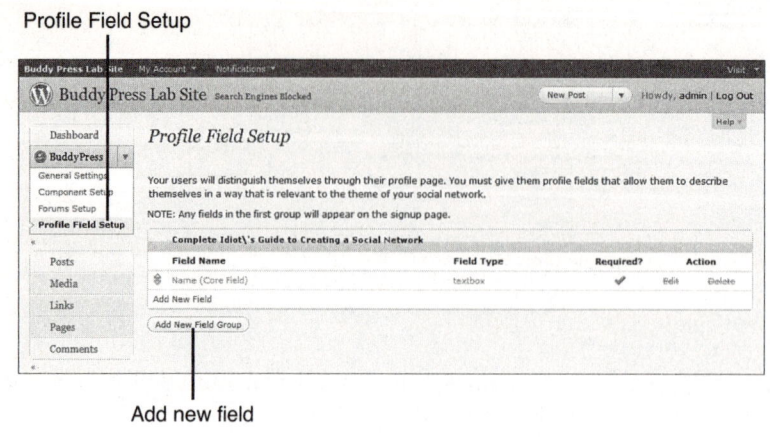

Profile Field Setup

Add new field

BuddyPress Profile Field Setup.

To create a new field, click **Add new field**. This takes you to the Add Field page. From here you can give your field a title and description. You can also decide where a field is required or optional. BuddyPress also gives you the functionality to decide if the answer will be put in a text box, a drop-down menu, a date box, or something else.

Figure 21.18

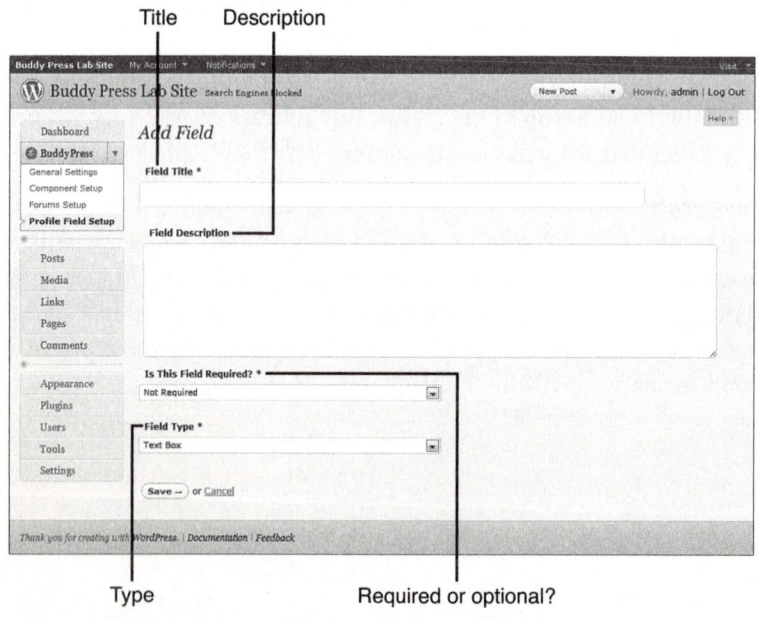

Title Description

Type Required or optional?

Use this form to create a profile field.

Let's create a couple of fields to illustrate how this form works. Suppose you ask members to share their cities. As in figure 21.19, the field name becomes "City" and the description reads "Please specify a city so that others can network with you and your company." This field is not required and can be answered in a text box. Be sure to click **Save** at the bottom of the screen to save your work.

Figure 21.19

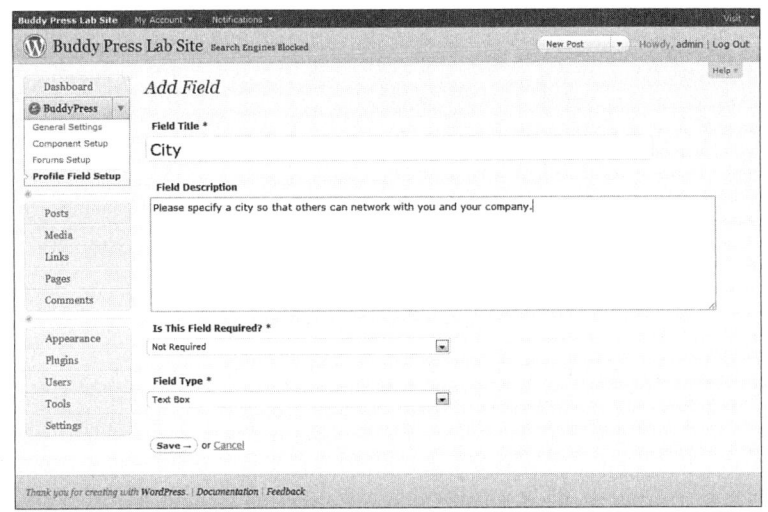

Creating a field called "City."

Next, you want to add a field called "I'm interested in …" to get a sense of what members hope to get out of the network. This time, select the Field Type "Drop Down Select Box" and enter in options that will appear in the drop-down menu. These options include "finding new clients," "creating a referral," or "ways to do business." You can add as many options as you like. You also get to select the default, or most common, option and you can determine the sequence the options will appear in the drop-down menu.

Figure 21.20

Creating a field using the Drop Down Select Box.

Don't forget to hit save when you're done. Each time you click save, you'll return to the Profile Field Setup screen. Continue creating new fields until you've added all the questions you desire.

Figure 21.21

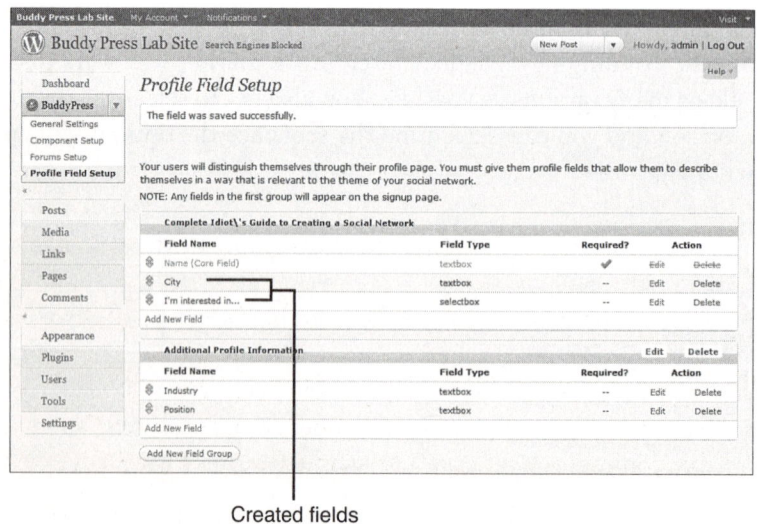

Profile Field Setup list with new fields added.

We could spend a lot of time experimenting with the Profile Field Setup options in your BuddyPress network. Hopefully these two quick examples illustrate how the profiles can be set up. Now, let's press on to some other features so you can get your community up and running.

> **CLOUD SURFING**
>
> For further information about BuddyPress visit www.wpmu.org. There you'll find reference documents, discussion forums, and daily tips to help you.

Once again, return to the dashboard links in the left column. Under the heading Appearance, click **Widgets** to select the sidebar options that will appear when people visit your site. The menu includes a variety of familiar features, from Groups and Calendar to RSS and Members.

Figure 21.22

A selection of widgets available for BuddyPress communities.

To select a widget, use your mouse to click and hold the title of the widget. Then drag it to the right of the screen and drop it under the Sidebar heading. Repeat this process for each widget you want to appear. In Figure 21.23, three widgets have been added to the sidebar—Recently Active Member Avatars, Recent Posts, and Groups. Visitors to this community will see those three features in the sidebar.

Figure 21.23

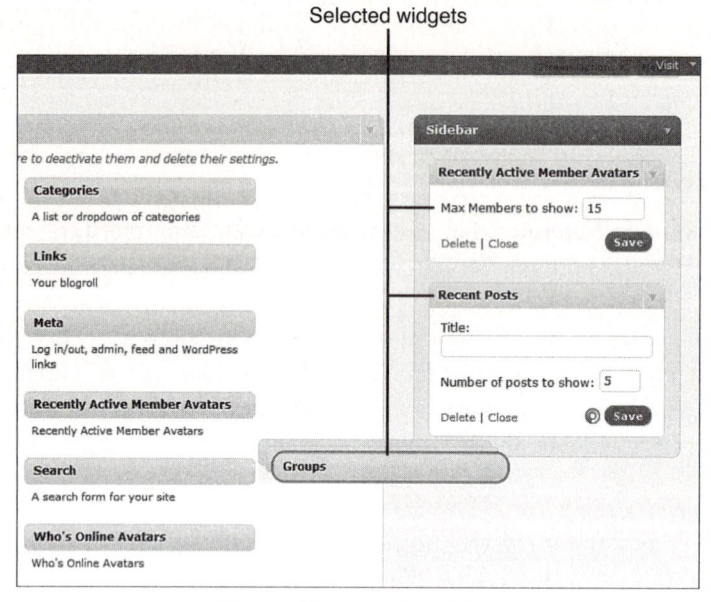

Three widgets in the sidebar.

And now your BuddyPress community is ready. I suggest you further explore the setup and refine your decisions before inviting members to join, but the basics of your community are now ready.

Figure 21.24

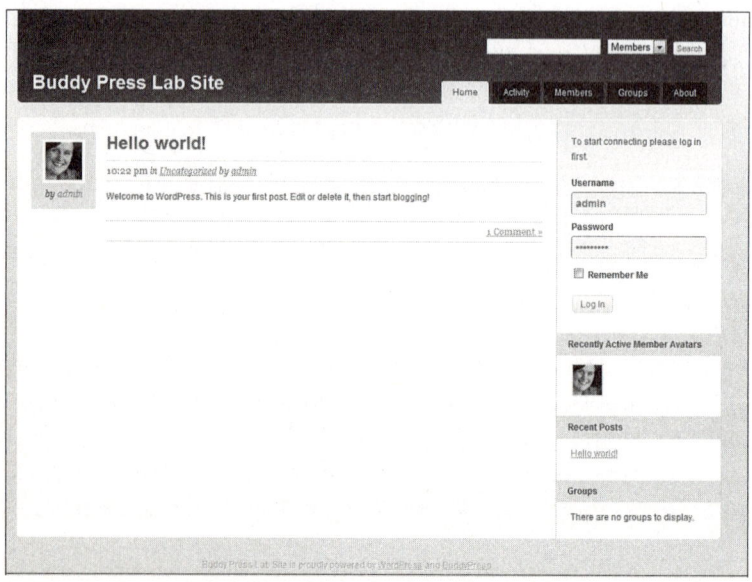

The community created in this tutorial.

The Least You Need to Know

- You must have a WordPress website to use BuddyPress.
- Download the free software at BuddyPress.org.
- BuddyPress is a WordPress plug-in.
- Adjust the color and design of your community by selecting a theme.
- Manipulate the features of your network in the dashboard controls for General Settings, Component Setup, Forums Setup, and Profile Field Setup.
- Control the appearance of your website by selecting and positioning appropriate widgets.

Chapter 22

KickApps Tutorial

In This Chapter

- Create a network on www.kickapps.com
- Explore the features available in KickApps communities
- See the KickApps Affiliate Center for customization and management
- Edit the appearance of a KickApps community with Site Styler or custom code
- Costs to continue your KickApps network after the free trial

To create a KickApps community, point your browser at www.kickapps.com. There you'll find a comprehensive introduction to all that KickApps has to offer and a list of the major brands that use the service, including NBC, NFL, Proctor & Gamble, and Qwest. Of course, KickApps isn't just for brands that are household names. They also work with thousands of smaller businesses to create their social networks. To try out this service free for 30 days, click **Start Free Trial**.

Figure 22.1

Get started at www.kickapps.com.

To create your network you'll need to answer six questions on the sign-up form. These include:

1. E-mail address
2. User name
3. Password
4. Network name
5. Captcha
6. Agree to Terms of Service

Once you've completed the sign-up form, click **Sign Me Up**.

Figure 22.2

Complete the form to create a KickApps network.

And with that simple process you have created your KickApps network. There may be a brief pause while your network is created. You'll see a message on the screen that says "We're working …" during this time.

Figure 22.3

Pause while your KickApps network is created.

You will be automatically directed to an administrator's view of your new community. The center of your screen will be filled with helpful information and links to get your network optimized as quickly as possible. I suggest you start with the video in the right column.

Figure 22.4

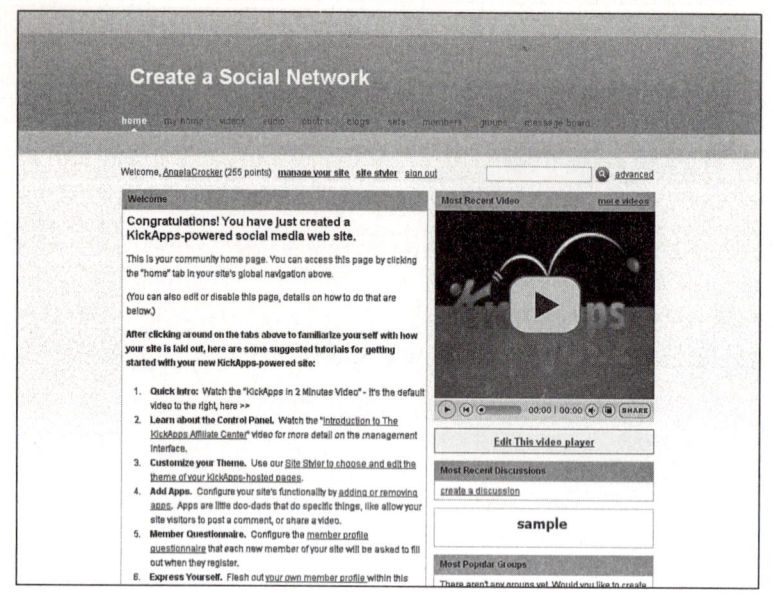

Helpful information to customize your KickApps community.

Next, explore the tabs at the top of your screen. They include:

- Home
- My Home
- Videos
- Audio
- Photos
- Blogs
- Sets
- Members
- Groups
- Message Board

These tabs represent the features that your members will have access to during their time within your network.

Figure 22.5

Navigate to network features using these tabs.

You'll notice as you click on the various tabs that each reveals a submenu of options. In Figure 22.6, I've clicked on the photos tab to reveal further links to the following:

- My photos
- Most recent (currently highlighted in Figure 22.6)
- Highest rated
- Most viewed
- Top favorites
- Most comments
- Add a photo

Look carefully for the "add a photo" tab as it's tucked off to the right.

KickApps automatically adds sample content when a network is created. This is helpful to provide a sense of how the network works. Once you've got a handle on the basics, be sure to delete the sample content. In Figure 22.6, we see two example images of the Empire State Building.

Figure 22.6

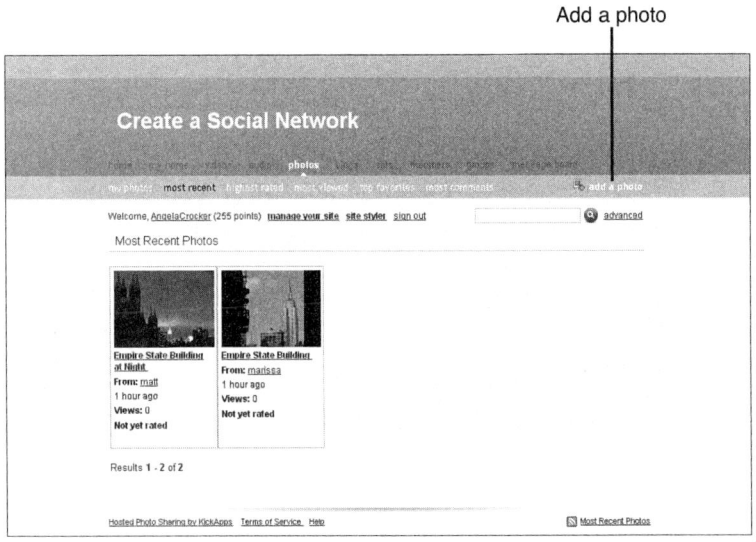

Example content is added to each new KickApps network.

You may notice that the Welcome line stays visible no matter what tab you are viewing. This line includes four links.

The first is your user name, in this case AngelaCrocker, with a link to your profile page. As with all networks, you can upload a profile picture, edit your biography, and leave a status update, called a comment on KickApps.

The second link reads "manage your site." This takes you to the KickApps Affiliate Center, which is also referred to as the AC. This is the KickApps dashboard where you can access the tools and design functions you need to manage your network.

Next up is the site styler link. This is where you can change the appearance of your KickApps network. We'll talk some more about that a bit later.

And, finally, we get to the sign-out link, which you can use when you are done for the day.

One more thing you'll notice in Figure 22.7 is that there are five members to this example network. You already know me, and the other four are members of the KickApps team who you can contact for assistance. Each of their profiles includes ways to contact them for help.

Figure 22.7

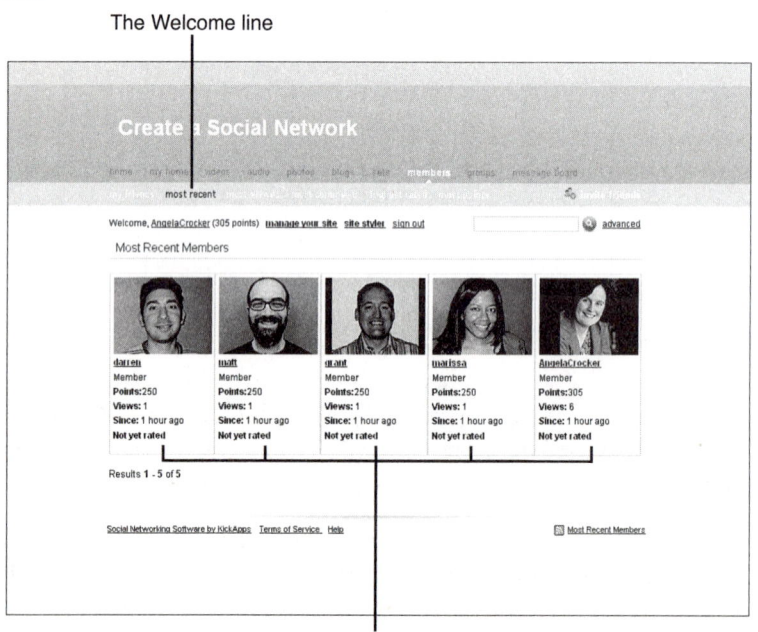

Example KickApps members directory.

Go ahead and click **manage your site** to visit the KickApps Affiliate Center (AC). Browse around the AC and you will discover links to help you configure and manage your community. You'll also be able to shop the App Studio for useful widgets and view comprehensive reports. To help familiarize you with all that's available in the AC, KickApps includes an introductory video. Once you've learned all you can from this clip, you can remove the module permanently.

Figure 22.8

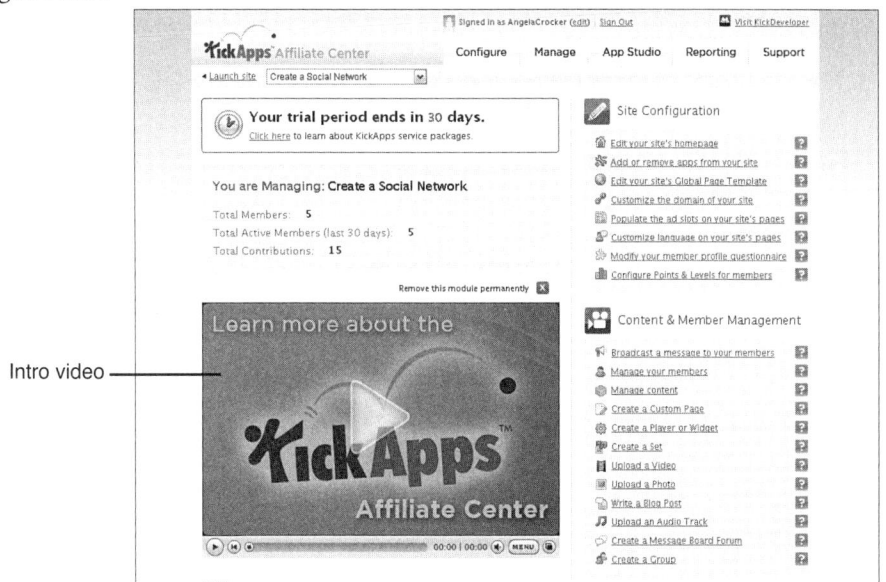

Explore the KickApps Affiliate Center.

Now let's return to your community page and click the **Site Styler** link in the Welcome line. In KickApps, Site Styler allows you to change the appearance of your social network. If you have no experience with web programming code, then you can use their what-you-see-is-what-you-get tool. Simply click on the desired theme from the Theme Gallery and see a preview on your site right away.

If you are comfortable with HTML, CSS, or Javascript, then click on the **Global Page Template** link and edit the header, body, and footer, as required. If you add CSS code, then you will no longer be able to use the Site Styler tool.

Figure 22.9

KickApps' Site Styler allows you to change the appearance of your community.

Figure 22.10

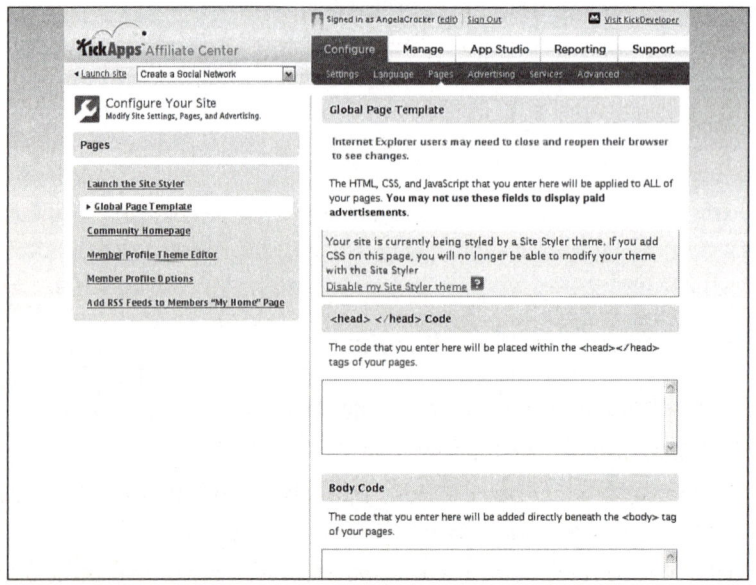

Use the Global Page Template to edit the appearance code.

Explore and play with KickApps robust tools as much as you can during your 30-day free trial. A countdown clock at the top of your Affiliate Center dashboard will let you know how many days you have left. If you want to continue with your community, then select a plan before your trial ends.

> **CLOUD SURFING**
>
> For further information visit kickdeveloper.com, the official help site of KickApps.

KickApps offers pricing plans for enterprise-level businesses. It also publishes a rate sheet appropriate for small- to medium-size organizations. The monthly cost varies depending on the level of service selected, with a Starter package at $9.95 per month up to Premium service for $299.95 a month.

Figure 22.11

All Plans Include NO Setup Fees	STARTER	BASIC	PRO	ADVANCED	PREMIUM
PRICE	$9.95/mo	$19.95/mo	$39.95/mo	$99.95/mo	$299.95/mo
PAGEVIEWS	2,500	5,000	10,000	20,000	50,000
TRAFFIC	5/GB	10/GB	30/GB	100/GB	300/GB
STORAGE	5/GB	5/GB	10/GB	20/GB	60/GB
DOMAIN	KickApps	Use Your Own	Use Your Own	Use Your Own	Use Your Own
SUPPORT CENTER	✓	✓	✓	✓	✓
24HR TICKETING				✓	✓
SITE BUILDER	✓	✓	✓	✓	✓
APP STUDIO	✓	✓	✓	✓	✓

Small Business & Personal Publishing — For starters to medium size customers

KickApps pricing for a small- to medium-size business.

The Least You Need to Know

- Try KickApps service at www.kickapps.com.
- KickApps offers a 30-day free trial.
- After sign-up, KickApps provides administrators with lots of helpful advice and links to optimize their network.
- KickApps populates each new network with sample content to allow new administrators to see the features in action.

- Use the KickApps Affiliate Center to explore customizations and management features available to your network.
- To continue using your network, you'll need to select a paid plan before your trial period ends.

Appendix A

Glossary

1ShoppingCart   An e-commerce solution providing a digital shopping cart for online purchases and an e-mail marketing system.

action   A click, a comment, or content made by a member of a network.

Alltop   A website that gathers or aggregates headlines from across the Internet. Users can subscribe to topics of interest.

API   Applied program interface. A protocol that allows programmers to write software that works seamlessly with existing software.

Attensity 360   A service that continually monitors and analyzes specific name brands in the social media sphere.

backup   The process of making a copy of a computer's software, files, and settings that can be used to restore the computer if needed.

Backupify   A tool used to automatically create a daily archive copy of data from online accounts such as Twitter, Flickr, Google Docs, Facebook, and other sites.

bandwidth   The technical term for the size of the pipe moving your information to and from you network.

Bing   A search engine developed by Microsoft.

Blogger   A blogging platform owned by Google.

BlogHer   A social network of women who blog.

Bloglines   An online service that helps users organize information of interest on the web, including websites, blogs, and social sites.

BuddyPress   A community-developed social networking platform designed to work with a WordPress website.

captcha   A trademarked security service that ensures an actual person is submitting a web form rather than an automated computer program trying to clog the network with automated accounts. This service requires the user to type in a distorted phrase or parts of an audio clip to confirm that he or she is a real person.

check-in   An action done on mobile social media services such as Foursquare and Gowalla. Users check in to announce their current location.

copyright   A form of legal protection for original work created by individuals.

Crowdvine   A social network platform that creates networks for communities or for specific events, particularly conferences.

custom label   Social network platforms that can build, deploy, and manage custom-made social networks. Platforms that offer this level of service include KickApps, ONEsite, and SocialGO.

Delicious   Previously known as del.icio.us, a social bookmarking site for storing and sharing weblinks of interest.

Digg   A service where users can share content of interest from across the web. Digg uses a thumbs-up or thumbs-down rating system.

Doodle   A scheduling tool that uses a quick poll of potential attendees to confirm time, date, and location details of a meeting or other event.

DropBox   A free application offering file sync and back-up services. Paid storage upgrades are also available.

e-commerce   Online sales transactions. Shoppers pay with a credit card or through PayPal, an online payment transfer system.

enterprise   Refers to large corporate-scale computing systems that have many types of computers, operating systems, and user needs that are managed by the company's IT department.

Etsy   A social network for those who love to purchase or sell hand-crafted and vintage-inspired items.

Eventbrite   An event-planning tool that can handle both registrations and payments.

Facebook   The world's largest online social network, with more than 500 million users worldwide.

fault tolerance   The process of building anything on a computer with an alternate way of accomplishing tasks in the event that the primary method should fail.

FeedBurner   *See* Google FeedBurner.

Flickr   The photo-sharing social network powered by Yahoo!.

Foursquare   A location-based microblogging social media tool where users check in at various locations to share tips, meet friends, and earn badges. *See also* Gowalla.

generic label   Social network platforms that offer a hosting service that includes the platform name. These services include Ning, Wall.fm, SocialGO, and KickApps.

Google   The world's largest search engine.

Google Alerts   A web service that sends users e-mails with search results for preselected words and phrases.

Google Analytics   A service that provides detailed information about website visitors.

Google Docs   A suite of office tools including a word processor, spreadsheet, calendar, and many other programs. Google Docs are stored on the web.

Google FeedBurner   A tool that shares audience data, such as the number of RSS subscribers, for website administrators to use in analyzing their efforts.

Google Reader   A tool to aggregate or gather web content of interest using RSS feeds.

Gowalla   A location-based microblogging social media tool. Users check in at various locations. *See also* Foursquare.

handselling   Happens when a sales clerk, in the real world or online, walks a customer through the features and benefits of a product suited to the needs he or she has expressed.

heads up display   A transparent computer screen that is available to users without having to change their point of view. Examples include a transparent display monitor, a helmet with visor, or even a pair of sunglasses.

Hootsuite   A social media tool that allows a person to manage multiple social media accounts from Twitter, Facebook, Blip.fm, and other platforms. Includes the ability to postdate content.

hosting   The process of making websites, blogs, networks, and any other Internet content available across the Internet by serving content from a dedicated business location other than yours.

InDesign   Part of the Adobe Suite used to edit and transform photographs and other images.

influence   How your views sway the opinions of others.

Infranview   Free, open source photo-editing software.

intellectual property   Anything created by an individual or a team including inventions, literary works, art in all its forms, symbols, concepts, designs, and much more. What comes from the mind is the property of that individual or team.

KickApps   A social networking platform offering both a do-it-yourself platform and custom social network design.

MarketingCharts   A source for news about online marketing and promotion.

Mashable   A website featuring news, blog posts, and other content related to social media, technology, and online marketing.

Master Minds   The brainchild of Napoleon Hill in his book *Think & Grow Rich*. A Master Mind group of about eight people join forces to share ideas, support one another, and freely express opinions in a safe, confidential environment. Such groups are usually facilitated by a moderator and result in a hybrid between a support group and a success circle.

Meetup   An event-planning service that aids online groups in planning and executing real-world events.

microblog   Text-based communication tools such as Twitter or Gowalla where the text communication is limited to 140 characters.

Mind Meister   A collaborative brainstorming tool that digitizes the thought clouds of the team into hierarchical relationships in a treelike structure.

Miso   A location-based social check-in tool for TV and movie watchers.

mobile technology Any computer, device, or system that enables users to connect to the Internet and each other while away from traditional wired computers and phones.

MySpace A social network similar to Facebook that is popular with music lovers and independent bands and musicians.

Ning A service for creating social networks. This platform is built on a self-service model.

Ning address The web address of a Ning network. These usually take the form of *nameofnetwork*.ning.com.

Ning ID A single ID a user can create to identify herself in all Ning networks. A Ning ID is simply a user name, often an e-mail address, and a password.

ONEsite A social network platform used to build customized communities and related microsites.

open source Software created from community-built code; anyone with programming knowledge can access, adapt, and use the software for free.

opt-in Gives participants the choice whether or not to receive certain kinds of information. Within a social network, they can usually opt in or, conversely, opt out of various notifications.

Paint Shop Pro Fully functional, midprice-range image-editing software.

Photofunia Offers a suite of fun photo-altering tools that enable users to create unique and memorable profile images and avatars.

Picasa A photo-sharing site where users can upload, view, comment, and rate pictures.

Ping.fm An online service to gather multiple social networks in one dashboard for easier engagement and monitoring.

plagiarism An infringement of intellectual property rights where another person's writing, ideas, or other work is presented as one's own.

PollDaddy A service to create an online survey. The system gathers the results for analysis.

PostRank   An online scoring system to rate and rank user-generated content anywhere online.

Radian6   A paid service that provides both social media analytics and a dashboard for engaging community members across multiple social media tools.

rate card   The menu advertisers review when buying ad space. It outlines the size of the ad space, the rates, frequent purchase discounts, and the technical details on how and when to deliver the ad.

reach   The size of your community; the number of members who have joined your network plus those you reach through social media outposts.

Really Simple Syndication (RSS)   A piece of website code that allows readers to share and subscribe to content.

Reddit   A social bookmarking site that allows users to post links of interest to share with other users.

RSS   *See* Really Simple Syndication.

scaleability   The process of adjusting hosting services to handle an increase or decrease in volume of data.

Search Engine Land   A respected news site for information related to the Internet.

search engine optimization   *See* SEO.

Second Life   A virtual reality world in which millions of real people don avatars and interact.

SEO   Search engine optimization. The process of creating content on a network, website, or blog that uses consistent keywords to make the web address appear in related search engine results.

Sharepoint   A collaborative work platform available from Microsoft.

Skype   Software that allows for free voice and video calls over the Internet.

slander   A comment is slander or libel if it demeans, berates, or otherwise harms the reputation of a person or brand. If the comment is made orally, it is considered slander, while written attacks are libel.

SmugMug   A photo- and video-sharing site on which users upload, view, rate, and comment on content.

Social Media Examiner A hub of news and education for social media professionals and marketing personnel.

Social Mention A real-time search engine that seeks out mentions of a person or brand across dozens of social tools.

SocialGO A social network platform used to build self-serve communities and custom build robust social networks.

SocialSafe A backup tool for the social network Facebook. It allows users to back up/save their status updates, photos, and friend connections.

static content Content on a website that does not change. It is constant (until it is edited for current content).

StumbleUpon A social bookmarking tool that allows users to rate content across the web. It also learns the habits and interests of users and suggests content of potential interest.

SugarSync Offers file sync and backup services.

Survey Monkey An online service for creating and conducting polls and questionnaires. It includes features to review the gathered data in real time in a variety of graphic layouts.

tagging The process of putting an electronic bookmark of sorts on an image, a video, or text that indicates who or what's in the content. The tags make it easy to record the who, what, and where for any content and can alert people and brands that they have been featured.

TechCrunch A blog and respected web resource for information about technology and gadgets.

Trackur An online social media monitoring tool.

trademark A type of intellectual property that legally protects the representation of a company's brand through text, logo, or a combination of both.

Twitter A microblogging social media platform wherein users can send and review brief 140-character messages, or "tweets."

TypePad A blogging service that offers free blogs to individuals.

URL   Uniform Resources Locator. More simply, it's a web address that you type into your browser to go to a particular website.

Vimeo   A video-sharing website that allows users to view, upload, rate, and comment on videos.

Vocus   A public relations firm that offers a media database, news distribution, and social media monitoring services.

voice   A theatrical term that refers to the character and feel of a particular way of speaking. By changing the voice, companies can change the way their brands are perceived.

Wall.fm   A social network builder developed by Skalfa eCommerce.

white label   Social network platforms that allow administrators to build the community on their own domain name.

widgets   Bits of add-on software found in all sorts of computer technology. Add-on features, color packages, badges, and many other tools can be provided as widgets.

wiki   Stems from Wikipedia, an online encyclopedia created by users. The short form "wiki" has come to be a casual term for any online collection of knowledge compiled and made available for easy reference.

Wordle   A service that generates word clouds (also known as tag clouds) wherein a list of words is graphically represented, with the size of words related to the number of times that word appears in a list of text.

WordPress   A free blogging platform that can be hosted either within WordPress or hosted on your own domain.

Xitti   An adult-oriented social network builder developed by Skalfa eCommerce using the same technology used to power Wall.fm.

YouTube   A video-sharing website that allows users to view, upload, rate, and comment on videos.

Appendix B

Resources

Social networks are wide-reaching tools that cover many topics, from technology to marketing. This field is ever-changing, with new features, new services, and new technology shaping the future of networks. This appendix provides additional resources you can use as you continue your journey to create and maintain a social network of your own.

Print Publications

Abernethy, Jennifer. *The Complete Idiot's Guide to Social Media Marketing.* Indianapolis: Alpha Books, 2010.

Bamberg, Matthew, Kris Krug, and Greg Ketchum. *Killer Photos with Your iPhone,* Boston: Course Technology, a Part of Cengage Learning, 2011.

Banks, Michael A. *Blogging Heroes: Interviews with 30 of the World's Top Bloggers.* Indianapolis: Wiley Publishing Inc., 2008.

Barefoot, Darren and Julie Szabo. *Friends with Benefits: A Social Media Marketing Handbook.* San Francisco: No Starch Press, 2010.

Brogan, Chris and Julien Smith. *Trust Agents: Using the Web to Influence, Improve Reputation, and Earn Trust.* Hoboken: John Wiley & Sons, Inc., 2009.

Clapperton, Guy. *This Is Social Media: Tweet, Blog, Link and Post Your Way to Business Success.* Chichester: Capstone Publishing Ltd., 2009.

Comm, Joel. *Twitter Power 2.0: How to Dominate Your Market One Tweet at a Time.* Hoboken: John Wiley & Sons, Inc., 2010.

Godin, Seth. *Meatball Sundae: Is Your Marketing Out of Sync?* New York: Portfolio—Penguin Group (USA), 2007.

Kraynak, Joe and Mikal E. Belicove. *The Complete Idiot's Guide to Facebook*. Indianapolis: Alpha Books, 2010.

Mac, Amber. *Power Friending: Demystifying Social Media to Grow Your Business*. New York: Portfolio—Penguin Group (USA) Inc., 2010.

McPhedries, Paul. *The Complete Idiot's Guide to Creating a Website*. Indianapolis: Alpha Books, 2008.

O'Reilly, Terry and Mike Tennant. *The Age of Persuasion: How Marketing Ate Our Culture*. Toronto: Alfred A. Knopf Canada, 2009.

Patterson, Sally J. and Janel M. Radtke. *Strategic Communications for Nonprofit Organizations: Seven Tips to Creating a Successful Plan. Second Edition*. Hoboken: John Wiley & Sons, Inc., 2009.

Plumley, George. *WordPress: 24-Hour Trainer: Watch, Read, and Learn How to Create and Customize WordPress Sites*. Indianapolis: Wiley Publishing, Inc., 2010.

Qualman, Erik. *Socialnomics: How Social Media Transforms the Way We Live and Do Business*. Hoboken: John Wiley & Sons, Inc., 2011.

Sabin-Wilson, Lisa. *BuddyPress for Dummies*. Indianapolis: Wiley Publishing Inc., 2010.

Sagoola, Dom. *140 Characters: A Style Guide for the Short Form*. Hoboken: John Wiley & Sons, Inc., 2009.

Stratten, Scott. *UnMarketing: Stop Marketing. Start Engaging*. Hoboken: John Wiley & Sons, Inc., 2010.

Treadaway, Chris and Mari Smith. *Facebook Marketing An Hour A Day*. Indianapolis: Wiley Publishing, Inc., 2010.

Weber, Larry. *Marketing to the Social Web*. Hoboken: John Wiley & Sons, Inc., 2007.

Social Network Services

BuddyPress (buddypress.org)
A plug-in for creating a social network on a WordPress website. See tutorial in Chapter 21.

CrowdVine (www.crowdvine.com)
A social network service that specializes in building communities for conferences and events.

Dlinked (www.dlinked.com)
Currently in development, a new social network service.

Diaspora (www.joindiaspora.com)
A privacy-aware, user-controlled, open source social network service.

GoingOn (www.goingon.com)
A social network service focused on communities for educational purposes.

Groupsite (www.groupsite.com)
A social network service targeting communication and organizations requiring team collaboration.

KickApps (www.kickapps.com)
A social network service focused on "global brands, media and entertainment companies, sports leagues and teams, small businesses, and non-profits." See Chapter 22 for a tutorial.

Ning (www.ning.com)
A social network service "for the world's organizers, activists, and influencers." See Chapter 18 for a tutorial.

ONEsite (www.onesite.com)
A social network service that specializes in custom communities.

SocialGO (www.socialgo.com)
A social network service focused on global brands and large-scale enterprises. See Chapter 20 for a tutorial.

Wall.fm (wall.fm)
A social network service focused on community groups, small businesses, and others displaced by Ning's business decision to charge for all networks. See Chapter 19 for a tutorial.

Xitti (xitti.com)
A social network service for adult content, from the makers of Wall.fm.

Zocku (my.zocku.com)
A social network service for adult content, from the makers of SocialGO.

Help with Featured Social Network Services

The following websites offer assistance for those using one of the social network services featured in this book:

Ning Help Community (help.ning.com)

Wall.fm Help Community (wall.fm/help.php)

WordPress and BuddyPress Help Community (wpmu.org)

SocialGO Owners Network (owners.socialgo.com)

SocialGO Help (help.socialgo.com/home)

KickApps Help (www.kickdeveloper.com)

Social Networking News and Tips

The Age of Persuasion CBC Radio—Terry O'Reilly (www.cbc.ca/ageofpersuasion)
A podcast that talks about marketing and communication issues, many of which relate to social networking.

Beachcomber Communications (beachcombercommunications.com)
The author's website, filled with social networking tips and information as well as a lab site BuddyPress community.

Boing Boing (boingboing.net)
A blog for all things geeky and technical.

Click—The Conversation Prism (theconversationprism.com/click)
An infographic about the many dimensions of social networking and the tools used for each facet.

Howcast (www.howcast.com)
A source for how-to videos on social networking and social media–related topics.

Joel Comm—Social Media Expert (joelcomm.com)
A blog and other resources regarding social media tools, particularly Twitter.

KnowEm (knowem.com)
A directory of top social networks grouped by industry.

MarketingCharts (www.marketingcharts.com)
A resource for social media and social networking–related research and statistics.

Mashable (mashable.com)
A blog filled with social networking–related trends and research.

Search Engine Land (searchengineland.com)
A blog focused on web design, search, and social networking issues.

SeeHowTwo.com (seehowtwo.com)
A WordPress video tutorial site.

Social Marketing Compass (www.flickr.com/photos/briansolis/3987986119)
An infographic about the many dimensions of social networking, and the tools used for each facet.

Social Media Examiner (www.socialmediaexaminer.com)
An online magazine chock-full of great information on social media tools, issues, and industry news.

Techcrunch (techcrunch.com)
A blog filled with information on social networking issues, technology, and tools.

What Is RSS? (www.whatisrss.com)
An introduction to RSS (Really Simple Syndication), with answers to common questions.

ZDNet.com (www.zdnet.com)
A blog with a wide-reaching technical focus, including some social networking content and great help forums.

Social Media Tools

Alltop (www.alltop.com)
A site developed by Guy Kawasaki, noted author and speaker, that provides links to content of interest from across the web. Users can create customized Alltop experiences suited to their interests.

Audioboo (audioboo.fm)
A web-based and mobile service that allows users to record audio podcasts for social sharing.

bit.ly (bit.ly)
A simple URL shortener that allows users to take long and complex web addresses and abbreviate them for easier sharing.

Blip.fm (blip.fm)
A social media tool for sharing audio files, most often songs, accompanied by short messages.

Blogger (www.blogger.com)
Google's blogging platform.

BlogTalkRadio (www.blogtalkradio.com)
A service that allows users to broadcast their own radio programs over the Internet.

Delicious (www.delicious.com)
A social bookmarking tool; useful for saving bookmarks to websites of interest and also for browsing web content.

Digg (www.digg.com)
A social bookmarking tool where users can rate content with a thumbs-up (they dig it) or a thumbs-down (they don't).

Facebook (www.facebook.com)
The world's largest social network, with over 500 million active users.

Foursquare (foursquare.com)
A location-based check-in social media tool with game interactivity to achieve Mayorships, earn badges, and score points.

Gowalla (www.gowalla.com)
A location-based check-in social media tool with game interactivity to explore communities and earn related badges.

Hootsuite (hootsuite.com)
A service for managing multiple social media accounts on Twitter, Facebook, Blip.fm, and other social sites.

LinkedIn (www.linkedin.com)
A social network for professionals that includes an online directory of contacts and opportunities for dialogue.

Miso (gomiso.com)
A social check-in service for sharing television and movie experiences.

NetworkedBlogs (www.networkedblogs.com)
A tool used to publish blogs on social media sites such as Facebook.

Reddit (www.reddit.com)
A social bookmarking tool for sharing links of interest.

StumbleUpon (www.stumbleupon.com)
A social bookmarking site that takes information about users, their friends, and strangers with similar interests and recommends content of interest.

Twitter (twitter.com)
A microblogging tool for sharing 140-character messages called tweets.

TypePad (www.typepad.com)
A blogging platform.

WordPress (wordpress.com and wordpress.org)
An open source platform used to create blog websites; it's required to run the BuddyPress plug-in social network service.

Audio and Video Resources

Flickr (www.flickr.com)
A social media tool for sharing photos; run by Yahoo!.

IrfanView (www.irfanview.ca)
A free, open source image- and photo-editing software package.

Paint Shop Pro (www.corel.com/paintshoppro)
Paid image- and photo-editing software that provides robust tools at a mid-range price.

PhotoFunia (photofunia.com)
A site to create fun variations of a head shot, including sketches, mug shots, billboards, and wanted posters.

Photoshop (www.adobe.com/photoshop)
Paid image- and photo-editing software and part of the Adobe suite of desktop publishing tools.

Picasa (picasa.com)
Google's photo-sharing and -editing software.

SmugMug (www.smugmug.com)
A photo- and video-sharing site.

Vimeo (www.vimeo.com)
A video-sharing and distribution site.

YouTube (www.youtube.com)
A video-sharing and distribution site, and the world's second-largest search engine.

Other Helpful Online Tools

DropBox (www.dropbox.com)
A tool for online file backup, file sync, and file sharing.

EventBrite (www.eventbrite.com)
An event-planning and registration management tool.

Evernote (www.evernote.com)
A tool to capture text, audio, video, and photo notes, and tag them for future reference.

Google AdSense (www.google.com/adsense)
Google's advertising program for publishers selling advertising space on websites.

Google AdWords (www.google.com/adwords)
Google's advertising program for advertisers seeking advertising space on websites.

Google Alerts (www.google.com/alerts)
Google's tool to monitor keywords and phrases that have been indexed by Google's search engine.

Google Docs (www.google.com/docs)
Google's online office tools for creating text documents and spreadsheets.

Google Feedburner (www.feedburner.com)
Google's RSS feed-generated management tool for blogs and websites.

Google Reader (www.google.com/reader)
Google's service to organize and display RSS subscriptions.

MeetUp (www.meetup.com)
A social site the helps people with like interests organize real-world events.

Mind Meister (www.mindmeister.com)
An online mind-mapping and brainstorming tool.

Polldaddy (www.polldaddy.com)
An online tool to conduct polls and surveys. *See also* Survey Gizmo and SurveyMonkey.

SugarSync (www.sugarsync.com)
A remote file sync and backup service.

Survey Gizmo (www.surveygizmo.com)
Online software to create simple surveys, complex surveys, evaluations, and polls. *See also* Polldaddy and SurveyMonkey.

SurveyMonkey (www.surverymonkey.com)
A popular online tool to conduct polls and surveys. *See also* Polldaddy and Survey Gizmo.

Wordle (www.wordle.net)
A tool to create graphic depictions of groups of words, called word clouds.

Social Network Monitoring Tools

Alexa (www.alexa.com)
A site to check your website's global ranking.

Attensity 360 (www.attensity360.com)
A tool to monitor brand reputations on the Internet.

Google Analytics (www.google.com/analytics)
A tool to quantify and review a website's visitors.

PostRank (www.postrank.com)
A social media monitoring service.

Radian6 Social Media Monitoring and Engagement (www.radian6.com)
A paid tool for social media monitoring and social media engagement.

Social Mention (www.socialmention.com)
A tool for tracking mentions of a name or brand across dozens of social sites.

Social Network Comparison Chart

Appendix C

The following chart provides an overview of the six social network platforms featured in this book. At a glance, you can see general information about each service and how it compares to others. While every effort has been made to ensure the accuracy of this information, the featured platforms are at liberty to modify their product offerings, rates, and terms of use at any time.

Type	Ning	Wall.fm	BuddyPress	SocialGO	KickApps	ONEsite
Generic label	Yes	Yes	No	Yes	Yes	No
White label	Yes	Yes	Yes	Yes	Yes	Yes
Custom label	No	No	No	Yes	Yes	Yes

Setup	Ning	Wall.fm	BuddyPress	SocialGO	KickApps	ONEsite
Network name	Yes	Yes	Yes	Yes	Yes	No
Network address	Yes	Yes	No	Yes	Yes	No
Connect your own domain	Yes	Yes	Yes	Yes	Yes	Yes
Privacy control	Yes	Yes	Yes	Yes	Yes	Yes
Tagline	Yes	Yes	Yes	Yes	Yes	Yes
Description	Yes	No	Yes	Yes	Yes	Yes
Keywords	Yes	No	No	No	Yes	Yes
Language options	Yes	No	No	No	Yes	Yes

Basic Features	Ning	Wall.fm	BuddyPress	SocialGO	KickApps	ONEsite
Membership	Yes	Yes	Yes	Yes	Yes	Yes
User profiles	Yes	Yes	Yes	Yes	Yes	Yes
Relationships	Yes	Yes	Yes	Yes	Yes	Yes
Communications						
Status updates	Yes	Yes	Yes	Yes	Yes	Yes
Activity feed	Yes	Yes	Yes	Yes	Yes	Yes
Chat	Yes	Yes	Yes	Yes	Yes	Yes
Groups	Yes	Yes	Yes	Yes	Yes	Yes
Forums	Yes	Yes	Yes	Yes	Yes	Yes
Comments	Yes	Yes	Yes	Yes	Yes	Yes
Messages	Yes	Yes	Yes	Yes	Yes	Yes
Content						
Music	Yes	No	Plug-in	Plug-in	Custom	Custom
Notes	Yes	No	Plug-in	No	Custom	Custom
Photos	Yes	Yes	Plug-in	Yes	Custom	Custom
Videos	Yes	Yes	Plug-in	Yes	Custom	Custom
Links	No	Yes	Yes	Yes	Custom	Custom

Advanced Features	Ning	Wall.fm	BuddyPress	SocialGO	KickApps	ONEsite
Share (Facebook, Twitter)	Yes	Yes	Plug-in	Yes	Yes	Custom
Blogging and Microblogging	Yes	Yes	Yes	Yes	Yes	Custom
RSS	Yes	Yes	Plug-in	No	Yes	Custom
Calendar	Yes	Yes	Plug-in	Yes	Yes	Custom
Birthdays	Yes	No	Plug-in	Yes	No	Custom
Events	Yes	Yes	Plug-in	Yes	Yes	Custom
Notifications	Yes	No	Plug-in	No	No	Custom
Tagging	Yes	Yes	Plug-in	No	Yes	Custom
Polls	Yes	No	No	No	No	Custom
Ratings	Yes	Yes	Plug-in	No	No	Custom
Badges	Yes	No	Plug-in	No	No	Custom
Import contacts	Yes	Yes	Plug-in	No	No	Custom

Administration	Ning	Wall.fm	BuddyPress	SocialGO	KickApps	ONEsite
Setup time	minutes	minutes	minutes	minutes	minutes	6–8 weeks
Appearance	Custom	Static	Custom	Custom	Custom	Custom
Themes	52 options	4 options	limited options	Purchase $20–$40	Custom	Custom
Admin dashboard	Yes	Yes	Yes	Yes	Custom	Custom
Maintenance page	No	Yes	No	No	No	Custom
E-commerce	Yes	No	No	Yes	No	Yes
Platform advertising	Yes	Yes	No	Yes	No	No
Your own advertising	No	No	Yes	Yes	Yes	Yes
Moderation	No	Yes	Plug-in	No	Yes	Custom
Text box	Yes	Yes	No	No	No	Custom
Contests	No	No	No	No	Custom	Custom
Description	Yes	No	Yes	Yes	Yes	Yes
Integrated sign-on	No	Yes	No	No	Custom	Custom
API	Yes	No	Yes	Yes	Yes	No
Mobile	No	No	No	Custom	Custom	Custom
Widgets/plug-ins	Yes	Yes	Yes	Yes	Custom	Custom

Help	Ning	Wall.fm	BuddyPress	SocialGO	KickApps	ONEsite
Forum	Free	Free	Free	Free	No	Paid
Instant chat	n/a	n/a	n/a	Free	No	n/a
E-mail	Paid	Free	n/a	Free	Yes	Paid
Phone	Paid	n/a	n/a	n/a	No	Paid
Dedicated	Fee	n/a	Paid	Paid	Paid	Paid

Costs	Ning	Wall.fm	BuddyPress	SocialGO	KickApps	ONEsite
Free option	No	Yes	Yes	Yes	No	No
Lowest cost package	$2.95/month	Free	Free	Free	$9.95/month	Quote
Highest cost package	$49.95/month	Free	Free	$149.95/month	$39.95/month	Quote
Further fees	Options	Options	Technician	Options	Options	Options
Free trial	No	Yes	Yes	Yes	Yes	No
Included storage	n/a	n/a	n/a	1GB–10GB	Quote	Quote
Included bandwidth	n/a	n/a	n/a	10GB–100GB	Quote	Quote

Worksheet for Creating a Social Network

Appendix D

As you work through this book, it is helpful to keep your goals, priorities, and budget in mind. I suggest you use this worksheet to make note of your decisions and any special considerations related to your network. A free downloadable PDF version can be printed from www.angelacrocker.com.

Network Name _____

Network Location _____

Types of Connections (Chapter 2): Note the audience, or audiences, you are trying to reach.

- ❏ Business to business
- ❏ Business to consumer
- ❏ Peer to peer
- ❏ Community

Social Network Objectives (Chapter 2): Select a primary, a secondary, and, maybe, tertiary objectives for your community.

- ❏ Influencing _____
- ❏ Organizing _____
- ❏ Education _____
- ❏ Rallying _____
- ❏ Evangelizing _____
- ❏ Fundraising _____
- ❏ Sales _____

❑ Convenience _____
❑ Eliminating geographical borders _____
❑ Just for fun _____

Features (Chapter 4): Note those features your network needs and those you desire, as well as the features you do not require.

Features	Need	Wish For	Don't Need
Activity			
Members			
Photos and videos			
Tagging			
Forums			
Events			
Groups			
Polling			
Ratings			
Blog			
Chat			
Music			
Description			
Notes			
Text box			
RSS			
Badges			
Birthdays			

Free Trials:

- ❏ Is there a free trial available? _____
- ❏ How long does the free trial last? _____
- ❏ Note your free trial expiration date. _____

Social Network Service Pricing (Chapter 5): What are you willing to pay for your social network service each year?

- ❏ $0
- ❏ Less than $100
- ❏ Less than $500
- ❏ $500 or more

Back Office Costs (Chapter 5): As you explore the back office costs, note those costs that will affect your budget.

- ❏ Hosting _____
- ❏ Fault tolerance _____
- ❏ Volume of storage _____
- ❏ More bandwidth _____
- ❏ Enhanced functionality _____
- ❏ Backups and restoration _____

Other Costs: What other expenses will your network incur?

- ❏ Mobility _____
- ❏ Other _____

Content Ratio (Chapter 10):

- ❏ Referenced content _____%
- ❏ Original content _____%

Gathering Content (Chapter 10): Note the places where you will find content of interest to your community. Be specific.

- ❏ Reports and research _____
_____

- ❏ Opinions _____
_____

- ❏ Dialogue _____
_____

- ❏ Links _____
_____

- ❏ Google Alerts _____
_____

- ❏ Bookmarking accounts _____
_____

- ❏ Photo ideas _____
_____

- ❏ Photo sharing account _____
_____

- ❏ Video ideas _____
_____

- ❏ Video sharing account _____
_____

Social Network Services (Chapter 6): Which social network service did you select?

- ❏ Ning
- ❏ Wall.fm
- ❏ SocialGO
- ❏ BuddyPress
- ❏ KickApps
- ❏ ONEsite
- ❏ Other _____

Social Media Outposts (Chapter 13): What social media outposts will you activate?

- ❏ Facebook
- ❏ Twitter
- ❏ Foursquare
- ❏ LinkedIn
- ❏ Special interest communities _____
  _____
- ❏ Others _____
  _____

My Daily Routine: Make a contract with yourself to participate in your community each day. What will you do?

❏ I commit to: _____

_____
_____
_____
_____
_____
_____
_____
_____
_____
_____
_____
_____
_____
_____
_____
_____
_____
_____
_____
_____
_____
_____
_____

Index

Numbers

1ShoppingCart.com, 25, 201
140-character biographies, user profiles, 119-120

A

About tab (BuddyPress), 273
AC (Affiliate Center), KickApps, 293
acquaintances, relationships, 125
actions, 215
active listening, 169
activity feature, 51-52
adaptation, 241
Admin Centre (SocialGO), 267
administrative check-ups, 238
AdSense (Google), 205
AdTech, 209
advertisements, selling, 207-209
advertisers, rate cards, 207
advertising, 201-205
   Google AdSense, 205
   Google AdWords, 205-207
AdWords (Google), 205-207
Affiliate Center (AC), KickApps, 293
affiliate marketing, 209-210
Affiliate Summit, 209
Alexa.com, 242
Alli Community, 26
Alltop.com, 148

Analytics (Google), 220-221
annual check-ups, 238
anonymity, members, 229-231
appearance, customizing, 109
Apple, 155
assessments, success metrics, 223-224
Audio Video Interleave, 155
audio-video editing software, 154-155
authenticity, content, 233-234
Autism Speaks network page, 202
availability, names, 100-102
avatars, user profiles, 120-123

B

BabyVibe, 203
back office costs, 76-77
backups, 81-82
badges feature, 68-70
Ballpark Chasers, 54
bandwidth costs, 80-81
befriending, 125-126
benefits, members, articulating, 163
biographies, user profiles, 119-120
birthdates, 115
birthdays feature, 70
Blip.fm, 194
blog feature, 61-63
Blogger, 62
BlogHer, 3, 62

blogs
    microblogs, 178-179
    success metrics, 218
Blum, Manuel, 37
Book Broads, The, 7, 99
breaking news, sharing, 174
BuddyPress, 12-13, 32, 40-42, 109, 269
    communities, 284
    Component Setup, 278
    creating forums, 278-279
    free services, 75
    general settings, 277
    installing, 273-276
    live demonstration, 270
    navigation tabs, 270-273
    profiles, 5, 280-283
    themes, 276
    widgets, 284
budgets, 74-76
business to business connections, 15
business to consumer connections, 16

C

CafeMom.com, 194
calendar, success metrics, 218
CAN-Spam Act, 209
Canadian Women in Communications (CWC), 16-17
captchas, 37
Carnival Cruise Lines, Funville social network, 4, 97
catchphrases, Wall.fm, 254
chat feature, 63
check-in services, 69-70
Club CK, 239-240
comments
    libel, 179
    moderating, 178-180
    negative, 171
    slander, 179
    statistics, 180
    success metrics, 218
common objections, determining, 165-166
communications, 163-164
    active listening, 169
    comments, moderating, 178-180
    direct communicator style, 164
    facilitating dialogue, 169-172
    feedback, 175-176
    in person, 180-182
    membership benefits, 163
    one-on-one, 177-178
    peaceful collaborator style, 164
    relationships, 160-161
    sharing information, 172-175
    spirited contributor style, 164
    success metrics, 217
    systematic methodist style, 164-165
    systemwide messages, 180
communities
    BuddyPress, 284
    influence, 214
    reach, 214
    success metrics, size, 225-226
Component Setup (BuddyPress), 278
Connected Peace Corps community, 60
connections, 15
    business to business, 15
    business to consumer, 16
    community, 17-18
    peer to peer, 16-17
    professional versus personal, 18
    social networks, 5
content, 130-131
    authenticity, 233-234
    copyrights, 132-133
    crowd sourced, 148
    moderation, 135-136
    plagiarism, 133
    referenced, 131-132
    success metrics, 218
    uploading, 133-135

copyrights
    content, 132-133
    music, 64
costs, 73-76
    additional functionality, 83-85
    back office, 76-77
    backups, 81-82
    bandwidth, 80-81
    budgets, 74-76
    fault tolerance, 82-83
    hosting, 77-79
    mobility, 85-86
    restoration, 81-82
    time, 86
    volume of storage, 79-80
Cranbury, Sean, 187
Creative Commons License, 99
Crocker, Angela, 254
crowd sourced content, 148
Crowdvine, 32, 48
custom label network services, 13-14, 42-44
    KickApps, 44-45
    ONEsite, 46-48
customer service resources, 90
customization services, 89-90
CWC (Canadian Women in Communications), 16-17

D

daily check-ups, 238
dashboards
    Ning, 251
    Wall.fm, 38-39
data gathering, success metrics, 220-223
Delicious.com, 148
description feature, 64
dialogue
    facilitating, 169-172
    sharing, 139-140

Diaspora social media network, 186
Digg.com, 61, 148
digital cameras, 149-150
direct communicator style, 164
domain names, 77
    availability, 100-102
    formats, 34
    length, 104-105
    memorable, 102-104
    Ning, 40
    spelling, 105-106
    trademarks, 107
    Wall.fm, 40
Domino's Pizza Chicago Twitter account, 189
Doodle.com, 60
drag-and-drop navigation, Ning, 35
DropBox, 133

E

e-commerce, 25, 199-201
e-mail addresses, user profiles, 116
English Companion community, 34
enterprise computing, 46
etiquette, 6-7
Etsy, 3
events, promoting, 174
events feature, 57-58
    success metrics, 218
Evernote.com, 149
everyone-knows-everyone model, 52

F

Facebook, 3, 134, 183
    advertising revenue, 11
    Insights data, 10
    limitations, 9-11
    popularity, 9
    social media plans, 186-189

FanVoice (NBA), 57
fault tolerance, costs, 82-83
features, 49-50
    activity, 51-52
    badges, 68-70
    birthdays, 70
    blog, 61-63
    chat, 63
    choosing, 88
    description, 64
    events, 57-58, 218
    forums, 56-57
    groups, 59
    members, 52-53
    music, 64
    Ning, 35, 50
    notes, 64
    photos, 53-55
    polling, 59-60
    ratings, 60-61
    RSS (Really Simple Syndication), 66-68
    tagging, 55-56
    text box, 65
    usage, 238
    videos, 53-55
feedback, responding, 175-176
Feedburner (Google), 67
File Transfer Protocol (FTP), 133-134
Fiskar, 18
Flickr, 3, 8, 152
Food2, 44
forums, BuddyPress, creating, 278-279
forums feature, 56-57
Forums tab (BuddyPress), 272
Foursquare, 179
    social media plans, 192-193
Fox Television social network, 47
free social network services, 75
free trials
    Ning, 248
    SocialGO, 264-265
friending, 125-126
FTP (File Transfer Protocol), 133-134
fundraising, 25

G

general settings, BuddyPress, 277
generic label network services, 12, 33-34
    Ning, 35-36
    Wall.fm, 36-39
Get Started Now button (Ning), 245-246
GetUrGoodOn, 104
Global Page template (KickApps), 294-295
global positioning satellites (GPS), check-in services, 70
GoingOn, 32
Google
    search terms, 141-146
    AdSense, 205
    AdWords, 205-207
Google Alerts, sharing links, 141-146
Google Analytics, 220-221
Google Docs, 133
Google Feedburner, 67
Gore-Tex social network, 45
Gowalla, 192
groups, 126-127
groups feature, 59
    success feature, 217
Groups tab (BuddyPress), 271
Groupsite, 32, 48

H

handselling, 197-198
Harlem Globetrotters social network, 45
hashtags (Twitter), 191
Haystack, 32
heads up displays, 237
help (technical), 91-92

HootSuite, 134
Hopper, Nicholas J., 37
hosting websites, 33
    costs, 77-79
house icons, Wall.fm, 38
H&R Block technical support, 63
H&R Block: Ask a Tax Question feature, 85

I-J

icons, user profiles, 120-123
IDs
    Ning, 35
    Wall.fm, 37
images, user profiles, 120-123
in-person communications, 180-182
Indexer's Network, 208
influence, communities, 214
information, sharing, 172-175
Insights data (Facebook), 10
installation, BuddyPress, 273-276
interest-specific communities, 3
interfaces, services, 93
IP addresses, 230

K

Karen's Linguistic Issues, 106
Kelley, Kevin, 235
keywords
    searches, 241-242
    tags, 56
KickApps, 12-13, 32-34, 40, 44-45, 201, 287-292
    AC (Affiliate Center), 293
    Global Page template, 294-295
    levels of service, 295
    navigation tabs, 290-291
    Site Styler, 294
KickDeveloper.com, 295

Knitting Network, 22
Knowem.com, 184

L

Lane Bryant, Inside Curve community, 162
Legal Information Institute, 135
length, names, 104-105
levels of service
    KickApps, 295
    Ning, 245-246
    SocialGO, 264
Levi's jeans social community, 189
libel, 179
LinkedIn, 183
    social media plans, 193-194
    special-interest communities, 194
links, sharing, 140-149
LiveNation.com, 162
logos, user profiles, 120-123
Lynyrd Skynyrd, Skynyrd Nation, 97

M

marketing, 201-205
    affiliate, 209-210
    competition analysis, 211
    Google AdSense, 205
    Google AdWords, 205-207
    relationships, 211-212
    selling advertisements, 207-209
    sponsorships, 210-211
measurables, 220
    success metrics, 216-220
members, 113
    anonymity, 229-231
    articulating benefits, 163
    birthdates, 115
    determining common objections, 165-166
    ease of joining, 113-115

facilitating dialogue, 169-172
feedback, 175-176
in-person communications, 180-182
inviting, 176-177
IP addresses, 230
moderating comments, 178-180
one-on-one interaction, 177-178
overcoming reluctance, 165-167
participation, 161-163
privacy policy, 232-233
quality versus quantity, 234-235
safety concerns, 231-232
security, 231-232
sharing information, 172-175
superusers, 177
systemwide messages, 180
terms of use, 232-233
user profiles, 115-116
    avatars, 120-123
    biographies, 119-120
    details, 123
    icons, 120-123
    logos, 120-123
    organizational, 116
    personal, 116
    photographs, 120-123
    relationships, 123-127
    strong passwords, 118-119
    unique names, 117-118
    valid e-mail addresses, 116
welcoming, 167-168
members feature, 52-53
Members tab (BuddyPress), 270-271
memorable names, 102-104
messages
    success metrics, 218
    systemwide, 180
metrics (success), 213-215, 220, 227
    assessments, 223-224
    community size, 225-226
    data gathering, 220-223
    measurables, 216-220
    monetary, 224-225
    quality of interactions, 227
microblogs, 178-179
    success metrics, 218
microsites, 46
Mind Meister, 98-99
mobile technology, 85
mobility costs, 85-86
moderating comments, 178-180
moderating content, 135-136
monetary success, metrics, 224-225
monthly check-ups, 238
music, sharing, 64
music feature, 64
My Godly Place, 24
My Sun community, 127
MySpace, 3

N

names, user profiles, 117-118
naming social networks, 97-100
    availability, 100-102
    length, 104-105
    memorable, 102-104
    spelling, 105-106
    trademarks, 107
NASCAR social network, 46
navigation tabs, KickApps, 290-291
negative comments, 171
Nerd Merit Badges, 70
news, sharing, 174
News tab (BuddyPress), 272
Ning, 12, 32, 40, 109, 245-252
    badges feature, 69
    dashboard, 251
    discounts, 245
    domain names, 40
    drag-and-drop navigation, 35

features, 35, 50
fees, 36
free trials, 248
generic label services, 35-36
Get Started Now button, 245-246
IDs, 35
levels of service, 245-246
payment plans, 249
Ning network, 208
notes, success metrics, 218
notes feature, 64

O

obscurity, members, 229-231
off-topic conversations, permitting, 20
one-on-one interactions, 177-178
ONEsite, 12-14, 32, 43-48, 201
    microsites, 46
open source software, 42
OpenWack.org, 36
opinions, sharing, 139
opt-ins, 116
organizational user profiles, 116
Orkut, 32
outreach, success metrics, 219
Oxwall, 36

P

Panasonic social network, 47
participants. *See* members
participation, members, 161-163
passwords, user profiles, 118-119
patience, 182
payment plans, Ning, 249
PayPal, 25
peaceful collaborator communication style, 164
peer to peer networks, 16-17

PeoplePodcastProject, 198
personal user profiles, 116
photo-editing software, 151
photo-sharing accounts, 152
Photofunia.com, 123
photographs
    photo-editing software, 151
    sharing, 149-152
    taking, 150-151
    user profiles, 120-123
photos feature, 53-55
Picasa, 152
plagiarism, 133
plug-ins, 42
Polldaddy.com, 60
polling feature, 59-60
Port Coquitlam Soccer, 21
Posting Up social network (Detroit Pistons), 59
privacy policies, 232-233
privacy settings, 107-108
products, selling, 199-201
profiles (user), 115-116
    avatars, 120-123
    biographies, 119-120
    BuddyPress, setting up, 280-283
    details, 123
    icons, 120-123
    logos, 120-123
    organizational, 116
    personal, 116
    photographs, 120-123
    relationships, 123-127
    strong passwords, 118-119
    unique names, 117-118
    valid e-mail addresses, 116
proselytizing, 23-25
protocols, 6-7
publicists, 160
publicity stunts, 161

Q-R

quality members, 234-235
quality of interactions, success metrics, 227
quarterly check-ups, 238
QuickTime, 155

rate cards, advertisers, 207
ratings feature, 60-61
reach, communities, 214
Reddit.com, 148
Redhead Business Management, 122
referenced content, 131-132
relationships
    contacting, 160-161
    criteria, 159
    marketing, 211-212
    user profiles, 123-127
reluctance, membership, overcoming, 165-167
reports, sharing, 138-139
Republicanville, 24
research, sharing, 138-139
restoration costs, 81-82
Richardson, Peggy, 121-241
RSS (Really Simple Syndication) feature, 66-68

S

safety, members, 231-232
search, 241
search engines, 242
searches
    Google, 141-146
    keywords, 241-242
    search engines, 242
Second Life online community, 230
security, users, 231-232
SeeHowTwo.com, 69
Segway.com, 173
selling
    advertisements, 207-209
    products, 199-201
semi-annual check-ups, 238
servers, 77
services, 12, 31-33
    choosing, 87-93
    comparing, 48
    custom label, 13-14, 42-44
        KickApps, 44-45
        ONEsite, 46-48
    customer service resources, 90
    customization, 89-90
    features, 88
    generic label, 12, 33-34
        Ning, 35-36
        Wall.fm, 36-39
    interfaces, 93
    technical help, 91-92
    trial offers, 93-94
    white label, 13, 39-40
        BuddyPress, 42
        SocialGO, 40-42
Shards of Orn, The, 231
Sharepoint, 133
sharing, 129-130, 137
    dialogue, 139-140
    links, 140-149
    opinions, 139
    photographs, 149-152
    reports, 138-139
    research, 138-139
    videos, 153-156
sharing information, 172-175
sharing music, 64
Shupe, Renee, 122
Site Styler (KickApps), 294
six-month check-ups, 237-241
Skalfa eCommerce, Wall.fm, 36

slander, 179
SmartGirlPolitics, 58
SMEs (subject matter experts), 175
Smith, Mari, 11
SmugMug, 152
social media plans, 184-186
   daily routines, 194-195
   Facebook, 186-189
   Foursquare, 192-193
   LinkedIn, 193-194
   special-interest communities, 194
   Twitter, 189-191
social media versus social networks, 8
social networks, 3-4, 15, 97, 113
   adaptation, 241
   BuddyPress, 269-284
   connections, 5, 15
      business to business, 15
      business to consumer, 16
      community, 17-18
      peer to peer, 16-17
      professional versus personal, 18
   content, 130-131
   copyrights, 132-133
   costs, 73-76
      additional functionality, 83-85
      back office, 76-77
      backups, 81-82
      bandwidth, 80-81
      budgets, 74-76
      fault tolerance, 82-83
      hosting, 77-79
      mobility, 85-86
      restoration, 81-82
      time, 86
      volume of storage, 79-80
   customizing appearance, 109
   ease of joining, 113-115
   etiquette, 6-7
   Facebook, limitations, 9-11

features, 49-50
   activity, 51-52
   badges, 68-70
   birthdays, 70
   blog, 61-63
   chat, 63
   description, 64
   events, 57-58
   forums, 56-57
   groups, 59
   members, 52-53
   music, 64
   notes, 64
   photos, 53-55
   polling, 59-60
   ratings, 60-61
   RSS (Really Simple Syndication), 66-68
   tagging, 55-56
   text box, 65
   videos, 53-55
KickApps, 287-295
moderation, 135-136
naming, 97-100
   availability, 100-102
   length, 104-105
   memorable, 102-104
   spelling, 105-106
   trademarks, 107
Ning, 245-252
objectives, 19
   convenience, 27
   education, 21-22
   eliminating geographic borders, 27
   fun, 27
   fundraising, 25
   influence, 19-20
   inspiration, 22-23
   organization, 20-21
   proselytizing, 23-25
   sales, 25-26

origins, 8
privacy settings, 107-108
protocols, 6-7
referenced, 131-132
services, 12, 31-33
    BuddyPress, 42
    comparing, 48
    custom label, 13-14, 42-48
    generic label, 12, 33-39
    KickApps, 44-45
    Ning, 35-36
    ONEsite, 46-48
    SocialGO, 40-42
    Wall.fm, 36-39
    white label, 13, 39-42
sharing, 129-130
six-month check-ups, 237-241
SocialGO, 263-267
sponsorships, 210-211
strategic alliances, 7-8
transparency, 234
uploading, 133-135
user profiles, 115-116
    avatars, 120-123
    biographies, 119-120
    details, 123
    icons and logos, 120-123
    organizational, 116
    personal, 116
    photographs, 120-123
    relationships, 123-127
    strong passwords, 118-119
    unique names, 117-118
    valid e-mail addresses, 116
versus social media, 8
Wall.fm, 253-261
SocialGO, 12, 32-34, 40-42, 201, 263-267
    Admin Centre, 267
    adult content, 39
    free services, 75
    free trial, 264-265
    introductory video, 40
    levels of service, 264
    network configuration, 265
    Widget Store, 41
    widgets, 41
SocialMediaExaminer.com, 132
Society for the Prevention of Cruelty to Animals (SPCA), 104
software
    audio-video editing software, 154-155
    open source, 42
    photo-editing, 151
SPCA (Society for the Prevention of Cruelty to Animals), 104
spelling, domain names, 105-106
spirited contributor communication style, 164
sponsorships, 210-211
static content, websites, 64
Stelzner, Mike, 132
Stone Temple Pilots community, 84
storage costs, 79-80
strangers, relationships, 124
strategic alliances, 7-8
strong passwords, user profiles, 118-119
StumbleUpon, 146-148
subject matter experts (SMEs), 175
success metrics, 213-215, 220, 227
    assessments, 223-224
    community size, 225-226
    data gathering, 220-223
    measurables, 216-220
    monetary, 224-225
    quality of interactions, 227
superusers, 177
surveys, creating, 240
systematic methodist communication style, 164-165
systemwide messages, 180

Index

T

tagging feature, 55-56
taglines, Wall.fm, 254
tags, 56
Tasty Kitchen, 13
technical help, 91-92
terms of use, 232-233
text, sharing, 137
    dialogue, 139-140
    opinions, 139
    reports, 138-139
    research, 138-139
text box feature, 65
themes
    BuddyPress, 276
    Wall.fm, 255-256
trademarks, domain names, 107
transparency, 234
trial offers, 93-94
TweetDeck, 134
Twitter, 8, 134, 179, 183, 190
    hashtags, 191
    social media plans, 189-191
    text box feature, 65
TypePad, 62

U

Uniform Resource Locators (URLs), 12
unique names, user profiles, 117-118
United States CAN-Spam Act, 209
upcoming events, promoting, 174
uploading content, 133-135
URLs (Uniform Resource Locators), 12
user profiles, 115-116
    See also members
    anonymity, 229-231
    avatars, 120-123
    biographies, 119-120
    details, 123
    icons and logos, 120-123
    IP addresses, 230
    organizational, 116
    personal, 116
    photographs, 120-123
    privacy policy, 232-233
    relationships, 123-127
    safety concerns, 231-232
    security, 231-232
    strong passwords, 118-119
    terms of use, 232-233
    unique names, 117-118
    valid e-mail addresses, 116

V

valid e-mail addresses, user profiles, 116
video cameras, 153
video-sharing accounts, 155-156
videos, sharing, 153-156
videos feature, 53-55
Vimeo, 155
voice, 116
volume of storage costs, 79-80
von Ahn, Luis, 37

W

Wall.fm, 12, 32, 40, 109, 201, 253-261
    adult content, 39
    catchphrases, 254
    dashboard, 38-39
    domain names, 40
    free services, 75
    generic label services, 36-39
    home page, 253
    house icon, 38
    IDs, 37
    taglines, 254
    themes, 255-256

WD-40 Buzz activity feed, 51
websites
    domain name formats, 34
    hosting, 33
    static content, 64
weekly check-ups, 238
WEGO Health network, 108
welcoming members, 167-168
white label network services, 13, 39-40
    BuddyPress, 42
    SocialGO, 40-42
Whole Foods Market Twitter account, 189
Widget Store (SocialGO), 41
widgets
    BuddyPress, 284
    SocialGO, 41
Windows Media Format, 155
WizardofeBooks.com, 241
Wizards of the Coast community, 53
Wordle, 99-100
WordPress, 42, 62
World Theatre Day, 23
World Wrestling Entertainment (WWE) social network, 14, 43

X-Y-Z

Xitti, 32, 39

YouTube, 3, 8, 155

ZDNet, 91
Zocku, 32, 39
Zootopia, 105

CHECK OUT THESE BEST-SELLERS

More than 450 titles available at booksellers and online retailers everywhere!

Grammar and Style, Second Edition	Word Search Puzzles	Glycemic Index Weight Loss, Second Edition	World Religions, Third Edition	The Perfect Resume, Fifth Edition
978-1-59257-115-4	978-1-59257-900-6	978-1-59257-855-9	978-1-59257-222-9	978-1-59257-957-0
U.S. History Graphic Illustrated	Calculus, Second Edition	Positive Dog Training, Second Edition	Personal Finance in Your 20s & 30s, Fourth Edition	Organizing Your Life, Fifth Edition
978-1-59257-785-9	978-1-59257-471-1	978-1-59257-483-4	978-1-59257-883-2	978-1-59257-966-2
Learning Spanish, Fifth Edition (CD Included)	Wine Basics, Second Edition	Microsoft Windows 7	Music Theory, Second Edition (CD Included)	Walt Disney World
978-1-59257-908-2	978-1-59257-786-6	978-1-59257-954-9	978-1-59257-437-7	978-1-59257-888-7

ALPHA

idiotsguides.com

Find us on
facebook®

facebook.com/completeidiotsguides

Become a fan and get updates on upcoming titles, author book signing events, coupons, and much more!

ALPHA